1993

Faulkner and the Short Story
FAULKNER AND YOKNAPATAWPHA
1990

Faulkner and the Short Story

FAULKNER AND YOKNAPATAWPHA, 1990

EDITED BY
EVANS HARRINGTON
AND
ANN J. ABADIE

UNIVERSITY PRESS OF MISSISSIPPI
Jackson and London

95 94 93 92   4 3 2 1

The paper in this book meets the guidelines for permanence and durability
of the Committee on Production Guidelines for Book Longevity of the Council
on Library Resources.

Library of Congress Cataloging-in-Publication Data

Faulkner and the short story : Faulkner and Yoknapatawpha, 1990 /
   edited by Evans Harrington and Ann J. Abadie.
        p.   cm.
   Lectures presented at the 17th Annual Faulkner and Yoknapatawpha
Conference, Oxford, Miss., July 29–Aug. 3, 1990.
   Includes index.
   ISBN 0-87805-606-8 (alk. paper). — ISBN 0-87805-607-6 (pbk. :
alk. paper)
   1. Faulkner, William, 1897–1962—Criticism and interpretation—
Congresses.   2. Yoknapatawpha County (Imaginary place)—Congresses.
3. Short story—Congresses.   I. Harrington, Evans.   II. Abadie, Ann J.
PS3511.A86Z783211275   1992
813'.52—dc20   92-35761
                                                                    CIP

British Library Cataloging-in-Publication data available

IN MEMORIAM,

Carvel Collins
1912-1990

James Hinkle
1924-1990

Elizabeth M. Kerr
1905-1990

Contents

Introduction   ix
EVANS HARRINGTON

A Note on the Conference   xiv

Shortened Stories: Faulkner and the Market   3
JOHN T. MATTHEWS

Faulkner's Short Story Writing and the Oldest Profession   38
JAMES B. CAROTHERS

Beyond Genre? Existential Experience in Faulkner's Short Fiction   62
HANS H. SKEI

"Carcassonne," "Wash," and the Voices of Faulkner's Fiction   78
DAVID MINTER

"Ad Astra" through New Haven: Some Biographical Sources of
Faulkner's War Fiction   108
CARVEL COLLINS

Contending Narratives: *Go Down, Moses* and the Short Story
Cycle   128
SUSAN V. DONALDSON

Knight's Gambit: Poe, Faulkner, and the Tradition of the
Detective Story   149
JOHN T. IRWIN

Faulkner's Short Stories and Novels in China   174
TAO JIE

Go Down, Moses and the Ascetic Imperative   206
ROBERT H. BRINKMEYER, JR.

"He Come and Spoke for Me": Scripting Lucas Beauchamp's
Three Lives   229
PHILIP M. WEINSTEIN

Faulkner's Advice to a Young Writer   253
  JOAN WILLIAMS

Soviet Perceptions of Faulkner's Short Stories   263
  SERGEI CHAKOVSKY/MAYA KORENEVA/EKATERINA STETSENKO/
  TATIANA MOROZOVA/TAMARA DENISOVA

Contributors   286

Index   291

Introduction

From contributors to this volume we learn that the first works by Faulkner to be published in Chinese and in Russian were his short stories. As the contributors point out, the reason was a very practical one: Faulkner is hard to translate, and short stories are short. For similar practical reasons, most readers of Faulkner everywhere probably first encounter him in one of his short stories. Publishers of anthologies of American literature, and therefore their editors, have to conserve space. Publishers of short story collections need to pay the lowest royalty fees. Teachers can demand only so much reading of their students. Therefore, "A Rose for Emily," "Barn Burning," and/or "That Evening Sun."

And though aficionados of Faulkner tend to forget it, and to groan about the monotonous appearance of these chestnuts in anthology after anthology, first encounters with them are often enthralling, frequently turning readers into aficionados who groan about them as chestnuts. In my case, here in Mississippi on New Year's morning, 1949, the story (not a chestnut then) was "That Evening Sun," the most powerful reading experience I have ever had. Three times I laid it aside, unable to bear the terror and hopelessness of Nancy; and the next year, in a graduate course under Harry Modean Campbell, I wrote a forty-page analysis of it, trying to find out how Faulkner had achieved this unprecedented effect on me. I never satisfied myself with an answer to that question, but I became a devoted Faulkner reader—and I learned more about effective storytelling than I have in any other endeavor.

But the importance of Faulkner's short stories is not just the pragmatic one suggested here. The number of his short story masterpieces, estimated at a dozen by one of the contributors to this volume, rivals or exceeds those of most writers known especially for their short stories, such as Poe. And it is hard to think of another writer of novels—Henry James is a possibility—whose achievement in both novel and short story equals Faulkner's. Given this primary importance of Faulkner's short stories, it seems a testament to the power and richness of his novels that he is generally considered "The Novelist as Short Story Writer," as Hans Skei, a contributor to this volume and one of the most knowledgeable students of Faulkner's short stories, phrases it.[1] And it is somewhat embarrassing to at least this administrator of the University of Mississippi's annual Faulkner and Yoknapatawpha Conference that it was not until our seventeenth conference—at which the following papers were presented in the summer of 1990—that we got around to focusing on Faulkner as short story writer.

Given the opportunity, however, our speakers brought profound, original insights to the subject. John T. Matthews, in "Shortened Stories: Faulkner and the Market," merely begins with the well-known fact of Faulkner's frustration and resentment of commercial restrictions by mass market magazines, and demonstrates convincingly the surprising circumstance that the compression and curtailment required by magazines like the *Saturday Evening Post* actually helped Faulkner to put in the foreground criticisms of commercialism which in a longer, more detailed account might have been relegated to background. In "There Was a Queen" and "Mule in the Yard," for instance, "the [commercially requisite] sundering of fiction from context releases the actors to dispute or challenge the [commercial] determinants of their behavior."

James B. Carothers, in "Faulkner's Short Story Writing and the Oldest Profession," carefully and ironically investigates Faulkner's frequently expressed feeling that writing for the mass markets was whoring, and concludes that perhaps it was whoring but that we should take a "charitable view" of both sexual and literary prosti-

tutes, including Faulkner, because otherwise, as readers of his stories, we would cast ourselves as voyeurs like Popeye in *Sanctuary*.

Hans Skei suggests, in "Beyond Genre? Existential Experience
in Faulkner's Short Fiction," that the short story is particularly
suited to the rendering of that kind of experience denoted by the
current term existential—experiences that pose "questions regarding choice, freedom, suffering, anxiety, absurdity, death, but
also . . . the struggle to create oneself"—and demonstrates how
Faulkner effectively creates such stories in some of his early
sketches and stories, notably "The Hill" and "Mountain Victory."

In a deeply informed, beautifully expressed meditation on
Faulkner's development as a writer, David Minter, in "'Carcassonne,' 'Wash,' and the Voices of Faulkner's Fiction," demonstrates how Faulkner discovered in early stories like "Carcassonne"
that he could "commit himself to what James called *the real* and
the romance, making interplay his mode and his goal, and resolution a thing to be deferred rather than forced." Later, in a story
like "Wash" this use of interplay achieved a powerful story, but,
still later, in *Absalom, Absalom!* Faulkner enriched the account of
Wash Jones even more by pushing even further his use of interplay and postponement of resolution. The interplaying voices of
Faulkner's fiction speak to our own need for the real and romance,
giving Faulkner's works a rare power.

The late Carvel Collins was to have delivered a paper at this
conference, but he died in April 1990. His good friend and
admirer, Lawrence Wells, delivered a eulogy for him and read
his paper, "'Ad Astra' through New Haven: Some Biographical
Sources of Faulkner's War Fiction." As always, Carvel Collins
provided in this last contribution to knowledge about William
Faulkner information only he possessed.

As John Matthews found in the constrictions required by mass
magazines an unexpected strength for Faulkner's fiction, Susan V.
Donaldson, in "Contending Narratives: *Go Down, Moses* and the
Short Story Cycle," finds that the seven stories of *Go Down,*

Moses derive vitality and significance by struggling against the patriarchial narrative of the McCaslin family which dominates *Go Down, Moses* as a whole.

In *"Knight's Gambit*: Poe, Faulkner, and the Tradition of the Detective Story," John T. Irwin presents a subtle, many-faceted analysis of Faulkner's use of the tradition of the detective story begun by Edgar Allan Poe.

Though Chinese scholar Tao Jie discusses both "Faulkner's Novels and Short Stories in China," general knowledge about the reception of Faulkner's work in China is so scant that her in-depth discussion is highly rewarding. General knowledge is equally scant about the reception of Faulkner's work in the Soviet Union, so that the comments about "Soviet Perceptions of Faulkner's Short Stories" by five Soviet scholars are equally rewarding.

Two final discussions of *Go Down, Moses*—which drew the bulk of attention in the 1990 conference, as one or another Faulkner work does each year—are fresh and thought-provoking. Robert Brinkmeyer, in *"Go Down, Moses* and the Ascetic Imperative," contrasts as two extremes of asceticism Ike McCaslin's eremitic withdrawal from his tainted heritage and Adolph Hitler's cenobitic creation of a "community . . . based on a monastic ideal." Both were failures, of course, and Brinkmeyer suggests that Faulkner himself saw a mean, a middle way, in two characters in *Go Down, Moses*: Molly Beauchamp, with her willingness to sacrifice for the well-being of the community, but her sturdy insistence on what she is convinced is right; and Gavin Stevens, with his, albeit flawed, "commitment to working within the community and its structures, doing his best at helping others."

Philip Weinstein, in "'He Come and Spoke for Me': Lucas Beauchamp's Three Lives," concentrates most of his discussion on *Go Down, Moses*, but he begins with Faulkner's magazine story about Lucas Beauchamp and concludes with his treatment of Lucas in *Intruder in the Dust*. He examines with a clear, unsparing, but never harsh eye what he finds to be Faulkner's failure to render or even finally allow the black part of Lucas Beauchamp.

Joan Williams, a highly accomplished writer in her own right and one too often thought of only as someone to whom Faulkner was drawn, read her story "The Morning and the Evening" at the conference. Her remarks about Faulkner's advice to her about writing are printed here, a valuable addition to the volume.

Evans Harrington
The University of Mississippi
Oxford, Mississippi

NOTE

1. *William Faulkner: The Novelist as Short Story Writer* (Oslo: Universitetsforlaget, 1985).

A Note on the Conference

The Seventeenth Annual Faulkner and Yoknapatawpha Conference sponsored by the University of Mississippi in Oxford took place from July 29 through August 3, 1990, with over 250 persons from forty-one states and seven foreign countries in attendance. The six-day program on the theme "Faulkner and the Short Story" featured the lectures collected in this volume. The literary scholars who delivered the lectures also led panel discussions on "The Stories and the Faulkner Canon" and "Faulkner's Stories and the World Outside" during sessions for small groups.

Sunday was perhaps the busiest, most varied beginning the conference has ever had. The University Museums presented "Faulkner's Mississippi," an exhibition, with gallery lecture, by photographer William Albert Allard. Afterwards, at Faulkner's home, Rowan Oak, Joan Williams presented the third annual Eudora Welty Awards to two young Mississippi writers, Edward T. Chaney of Jackson and Julie Barnes of Fulton, and George Plimpton announced the winners of the first Faux Faulkner write-alike contest, coordinated by the author's niece, Dean Faulkner Wells, and sponsored by American Airlines' *American Way* magazine, Yoknapatawpha Press and its *Faulkner Newsletter*, and the University. First-place winner Saul Rosenberg, a Columbia University graduate student from London, England, read his entry, "Delta Faulkner," following an address by Plimpton. He and authors William Styron and Willie Morris judged the contest, which received more than 600 entries. After a buffet supper, held on the lawn of Dr. and Mrs. M. B. Howorth, Jr., and sponsored by *American Way*, the conference sponsors and the Yoknapatawpha Arts Council presented a musical comedy, *The Battle of Harrykin Creek*, based on Faulkner's story "My Grandmother Millard and

General Bedford Forrest and the Battle of Harrykin Creek."
Conference director Evans Harrington wrote the book and lyrics,
and Andrew Fox, professor of music theory at the University,
composed the score for the musical, which premiered at the 1976
conference. After the performance, Square Books hosted a party
for the cast and crew and for conference speakers and registrants.

Besides George Plimpton and Joan Williams, two other distinguished authors spoke at the conference. Willie Morris, writer-in-
residence and director of the Visiting Writers' Program at the
University of Mississippi, gave participants the benefit of his
concentration on Faulkner during his work on *Faulkner's Mississippi*, for which he wrote the text and William Eggleston provided
photographs. Elizabeth Spencer, native Mississippian and winner
of the American Academy of Arts and Letters Award of Merit
Medal for the Short Story, first read a freshly improvised account
of her journeys to Taylor and other rural Yoknapatawpha areas
during the conference and then read from her *Jack of Diamonds*.

"Oxford Women Remember Faulkner," a panel discussion mod-
erated by Chester A. McLarty, featured Mary McClain Hall,
Minnie Ruth Little, and Bessie Summers. Howard Duvall and
John Ramey served as panelists and M. C. Falkner as moderator
for sessions on "William Faulkner of Oxford." Other conference
activities included a slide lecture by J. M. Faulkner and Jo Mar-
shall, sessions on "Teaching Faulkner" conducted by Robert W.
Hamblin and Charles A. Peek, guided tours of North Mississippi,
the annual picnic at Rowan Oak, and a banquet at St. Peter's
Episcopal Church.

Faulkner books, manuscripts, photographs, and memorabilia
were displayed at the University's John Davis Williams Library,
and the Library's Department of Archives and Special Collections
mounted an exhibition of items of the Rowan Oak Papers, nearly
1,800 pages of handwritten working drafts and typescripts of
Faulkner's early novels and short stories found in a closet of his
home on August 31, 1970. Included in the papers are stories that
appeared in *The Unvanquished*, eight different versions of "Liz-

ards in Jamshyd's Courtyard," and the unpublished story "Rose of Lebanon." The University Press of Mississippi again in 1990 exhibited Faulkner books published by university presses throughout the United States. Also, the campus television station and Mississippi ETV aired films relating to Faulkner's life and work and film adaptations of his short stories.

The conference planners are grateful to all the individuals and organizations who support the Faulkner and Yoknapatawpha Conference annually. We offer special thanks to Dr. and Mrs. William C. Baker, Dr. and Mrs. M. B. Howorth, Jr., Dr. and Mrs. C. E. Noyes, Mr. Glennray Tutor, Mr. Richard Howorth of Square Books, St. Peter's Episcopal Church, the City of Oxford, the Yoknapatawpha Arts Council, participants in *The Battle of Harrykin Creek*, and *American Way*, the magazine of American Airlines, and its editor, Mr. Doug Crichton.

Faulkner and the Short Story
FAULKNER AND YOKNAPATAWPHA
1990

Shortened Stories: Faulkner and the Market

John T. Matthews

Let the Post keep this second story until I finish the third and send it to *you* before you talk price, because I think the third story will be the most novel (damn the word) of all.[1]

Faulkner's private remarks about writing short fiction for mass market magazines never stray far from two themes: scorn for the commercialism of the popular medium and cold-blooded calculation about how to take advantage of it. He complains sharply about the simplicities and curtailments urged upon his fiction by writing for national magazines like the *Saturday Evening Post, Scribner's,* the *American Mercury,* and others. Faulkner's resentment at having to finance his longer fiction by writing short stories erupts parenthetically in the letter from which I quoted above. He suggests that the *Saturday Evening Post* be offered a series of stories about the Sartorises (which would appear in book form later as *The Unvanquished*). In an earlier letter, Faulkner authorizes his agent to ask for $1,500 for "Ambuscade," but in this subsequent instruction he suggests holding back the first few stories until they can be offered as a group and so command a higher fee. Touting the appeal of the third story, "Raid," Faulkner accidentally puns on a word that betrays an extreme tension in his writing career at this moment: he plumps the story for being the most "novel," then damns the word for reminding him of the novel he is not writing because he has to convert some of his fictional property into quick cash. During

3

the period in which he wrote all his great short stories, Faulkner held that they interfered with his serious longer work, that novels were being put off to satisfy the story market's appetite for novelty.

Faulkner's brief against mass market short fiction rests on a number of accusations familiar to students of the short story. His complaints exemplify more widespread contemporary fears about the corruptive effects of the mass media on verbal artistry. Often desperate for money in the early thirties, Faulkner was driven to the marketplace. We know that he worked and reworked stories to tune them for the highest-paying magazines, and that he produced short stories at a fearsome rate during the period that followed the completion of *As I Lay Dying* in January of 1930. Faulkner's famous short story sending schedule suggests a Franklinian design on solvency through the typewriter.

His hopes were not misplaced, as we know, since Faulkner earned more from the sale of four short stories to the *Saturday Evening Post* than from his first four novels.[2] Until *Sanctuary* heated up Faulkner's notoriety and attracted Hollywood's bigger money (and intermittently thereafter when even studio contracts were inadequate to his needs), Faulkner essentially produced a double corpus of novels and short stories. Commonly the stories were extracted from longer work already in preliminary form, and so these sometimes became yet further intermediate stages in the evolution of Faulkner's novels, especially the Snopes material, which developed over thirty years. Faulkner demonstrably kept the two venues for his writing in communication, circulating material back and forth as he needed. But he also chafed under the constrictions of mass market requirements, modified what he wrote to a far greater degree in response to what outside authorities asked, and at least felt more himself as a writer in the novel's more capacious form.

I am less interested in addressing the rather tired question of Faulkner's greatness of achievement as a short story writer, than in examining what his vehement resistance produces within his writing project. Once we acknowledge the reasonable judgment that Faulkner wrote probably a half dozen first-rate stories and another dozen extraordinary ones, and that they might have earned him a fine if minor reputation on their own, I think evaluative criticism actually obscures a number of more instructive questions we might put to Faulkner's work.

Ranking Faulkner's achievement as a short story writer requires us either to pretend that the novels do not exist or to accept them as the frame of reference within which Faulkner's material develops. In the first instance we disfigure the coherence of Faulkner's complex writing project; surely the story writing, like his later work on filmscripts, both diverts and informs his novel writing. Faulkner segregated his marketing of stories and novels, but their composition clearly involved the practice of transforming, recasting, and rearranging a body of material that exceeded common generic boundaries: Yoknapatawpha encompasses sketches, short stories, a play, films, a trilogy, several paired novels, short story cycles, collections, the Viking anthology, expository addenda, and so forth. In the second instance—in asserting the achievement of the stories within Faulkner's whole oeuvre—we inevitably convert the stories into derivations or preliminary sketches of the longer work to which they point. Notice the way the volume of *Uncollected Stories* is arranged by grouping stories according to the novels they orbit. This is a perfectly sensible procedure, and it arises because Faulkner's greatest stories—"The Bear," "That Evening Sun," "Spotted Horses," and "Barn Burning"—all reappear (or preappear) in longer works. (One might argue that even two exceptions to the preceding list— "A Rose for Emily" and "Dry September"—do approximate subsequent novelistic material: Emily Grierson presages Rosa Coldfield, as Will Mayes does Joe Christmas or Lucas Beauchamp.) But Faulkner's extraction and segmentation of some of the Yoknapatawpha material into short form permits him to consider aspects of social and aesthetic developments in the New South that fade when they are absorbed into the master narratives that recon-

struct the mythical histories of the Sartorises, Compsons, Sut-
pens, and Snopeses.

What I would like to propose as an alternative route of exploration proceeds from the consequences of Faulkner's decision to
enter the mass market with his short fiction. We recall that
Faulkner's increasing difficulty in placing his novels at the outset
of his career led him to a partial renunciation of the market. In the
now-famous words of his introduction to a projected new edition
of *The Sound and the Fury*, Faulkner recalls, with some exaggera-
tion, the fate of his third novel, *Sartoris*:

> I wrote Sartoris. It took much longer, and the publisher refused it at
> once. But I continued to shop it about for three years with a stubborn
> and fading hope, perhaps to justify the time which I had spent writing
> it. This hope died slowly, though it didn't hurt at all. One day I
> seemed to shut a door between me and all publishers' addresses and
> book lists. I said to myself, Now I can write.[3]

Apparently freed from market prospects, the novelist can write a
book purely for his own delight and consumption: "Now I can
make myself a vase like that which the old Roman kept at his
bedside and wore the rim slowly away with kissing it" (710).

Such a private economy also appears to organize the experience
of writing his next novel, *As I Lay Dying*, which Faulkner called
his "tour-de-force." Faulkner's denial of market awareness does
accord with readers' reactions and with sales: these novels were no
bestsellers, and Faulkner could never have imagined for them the
10,000 buyers he expected for *Sanctuary*. He turned back to the
market, perhaps with equal vehemence, in composing *Sanctuary*
in 1929 after publishing *The Sound and the Fury*, in revising it in
1931, after publishing *As I Lay Dying*, and in launching his
campaign to place short stories in January 1930 after drafting *As I
Lay Dying*. Faulkner submitted more stories to the *Saturday
Evening Post* than any other magazine because it paid the highest
fees ("Red Leaves" fetched $750, for example); it could do so
because it had the widest circulation (and commensurate advertis-

ing revenues) though perhaps the lowest brow of any on Faulkner's list. What does it mean to Faulkner's writing for him to produce it under conditions he deeply resists yet to which he must subscribe?

My method will not be to examine the requirements of successful mass market fiction and then show their influence on what Faulkner wrote. Formulas inarguably exerted pressure on what the would-be story writer produced.[4] But any writer's conformity to generic or material constraint is complicated by resistances and critical reflections generated by such straitening. We should expect these effects to be all the more prominent in a writer like Faulkner, who tirelessly interrogates the premises of fictionmaking in all his work. I want to examine how a body of Faulkner's short fiction internalizes the conditions of the literary marketplace, and how several of his early short stories represent the circumstances of their own production. How do Faulkner's stories incorporate formally and thematically the sense of curtailment or abbreviation, the processes of aesthetic commodification, and the nature of mass cultural consumption? Do the stories practice forms of resistance to the market's demands? Can we see his short fiction challenge the conditions that enable it—in the spirit of ideological reflection we now recognize in his greatest novels?

MONEY AND THE MAGAZINES

When Faulkner submitted a story, probably "Red Leaves," to *Scribner's* early in 1930, his cover letter explained why it should be accepted:

> So here is another story. Few people know that Miss. Indians owned slaves, that's why I suggest that you all buy it. Not because it is a good story; you can find lots of good stories. It's because I need the money. . . . And that's why magazines get published, is it not? To get bought and re-bought. (SL 46–47)

Faulkner's flippancy hardly conceals his scorn for the commercialism of mass circulation, advertising-supported magazines. To

Faulkner, literary magazines differed only in degree from coarser variants that capitalized on the most basic desires. The worst of these were like the ones that showed up in Oxford's magazine store, which "carries nothing that has not either a woman in her underclothes or someone shooting someone else with a pistol on the cover" (*SL* 43).

The mass-circulation cultural magazines were not this bad, and some of them marked out relatively sophisticated audiences for themselves. Faulkner no doubt recognized the difference between the positions in the market of two of his favorite targets for submission—the *Saturday Evening Post* and *Scribner's*. The *Post* was edited by George Lorimer, whose political conservatism embraced isolationism, immigration limits, and anti-FDR sentiment, and whose editorship led the magazine to celebrate what its detractors characterized as "crass materialism" and heavily formulaic writing.[5] On the other hand, when Alfred Dashiell took over *Scribner's* in 1930, he immediately began both moving it toward the political left and reiterating its commitment to serious fiction by major writers. He serialized *Tender Is the Night*, for example, and his assistant wrote enthusiastic letters to Faulkner about *Scribner's* permanent interest in the Snopes stories: "We consider you one of the greatest writers alive and want to use everything of yours that is humanly possible."[6] But even when Faulkner was sympathetic with the higher mindedness or sophistication of magazines like *Scribner's* or Mencken's *American Mercury*, he held fast to his principle of looking for the best fee, and that usually meant trying the *Post* first.[7] As the "Red Leaves" letter makes clear, this was business.

Money determined many of the conditions associated with magazine publishing in the early twentieth century. The era of the cheap magazine had culminated at the turn of the century. Magazines became national in scope as they were transformed into instruments for market formation by large companies. It was advertising revenue that determined success; expanded circulation drove up desirability to advertizers but contributed little to the income of the magazines. Mass readership meant a reduction in the level of the contents' sophistication for most magazines, and it led to briefer articles and features for the modern consumer, who had less time for leisure, extended reflection, and singularity of attention.[8]

Faulkner registers these factors in remarks about his short story composition. It was very difficult for Faulkner to shorten narrative since his imagination tended toward expansion, layering, and repetition. Everyone will recall his complaint about Ben Wasson's cutting of the manuscript of *Flags in the Dust:* "A cabbage has grown, matured. You look at that cabbage; it is not symmetrical; you say, I will trim this cabbage off and make it art; I will make it resemble a peacock or a pagoda or 3 doughnuts. Very good, I say; you do that, then the cabbage will be dead." Wasson's laconic response measures the economic incentive to do just this kind of cutting: "Then we'll make some kraut out of it. . . . The same amount of sour kraut will feed twice as many people as cabbage."[9] In 1934 Faulkner says he is having trouble with the *Post* stories about the Sartorises because "I seem to have more material than I can compress" (*SL* 81). The requirement that fiction be short we may take to represent the violence to their work felt by many authors as they produced for mass circulation journals.

As mass media like the cheap magazine threatened to revolutionize cultural production as completely as other forms of modernization and mechanization were revolutionizing social institutions and economic relations, a few voices arose in protest. As the market grew crowded not only with weeklies and monthlies filled with short fiction and features but also with dozens of how-to books for cashing in on the escalating short story demands, at least one commentator linked the popularity of short fiction and the mechanization of everyday life.

In an impassioned if bizarrely impressionistic diatribe against the common magazine short story, Edward J. O'Brien addresses this problem in a book entitled *The Dance of the Machines: The American Short Story and the Industrial Age,* which appeared in

1929. In fact, the book is even more ambitious than its title suggests since it identifies some thirty attributes of the machine and finds their counterparts in the organization of the modern army and in the short story:

> American life has been chiefly shaped for our generation by the spiritual dictatorship of machinery, warfare, and magazines and newspapers of large circulation. To these shaping influences are now to be added the motion picture, the radio, the gramophone, the automobile, the corporation, queen-bee finance, and all forms of national and international advertising and propaganda.[10]

O'Brien lists traits of the machine such as interchangeability, standardization, impersonalization, mass production, homogenization, acceleration, and commodification (with the accompanying necessity of stimulating acquisitive desire). Such a description leads predictably to a characterization of the modern individual as similarly dehumanized and commodified (as both producer and consumer). O'Brien sees the emergence of the short story as the mechanistic literary form par excellence. O'Brien points to the following ingredients of the successful American short story. He points to its photographic accuracy; its conformity to pattern and manufacture by imaginative mass production; the "cheapness" of its stock characters, plots, and emotions; the interchangeability of its human types; the haste and brevity of the desired reading experience; the advertising environment that surrounds it page by page in the usual magazine format; its representation of current fashions and desires; its "mass production of public opinion and standards" (145); and the profound commodification of the cultural product. As an example of this last point, O'Brien cites an advertisement for *Liberty* magazine appearing in its own pages that trumpets increased circulation: "We know of no comparable record in the magazine business. Or in any business in a perishable product *where spoiled and unsold goods may be returned.*"[11]

As a cultural critic, O'Brien chooses to inveigh against the mechanization of fiction taking place in the modern magazine story. But as a practicing writer of fiction, Faulkner adopts a far more complex set of strategies for dealing with the market he occupied, manipulated, and resisted. O'Brien must have concurred that Faulkner's stories transcended the norm, for he selected stories by Faulkner for his *Best Short Stories of 1935* and *Best Short Stories of 1936*. I want to suggest in the balance of my paper how a number of Faulkner's early stories internalize and reflect critically upon the conditions under which short stories were produced and consumed in early modern American culture.

Obscene Letters

Many of Faulkner's earliest short stories reflect on their status as mass cultural products. One primary objective for a commodity is to establish its desirability in its market. National advertisers very early saw the advantage of binding together physical, financial, intellectual, and emotional desires in order to stimulate acquisitiveness and to suggest the pleasures of consumption. O'Brien sees that capitalist producers use the national magazines in such a way "that the consumer's desires have been artificially stimulated by national advertising, and in most cases even artificially created" (85). Like other participating students of the cultural marketplace, Faulkner understood that the saleable and the salacious were indivisible. *Sanctuary* proves it, but an earlier related story, "There Was a Queen," takes the erotics of commodified letters as a central theme.

Scribner's published "There Was a Queen" in January 1933. It recounts an episode in Narcissa Benbow Sartoris's widowhood in which she discovers that eleven obscene letters sent to her by a former bank bookkeeper thirteen years earlier have not disappeared with their author, who stole them back from her the evening he fled Jefferson. Instead, they have been recovered by the FBI agent working on the case. Mortified by their existence and the shame of having kept them, Narcissa offers to have sex with the agent in order to get them back. When she tells her dead husband's great aunt what she has done, the shock kills that last avatar of Sartoris pride.

From a variety of standpoints Faulkner investigates the binding together of the erotic and the economic in Narcissa's letters. In the first place, the letters originate from an ambivalent social and sexual position. Narcissa reminds Aunt Jenny Sartoris that "you remember that night after Bayard and I were married when somebody broke into our house in town; the same night that book-keeper in Colonel Sartoris' bank stole that money and ran away? The next morning the letters were gone, and then I knew who had sent them" (739). The bookkeeper—who remains unnamed in the story—produces the letters because he cannot more directly transgress the class lines that segregate the regal Sartoris women. The fictional romance that the letters must tell mediates and artificially gratifies socially prohibited desire. Thus they function like mass literature in stimulating desires for a vast array of pleasures that can be possessed only vicariously, voyeuristically, in the pages of the magazine. The story makes this connection explicitly but subtly when we notice what the daughter of Sartoris's black servant is doing as she discusses Narcissa's behavior with her mother: "[Elnora's] daughter Saddie sat at the table, eating from a dish of cold turnip greens and looking at a thumbed and soiled fashion magazine" (CS 729).

Narcissa has allowed the letters to soil her, too. They corrupt her in part because she consumes them vicariously as sexual attention. She keeps them, reading and rereading them in the privacy of her bedroom. The obscene letters fill up a vacancy in her life, producing and gratifying desire as a ritual of consumption. The materiality of the letters means that they can be enjoyed repeatedly; like other commodities they store up in physical form the labor of production and the pleasure of possession. The iterability of the consumer's reading, however, cannot be separated from a less pleasant consequence. Once the bookkeeper has retaken and then lost the letters, they become public property. Now the iterability of consumption permits the formation of a mass audience of impersonal readers: Narcissa says, "I thought of people, men, reading them, seeing not only my name on them, but the marks of my eyes where I had read them again and again. . . . It was like I was having to sleep with all the men in the world at the same time" (*CS* 739–40). Faulkner suggests the anxieties of both author and reader in the marketplace—that both will leave traces of the desires, emotions, identifications, and gratification that they purloin from letters.

One of the most striking effects of Faulkner's short stories is the extent to which they comprehend emancipatory social movements. Many critics have been tempted to read "There Was a Queen" strictly from Aunt Virginia Du Pre's perspective—as a shocked retreat from the vulgarities of a world bereft of tradition, dignity, and a firm sense of hierarchy.[12] Surely Aunt Jenny's proud defense of Sartoris virtue against Yankee opportunism, her household's unswerving belief in "quality" against "trash," and her insistence on racial purity against pressure from Jews, blacks, and others may seem to be endorsed by the story's tribute to her passing. All of Faulkner's provisional titles signal an era's eclipse, a point of passage: "An Empress Passed," "Through the Window," and "There Was a Queen."

But the fragmentary nature of the short story form—its necessary sense of compression, its severance from historical context, its foregrounding of moment and anecdote, its attention to minor or marginal phenomena—these attributes of its very *shortness* make it an effective vehicle for representing material often subordinate in more comprehensive fictional forms. In a provocative meditation on short story writing, William Carlos Williams muses on the opportunities short fiction presents the writer. Among them is the responsibility to portray the empirical reality that frames any work of fiction. Williams thinks about a story he wrote in 1932: "looking back upon it, what were the elements involved in my coming upon the short story as a means?—that is during The Depression?. . . I lived among these people. I knew them and saw the essential qualities, (not stereotype) the courage, the humor (an accident) the deformity, the basic tragedy of their lives—and the *importance* of it. . . . Why the short story? Not for a sales article but as I had conceived them. The briefness of their chronicles, its brokenness and heterogeneity—isolation, color. A novel was unthinkable."[13] The broken, brief form of the short story accommodates the heterogeneity and deformity of the lives of the underclasses. It should not surprise us that one of Williams's main examples is Gertrude Stein's cubistic *Three Lives*, particularly "Melanctha," which creates the subjectivity of a poor black female by dismantling traditional realistic narrative.

The abruptness with which Narcissa strikes her deal suggests an imaginative zone in which a great many new forms of behavior are being released. Aunt Jenny and the loyal black servant Elnora may uphold the unquestioned acceptance of tradition, for example, but the next generation of blacks stands ready to challenge former assertions. A comic interlude has Elnora trying to retell Aunt Jenny's legend of traveling from Carolina all by herself to rejoin her brother, John Sartoris: "All the way from Cal-lina, with Her folks all killed and dead except old Marse John, and him two hundred miles away in Missippi" (732).

> "It's moren two hundred miles from here to Cal-lina," Isom said. "Learnt that in school. It's nigher two thousand."
> Elnora's hands did not cease. She did not seem to have heard him.
> ". . . Then She begun to cry, and old Marse John holding her, after all them four thousand miles—"
> "It ain't four thousand miles from here to Cal-lina," Isom said. "Ain't but two thousand. What the book say in school." (732–33)

Isom speaks as a newly informed product of universal education in the South; his emancipation as a black depends on his correcting antebellum myth with the firm pressure of historical and geographical accuracy.[14]

The passing of queens like Aunt Jenny signals the break-up of an aristocracy whose pretense to exemption from the world of social change and economic exchange conceals their continued enjoyment of privilege as the product of oppression. Colonel Sartoris owned slaves and a plantation and then moved into banking. The story's perfectly realized conclusion disguises the violence of social reversal and eclipse marked by the death of Virginia Du Pre. Her moribund form sits "in the wheel chair beside the window framed by the sparse and defunctive Carolina glass" she has installed in her bedroom (742). But Elnora's behavior suggests the actual turbulence and confusion of new practices, such as Narcissa's brazen transaction. Elnora breaks off her sentence and disappears awkwardly from the scene the Sartorises have dominated: Elnora muses, "'I wished I knowed what been going on here this last week. . . .' [ellipses in original]. . . . Then she left the room. She did not go hurriedly, yet her long silent stride carried her from sight with an abruptness like that of an inanimate figure drawn on wheels, off a stage" (743). Syntactically and gesturally, the story figures the fragmentation, the leaving off, of a former world. This sensation of shortness in the ending underscores the abruptness of social change as viewed by those being displaced.

That the short story encourages the emergence of heterogeneity, as Williams claims, might be confirmed by the defensive posture of "There Was a Queen." The narrator, like Aunt Jenny, displays a hypersensitivity to the transgression of familiar divisions of the world. The story becomes a nightmare of lost distinctions. The narrator reveals that Elnora is Bayard Sartoris's half-sister, and thus the evident product of miscegenation; yet she insists that "I nigger and she [Narcissa] white" (732). Both she and Aunt Jenny struggle to uphold class divisions: "I just say to let quality consort with quality, and unquality do the same thing" (734). This distinction informs the more specific one between "Sartoris" and "outsiders," which in turn becomes the generalization differentiating Southerners, on the one hand, and Yankees and Jews on the other. However, all these categories threaten to collapse into each other. Whites act like blacks, quality like trash, Sartorises like non-Sartorises. The antebellum world, in which subtle difference made all the difference, appears in the laconic recognition of brother and sister at their reunion: "Old Marse John just said, 'Well, Jenny,' and she just said, 'Well, Johnny'" (733). In 1930, however, Isom bluntly summarizes a new order; Sartorises have no more quality than anyone else: "I don't see no difference" (732).

In my reading of "There Was a Queen" I have sought to identify several central features of mass market short fiction that Faulkner internalizes as the subject matter and aesthetic procedures of his work. The story meditates on the commodification and eroticization of the cultural product, on the practice of consumption, and on the emancipatory potential of the short form. In what follows I want to illustrate variations on these critical reflections in a number of other short stories from the same period.

GINGERSNAPS

When the unnamed Texan begins his auction in "Spotted Horses," he signals that a ritual of consumption will take place by taking a "new box of gingersnaps outen his pocket and [biting] the end offen it like a cigar" (US 168). All through his efforts to stimulate bidding, drive up prices, and sell out his stock, the Texan eats gingersnaps automatically. Once, he marks his surprise at a low bid by pausing emphatically: "He taken out that gingersnap box and held it up and looked into it, careful, like it might have been a diamond ring in it, or a spider" (US 170). The analogies belong to the narrator, the sewing-machine salesman Suratt, who measures precisely the distance between the consumers' delusions and reality—between a diamond ring and a spider. Like the Texan and Suratt, Faulkner will look carefully into the box in his early stories, from the multiple standpoints of producer, consumer, and skeptical critic.

Only when you read one of Faulkner's stories in the pages of the magazine in which it originally appeared can you appreciate the pressure of their commercial environment. "Spotted Horses" came out in the June 1931 issue of *Scribner's*; it was the featured and first piece in the number, and directly followed twenty-eight pages of advertising. The first eight of these pages were entitled "The Fifth Avenue Section of Scribner's," a touch that nicely insinuates how an advertising unit might be (mis)taken for one of the magazine's feature sections. After representing a cornucopia of toney products for the affluent reader, the ads shift to the production and consumption of writing. Virtually all of the remaining advertising pages offer to procure books or to teach readers how to become authors themselves. Think how difficult it would be to turn down the invitation on page 16: one trainee of the Newspaper Institute of America, already "encouraged by $100," asks, "How do you KNOW you can't WRITE?"

Scribner's stands on the restrained end of the advertising scale. The more commercial and more widely read *Saturday Evening Post* gobbled up advertising. Theodore Peterson reports that a "monument of sorts was the issue of the *Post* for 7 December 1929. Weighing nearly two pounds, the 272-page magazine contained enough reading matter to keep the average reader occupied for twenty hours and twenty minutes. From the 214 national advertisers appearing in it, Curtis [its publisher] took in revenues estimated at $1,512,000" (23). Reliance on this magnitude of advertising represented a significant historical turnabout, since most nineteenth-century magazine publishers rejected advertisements as cheapening their pages. But the mid-century industrial transformation that took manufacturing out of the home and small shop and created national companies also led to using national magazines as a way to formulate mass audiences for products. Advertising agencies appeared after the Civil War, and by the turn of the century most general magazines had begun "to seek and encourage advertising".[15]

As a prospective contributor, Faulkner must have registered these journals' drives to formulate mass markets both for consumer goods and for reading matter as a nationally distributed product. The format and basis of the general magazines constituting Faulkner's market for short stories appealed to an acquistive mentality. His stories provocatively reflect on the values and practices that frame them. If we return to "Spotted Horses," we might be in a position better to appreciate the performance of acquisition staged by the story.

"Spotted Horses" offers us a critical, because semidetached, perspective on the ritual of mass market transaction. To the men who yearn to buy and possess the spirited, almost otherworldly animals, the horses promise gratification that will somehow ease their disappointed lives. Marginalized by their poverty and incapacitated by the scale of the conditions causing it, the farmers look to the horses as embodiments of the furious, unfettered, hyper-masculine vitality that has forsaken them. The story suggests that Faulkner grasps what T. J. Jackson Lears has called the therapeutic ethos of the early culture of consumption. Americans suffered from "feelings of unreality" stemming "from urbanization and technological development; from the rise of an increasingly inter-dependent market economy; and from the secularization of liberal Protestantism."[16] To cure such anomie came the promise of self-fulfillment through consumption, especially as that promise informed the burden of modern advertising.

The lure of the horses cannot be separated from their flashy uselessness—that is, from their status as commodities. They are mainly indistinguishable from each other, and so might as well be mass produced, but they swirl with color like exotic parrots. They are nothing but image, worthless as work animals. Yet the Texan manages to get his clientele "hotted up" (US 171) by drawing on the mystifying power of group desire. Like successful advertising, the parade of the horses into town does nothing but announce their availability. The customers appear the next morning as if obeying subconscious instructions from a society that consumes. The horses sell because they are there to be bought. The counterweights of need and use are brushed off like Mrs. Armstid's restraining hand. The consumers seem helpless to resist the wasteful, lethal extravagance of purchasing what they want deeply but cannot use. Annexed by the market, they just buy.

Whatever the story's specific interest in the rise of the Snopeses, it is accompanied by the narrator's penetrating look into the heart of the modern mass market. He is himself a salesman, but one who prides himself on a humane and personal economic practice. Suratt tempers his behavior as a functionary of the marketplace by seeking only modest profits, by offering small charities to the needy, by affirming the priority of ties between "neighbors and kinfolks." What Faulkner sees through Suratt's eyes may be that even limited and skeptical engagement countenances the violence of the market. A truly critical look at this economic organization of modern life will have to make a place to express the real suffering of its victims—the "Ah-Ah-Ah-Ah-Ah" of this world's exploited, broken Armstids.

Nice justice must be responsible for placing the short story "Red Leaves" in the *Saturday Evening Post* (25 October 1930) at a time when the magazine had grown "fat" on advertising (Peterson 23). Recall that the bulk of the story involves the effort to track down the deceased Chief Issetibbeha's personal black slave so that he can be buried with his master for service in the hereafter. The slave has fled upon learning of the chief's death; the story recounts the Indians' patient outlasting of the black man, who surrenders some days after the chief's son and successor, Moketubbe, joins the hunt. Much of the story's macabre comedy derives from this figure, an obese, immobile, normally catatonic mass who must be hauled through the wilderness on his royal litter. Moketubbe's singular passion appears to be a pair of tiny red slippers purchased on a European tour by his father.

In the letter I quoted at the beginning of my paper, Faulkner remarks the novelty of this story about Indian slaveholders, a curiosity in slavery's peculiar history in America. Important as the story's representation of the Hydraheaded atrocity of antebellum slavery is, however, the context I have sought to establish for the short stories might also lead us to see it as a reflection on modern American society's enslavement to the principle of acquisition. To begin with, these Indians more resemble cigar store than ethnographic figures. Faulkner admitted that he knew little of Indian culture and essentially made up what he needed.[17] The society he made up caricatures his own. The two principal characters are a pair of Indians described as "squat men, a little solid, burgherlike; paunchy" (CS 313). One of them wears "an enameled snuffbox" in his ear (313).

These Indians prove among the most sophisticated and jaded consumers in all of Yoknapatawpha. Chief Issetibbeha acquires tastes for an astonishing array of finery—from imported French gilt beds to girandoles and slippers with red heels. The tribe's ultimate degeneration into decadence results from a fateful decision of Issetibbeha's father, however. In a loincloth-to-riches story, this self-made chief comes to be known as Doom, makes a fortune gambling in New Orleans, takes the Grand Tour through Europe, and returns to Mississippi as head man of his tribe. Disastrously, however, he marries his wife under the offices of "a combination itinerant minister and slave trader" (318). "After that, Doom began to acquire more slaves and to cultivate some of his land, as the white people did. But he never had enough for them to do" (318). Like their Indian masters, the "transplanted" Africans live in idleness; between them, these uncertain masters and unwilling slaves have created what the story calls "the Negro question" (319). Issitebbeha completes the imitation of the white slaveholder by turning his slaves into breeders. The chief's capital now derives from producing slaves for the market.

The third generation Moketubbe has been reduced to the "complete and unfathomable lethargy" (320) of the utterly sated consumer. Only the entirely useless, purely decorative red slippers rouse his attention. Encased in the prison of his engorged flesh, he is already dead. The slave, conversely, learns that his will to live exceeds his control, but he cannot protect even his bodily survival from the machine of possession. The black slave will lose his life because the rights of property in this culture extend even to the dead. The masters want everything and take it. In a moment of immense pathos, the starving captive is offered a last meal: "He put the food into his mouth and chewed it, but chewing, the half-masticated matter began to emerge from the corners of his mouth and to drool down his chin, onto his chest, and after a while he stopped chewing and sat there, naked, covered with dried mud, the plate on his knees, and his mouth filled with a mass of chewed food, open, his eyes wide and unceasing, panting and panting" (340). Appearing in the stuffed pages of the *Post* during the Depression, this becomes a remarkable image of the marginal man in a senselessly acquisitive society. His balked act of consumption indicts a social order—and the long history of its class and racial valences—that so extremely dooms some to surfeit and others to want.

"Lizards in Jamshyd's Courtyard" self-consciously contrasts several kinds of mass consumption and so comments on its own status as a work of art in the age of commodification. Between its magazine readership and the story's central spectacle—Henry Armstid's digging for buried treasure on the Old Frenchman's place—intervenes a represented audience, the hill folk who arrived at the end of each day to watch Armstid's delusion play itself out. They possess a quality of "holiday, of escape and of immolation like that of people going to the theater to see tragedy" (*US* 135). They watch silently with "the rapt and static interest of a crowd watching a magician at a fair" (137). Though Armstid's "monstrous" folly causes talk among them as they leave, no one will break the "decorum" of audience detachment in order to stop Henry or help his wife. The ritualized spectacle of Armstid's digging and his wife's hopeless assistance remains untouched by the "spectators"'s interest. Surely this *cordon sanitaire* reflects the safety of armchair consumption enjoyed by the readers of the *Post*, who are free to derive entertainment from the representation of misery.[18] By internalizing the act of passive consumption, Faulkner makes his audience his subject. The spectators themselves become a part of the spectacle beheld by the magazine audience: "From both directions they came up the valley, each in its own slow dust, with a quality profound and dramatic, like the painted barge which they hauled across the stage in Ben Hur" (*US* 135).[19]

Though the internal audience comprises Armstid's kindred peasants, their capacities to intervene have been largely neutralized by the new techniques of manipulation practiced by Flem Snopes in the hamlet. Flem remains silent and inscrutable, his power arising from the invisibility of his methods and motives. He is like a proto-corporate manager, everywhere evident but never seen exercising power. The narrator Suratt notes Flem's mystification of power: "That's what makes me so mad about it. . . . That he can set still and know what I got to work so hard to find out" (141).

The mass of the peasants can only digest Armstid's victimization. Surprisingly, the wily Suratt has also been tricked by Flem's ruse in salting the Old Frenchman's place grounds with buried coins and then concocting a faked interest in the property he eventually sells for his asking price. Though Suratt's humor supposedly constitutes an alternative to the harsh opportunism of Flem, in fact Suratt retails his humor as devotedly as his sewing machines and other goods. The narrator observes that he "achieve[s] his anecdote skillfully above the guffaws" (148) or that he goes about "getting his sober and appreciative laugh" (141). His humor aims to ingratiate the salesman; it is no mere routine, it is instrumental. To this extent Suratt's humor obscures his participation in the same market and practices as the inhuman Flem. The story spotlights Flem's coldblooded production of historical worth; he capitalizes on the newer South's credulous belief in the continuing value of the Old South. But the story downplays Suratt's implication in the process of making such contemporary history into amusing anecdotes, in part because this function too closely resembles the short story writer's. Faulkner uncomfortably broaches the resemblance between his and Suratt's retailing of Southern color, their fabrication of Southern material. With his narrator and accomplice, Faulkner too must "[fill] up the holes and [remove] the traces of their labor" (146).

One of Faulkner's most penetrating studies of cultural consumption turns up in "Dry September," a story ostensibly about the psychosexual basis of racial bigotry in the South. "Dry September" appeared in *Scribner's* in January of 1931. It recounts the apparent murder of a black man, Will Mayes, by an impromptu vigilante band of Jefferson townsmen, who act upon the white Minnie Cooper's allegation that something has happened to her. The narrator takes pains to point out immediately that no one ever verifies or even learns the specific accusation, but the defenders of female "honor" and racial "purity" do not care about justice: "McLendon whirled on the third speaker. 'Happen? What the hell difference does it make? Are you going to let the black sons get away with it until one really does it?'" (171–72).

McLendon's contradictory reasoning indicates the issue I want to pursue in the story, its consideration of how the mass media produce a reality suited to the desires of its consumers and also produce audience desires suited to its reality. McLendon and his fellows lynch Mayes because the collective fantasy of his action is truer than any factual evidence; the community grants greater authority to "the rumor, the story, whatever it was" (*CS* 169) as an image that now must be entertained than to the particular history of any individual. While vicious, even fatal gossip may be the blight of organic communities immemorially, but there is something new about 1930 Jefferson's response to a "spinster's" fantasies of racial transgression.

Late in the story we learn that Minnie Cooper breaks her seclusion after the "event" and Mayes's murder by joining some of her female friends for a movie:

> They reached the picture show. It was like a miniature fairyland with its lighted lobby and colored lithographs of life caught in its

terrible and beautiful mutations. Her lips began to tingle. In the dark, when the picture began, it would be all right. . . . So she hurried on before the turning faces, the undertones of low astonishment, and they took their accustomed places where she could see the aisle against the silver glare and the young men and girls coming in two and two against it.

The lights flicked away; the screen glowed silver, and soon life began to unfold, beautiful and passionate and sad, while still the young men and girls entered, scented and sibilant in the half dark, their paired backs in silhouette delicate and sleek, their slim, quick bodies awkward, divinely young, while beyond them the silver dream accumulated, inevitably on and on. (181).

This passage strikes to the heart of the American culture industry. The layers of vicarious gratification accumulate from the moment the customer enters the "fairyland" of the lobby. Only life "caught" in lithographs and then animated on the silver screen brings a tingle to Minnie's lips. Only the shadowy young men and women, who are themselves sublimating erotic desire into the consumption of standardized silver dreams, incarnate the unreality of youthful beauty made permanent.

Minnie's "accustomed place" as a moviegoer stems from her marginalization by a society that has eroticized the commodity as it has commodified eros. In her later thirties at the time of the story, Minnie had once taken a lover who quite publicly abandoned her. Now she shops for exotic lingerie with her friends in town, but she knows that she has lost her appeal: "she passed and went on along the serried store fronts, in the doors of which the sitting and lounging men did not even follow her with their eyes any more" (175). However, when the story of her "outrage" and its resolution reaches the ears of the public, she senses that she has temporarily restored her allure:

They entered the square, she in the center of the group, fragile in her fresh dress. She was trembling worse. She walked slower and slower, as children eat ice cream, her head up and her eyes bright in the haggard banner of her face, passing the hotel and the coatless drummers in chairs along the curb looking around at her: "That's the one: see? The one in pink in the middle." . . . Then the drug store, where even the young men lounging in the doorway tipped their hats and followed with their eyes the motion of her hips and legs when she passed. (181)

The narrator lingers on the psychopathology of consumption by describing to excess scenes of mediated sexual display and regard. The story in part identifies the capacity of mass market imaginative forms like cinema or magazines to stimulate sexual desire and then simulate gratification. On the way to the movies, Minnie actually ends up consuming the consumption of her story: "as children eat ice cream," she savors the feasting gaze of her audience. Even Minnie's friends crave a vicarious reliving: "'Do you feel strong enough to go out?' they said, their eyes bright too, with a dark glitter. 'When you have had time to get over the shock, you must tell us what happened. What he said and did; everything'" (180).

The brilliance of "Dry September" emerges not only in the power of Faulkner's analysis of cultural commodification, but also in his suggestion of critique. The last frame of the story portrays the head vigilante, McLendon, as he returns home late the night of the murder. He finds his wife waiting, "her face lowered, a magazine in her hands" (182). McLendon strikes her to impress his rage at what he considers her meddlesomeness. The vicarious, even voyeuristic indulgence of sexual passion objectifies women in this culture. There is no authorized place for their subjectivities, for desire as *they* might define it. McLendon's wife and other women in the stories get defined alternatively as objects of desire or obstacles to its fulfillment, but rarely as origins of desire.[20]

The sublimation of repressed instincts in the consumption of mass entertainment, however, does not survive "Dry September" unchallenged. Like the black slave's gagging in "Red Leaves," Minnie Cooper's vicarious gratification breaks down. As the silver dream accumulates, she begins to laugh hysterically. Her friends return her to home and try to hush her, but "soon the laughing

welled again and her voice rose screaming" (182). This utterance
marks the surplus of partial sublimation. It expresses the violence
done to blacks and women in American society as they become
agent and object of screened dramas of white male desires, desires played out vicariously in the products of the culture industry.

NEKKID MEAT

My final two illustrations of the impingement of mass market
consciousness on Faulkner's short story writing both take up
Snopesism. Though "Centaur in Brass" and "Mule in the Yard"
examine the relentlessness of Snopesian greed, they also both
stage defeats for Snopeses. In each case the victor belongs to a
group normally at great disadvantage: in "Centaur" two black
workers conspire to outwit their boss, Flem Snopes; in "Mule"
the widow Mannie Hait settles a longstanding inequity in a
business relation with I. O. Snopes. Yet the stories also divide in
their treatment of female subjectivity, an issue, as I have been
suggesting, crucial to the manipulation of desire in the mass
market.

"Centaur in Brass" appeared in the *American Mercury* in February 1932. The story briskly summarizes Flem's early successes
and his triumph over Suratt in the Frenchman's Place deal.
"Centaur" openly identifies Flem's excess: "that technically unas-
sailable opportunism which passes with country folks—and town
folks, too—for honest shrewdness" (*CS* 149). Later, as the anonymous narrator develps his anecdote, he bluntly refers to Flem's
"greed" in plotting to steal brass parts from the power plant he
supervises. Complicating his invariant acquisitiveness, however,
is Flem's necessary reliance on his victims to further his ends.

The story superimposes two triangular relations: one involves
Flem, his wife Eula, and his patron Major Hoxey; the other
involves the night and day shift power plant employees, Tom-Tom
and Turl, and Tom-Tom's wife. The first triangle fades into the
second, making the blacks' subplot a kind of reflection or working
out of the Snopesian foreground. The beautiful Eula Varner

Snopes mediates the business and personal relations between the present and would-be male powers of Jefferson. The town believes but cannot accept the fact that Flem apparently encourages adultery between his wife and his benefactor; the amicability of the whole affair seems unnatural: in fact, it seems to them "foreign, decadent, perverted" (151). These are exactly what this relation is not, however, because what the townspeople cannot see is the commodification of eros embodied in Eula's function.

The narrator describes Eula's entrancement of Hoxey as they chat in the restaurant Flem owns: "We could see her there behind the wooden counter worn glass-smooth by elbows in their eating generations: young, with the rich coloring of a calendar; a face smooth, unblemished by any thought or by anything else; an appeal immediate and profound and without calculation or shame" (150–51). Hoxey falls in love with a poster girl. The counter over which cash is exchanged for consumables articulates the relation between carnal and economic desire. In the light of Faulkner's many other stories about the modern commodification of eros, Eula's status must be taken as all too recognizable rather than "foreign." Eula's pathetic objectification in the field of Hoxey's and Flem's desires suggests the dynamic under which women become the vehicles of male sexual and fiscal appetite. Analyzing Eula's situation according to the gendering of subject and object as male and female in the mass market enables us to appreciate Faulkner's insight into the cultural *production* of erotics.

Flem plays off Tom-Tom's and Turl's fears for their jobs (during the Depression) as a means of getting one of them to hide his stolen brass and the other to transfer it to Flem's house. The plot founders when the notoriously amorous Turl shows up at Tom-Tom's house before his night shift in order to locate and transport the brass—only to discover Tom-Tom's bored and hospitable young wife. Frustrated after several weeks that Turl has made no progress in moving the brass, Flem finally realizes why Turl is diddling and tips off Tom-Tom, who arranges a surprise for his coworker. Sneaking up to the porch at sunset, Turl spies an accustomed form "in a white nightgown" lying on the cot. Turl "stoops over the cot and puts his hand on nekkid meat and says, 'Honeybunch, papa's done arrived'" (162). Except honeybunch turns out to be one enraged husband.

At this point the plot and the relations between the two black men threaten to burst into domestic sexual violence. Tom-Tom prepares for his confrontation with Turl by locking his wife in her bedroom, underscoring her status as his property. (He has been used to riding to church, for example, "with his new young wife beside him and a gold watch and chain" [156]). Tom-Tom's prosperity provides the basis of his sexual security, just as Turl's sexual opportunism arises from his economic motivation. The coworkers' fierce struggle over the woman comically collapses when the two near-victims of Flem's plot realize their common interest. It is as if the two men must work through the potential of sexual desire to divert the oppressed from their class interest. Tom-Tom chases Turl with a "nekkid knife" through the brush and right into a ditch. Turl recounts that the ditch "was about forty foot deep and it looked a solid mile across, but it was too late then. My feets never even slowed up. They run far as from here to that door younder out into nekkid air before us even begun to fall. And they was still clawing that moonlight when me and Tom-Tom hit the bottom" (165).

Like cartoon characters, these workers run right into a topographical depression before they realize there is nothing underneath them. They might end up killing each other over the diversion of sexual pleasure, but instead they hit bottom and "just sat there in the ditch and talked" (165). When they emerge, they have united to overthrow their boss. The two of them work together to return all of the contraband brass to the power plant, where they dump it into the boilers. Their act paralyzes Flem because he cannot recover the stolen property without indicting himself, nor can he avenge himself on his underlings without suffering their exposure of him.

This fable of black organization at the expense of white entre-

preneurial mastery reflects the anxieties of the racially and eco-
nomically advantaged in early thirties America. The narrator's
own bigotry—he once refers to "nigger nature" (165)—affiliates
him with the interests of those threatened by this anecdote of
insubordination. However, the story almost forgets about another
casualty of this skirmish between men, Tom-Tom's wife. After the
men settle their differences, Tom-Tom has her prepare a meal for
them—"the two grave, scratched faces leaned to the same lamp,
above the same dishes, while in the background the woman
watched them, shadowy and covert and unspeaking" (165). More
sharply than in Faulkner's novels, his stories demonstrate the
objectification and silencing of women in the theatre of male
desire. Tom-Tom's wife in a way stands in for Eula Snopes, and
both of them stand in for the financial objects that drive men. In
the modern culture of consumption, the erotic turns out to be a
pronounced sublimation of the economic. A text like "Centaur in
Brass" suggests that the age-old economic foundation of erotic
desire takes on particular clarification in capitalism's transition to
mass market practices.

SHOPPING BAGS

"Mule in the Yard," published in *Scribner's* in 1934, also recounts
an act of successful blackmail against a Snopes. In this case, a poor
townsman named Hait has worked for I. O. Snopes, a mule trader
who sells his stock to "farmers and widows and orphans black and
white for whatever he could contrive" (*CS* 252), and then arranges
to have Hait lead the remnant across the railroad tracks at an op-
portune moment. The railroad settles satisfactorily with Snopes
for his damages each time, until one day Hait meets his own end
in one of the crossing "accidents." At this point the railroad settles
with Hait's widow, Mannie, for $8,500 and apparently puts I. O.
on notice that he's reached the end of his line. Ten years later,
some of I. O.'s mules get loose in Mannie's yard, as they have
periodically in the interval; this time, however, in the ensuing

chaos one mule knocks a bucket of coals down the cellar steps, igniting the house and burning it down. Mannie curiously does not seek damages, but does offer to buy the mule. She offers I. O. ten dollars in cash for a mule he claims now costs $150. Mannie explains that I. O. failed to pay Hait his usual $50 for his last job, the one in which he loses his life, and that her offer is based on the difference between that debt and the $60 per mule value assessed by the company in all of its original settlements to I. O. Mannie takes the mule once the confused I. O. accepts the $10 bill from old Het, Mannie's ancient accomplice. When I. O. tries to nullify the deal, Mannie tells him where he can find his mule—though she fails to mention that she has shot it dead. "Dat's whut I call justice," concludes old Het (266).

What emboldens Mrs. Hait to take on the formidably successful Snopes? Her strength grows in part as she defines a position for herself in the marketplace; Mannie's success indicates the emancipatory potential of the market for enfranchising new subjectivities and desires. For example, the narrator points out that she wears shabby clothes and a "man's felt hat which they in the town knew had belonged to her ten years' dead husband. But the man's shoes had not belonged to him. . . . she had bought them new for herself" (250). Later, Mrs. Hait emerges from her burning house "wearing a new, dun-colored, mail-order coat, in one pocket of which lay a fruit jar filled with smoothly rolled banknotes and in the other a heavy, nickel-plated pistol" (258). Here is a shopper to be reckoned with.

Mannie has been indemnified monetarily for the loss of her husband's life and livelihood. That money becomes her weapon not only in outfitting herself for the future, but also in resisting male domination. She has sublimely ignored male advice that she bank her settlement; instead, she "departed with the money in a salt sack under her apron" (253). The money represents phallic empowerment in her society; she goes home and paints her house the color of the railroad station, whether in tribute or gratitude no one knows. Mannie seeks to respond to her confinement as a poor, purposeless widow—the invisible margin of her community.

When Mannie chooses her moment for retaliation, she intends to protest her very specific placement in oppressive regional, economic, and gender coordinates:

> "Them sons of bitches," Mrs Hait said, again in that grim, prescient voice without rancor or heat. It was not the mules to which she referred; it was not even the owner of them. It was her whole town-dwelling history as dated from that April dawn ten years ago when what was left of Hait had been gathered from the mangled remains of five mules and several feet of new Manila rope on a blind curve of the railroad just out of town; the geographical hap of her very home; the very components of her bereavement—the mules, the defunct husband, and the owner of them. (252)

Mannie's response challenges her disadvantage by seeking to complete the sort of transaction that could have spelled her emancipation. In other words, Hait and his wife, like anyone else in the underclass, could, according to the ideology of capitalist individualism, have left the wrong side of the tracks and made their way across—as Flem and his clan themselves have done. If they were blocked, it is because the ideology of individualism conceals the selective, arbitrary nature of success. Hait's is a case of bad timing.

Almost nothing survives of Hait but the suspension of his last payday. The story refers to his "mangled remains" (252), and to the detection of them as "foreign matter among the mangled mules and the savage fragments of new rope" (253). Hait represents the brutification of the working class, a point I. O. could not make clearer in his explanation to Mannie about why Hait never deserved to be paid:

> "But look! Here's where I got you. Hit was our agreement that I wouldn't never owe him nothing until after the mules was—"
> "I reckon you better hush yourself," Mrs. Hait said.
> "—until hit was over. And this time, when over had come, I never

owed nobody no money because the man hit would have been owed to wasn't nobody," he cried triumphantly. (262)

There could hardly be a more emphatic formulation of capitalism's prerogatives in separating labor from one's person and so commodifying it, in reducing human obligation to contractual letter, in calling the nonworker "nobody." Obscenely, in fact, I. O. goes on to protest that Mannie has actually profited unfairly from her loss: "I go to the worry and the risk and the agoment [sic] for years and years and I get sixty dollars. And you, one time, without no trouble and no risk, without even knowing you are going to git it, git eighty-five hundred dollars. I never begrudged hit to you" (263). Mannie forces capitalism to speak aloud its perverse definitions of loss, risk, and benefit.

On the other hand, Mannie's response, like Tom-Tom's and Turl's in "Lizards," uses the forward momentum of the market mentality to fell it. The mode of her response keeps strictly to business protocols. She accepts the valuation of the mule's seller (wittily implying that she will accept the ten-year-old payment of $50 while I. O. must accept the ten-year-old price of the mule). She plays her hand when I. O. finally puts himself in a vulnerable position (the townspeople point out to him that Mrs. Hait could sue him for damages to her house and that no jury would deny her). And she kills the mule while it is arguably her property, I. O. having accepted the cash briefly. I suggest that her scheme turns out to be less revenge than the symbolic completion of a long-deferred agreement.

In negotiating this financial settlement, Mannie proves resistant to mere sentimental or other "feminized" gratifications. When she loses her house, she refurbishes another with her own hands. She does have help, of course, with her anti-Snopes project, and old Het's function in the story indicates one last element in the awakening of female subjectivity that "Mule" portrays. Old Het treads through the story in her tennis shoes, carrying a shopping bag that she replaces in "an endless succession of the convenient paper receptacles with which [ten-cent stores] supply their customers for a few cents" (249). Het's shopping bag identifies a source of the women's common power: she uses the bag as a weapon against the the fugitive mule (251) and at the end of the story it becomes something I. O. "stumbled over" in his defeated last interview with his two adversaries. Like Mannie's purchases (or the magazines she stockpiles in her basement [256]), these shopping bags signal the capacity of economic enfranchisement to solidify female emancipation. Working together, the women confound a Snopes, just as, working together, the blacks do in "Centaur." Mannie and Het team "as though in invulnerable compact of female with female against a world of mule and man" (251). One would not want to exaggerate the achievement of these moments to forecast social transformations. Yet they do accurately delineate the forces and relations that pressure traditional white male ways. We ought to hear a complex set of promises and threats in old Het's closing remark on the women's job well done: "Gentlemen, hush! Ain't we had a day!" (264).

SHORTENED STORIES

Het's "endless succession of . . . convenient paper receptacles" returns us for a final time to the self-reflective properties of Faulkner's short stories. Short stories break up and mass reproduce Faulkner's fictional material; as he shipped off story after story in the early thirties, they must have seemed something like an endless succession of paper receptacles for his literary imagination. And yet the principle of condensation, interruption, fragmentation invades the stories' formal and stylistic features in such a way as to suggest the beneficial effects of such apparent violence to Faulkner's more typically expansive and accretive methods.

"Mule in the Yard" maintains high awareness of its status as a single moment. The narrator emphasizes that the mules appear suddenly; three or four times a year "they would become translated in a single burst of perverse and uncontrollable violence, without any intervening contact with time, space, or earth" (254).

The configuration of I. O., the mules, and Mannie freezes into a "tableau," we are told, a scene with the look of "a Spanish-Indian-American suttee" (256). The suttee suggests the framed, static moments common to many of the stories—moments staging funeral rites for the premodern South. What does losing "contact with time, space, or earth" accomplish for the short stories?

Because they must be broken off from the larger tracts of mythical and historical material they inevitably originate in, the stories carry with them—as a condition of their very formation—the traces of violent separation. Faulkner's own explanatory myths of Snopesism or the Sartoris code, as well as his reconstruction of Southern history in his longer fictions, must be partially sacrificed and disfigured by the law of short story composition. Such a process unleashes works that greatly advance Faulkner's critical reflection on the conditions and traditions that have produced him as an author.

The fragmentary nature of both *The Sound and the Fury* and *As I Lay Dying* incorporate the multiple-unit packaging of fiction in the age of the mass market. Both began literally as short stories, and continue as monstrosities of the form.[21] Such monstrosity, far from being a failure of aesthetic governance, powerfully contributes to the achievement of each book in challenging traditional representations of, respectively, the aristocracy's integrity and the laboring class's demoralization in the modern South. In the short stories we have examined, the sundering of fiction from context releases the actors to dispute or challenge the determinants of their behavior. Like photographs, the short stories segment and detach experience so as to defamiliarize and disrupt accepted structures of explanation. Floating like images in a fog, as "Mule in the Yard" suggests, such tableaux disrupt the production of the usual positions and places for subjects in a novelist's work. In the interstices of such cut up fiction, moments of reflection may be called for.

Consider, as a final point, the way the principle of rupture informs the following dispute between Mannie and I. O. Snopes:

"I don't know anything about hundred-and-fifty-dollar mules. All I know is what the railroad paid." Now Snopes looked at her for a full moment.

"What do you mean?"

"Them sixty dollars a head the railroad used to pay you for mules back when you and Hait—"

"Hush," Snopes said; he looked about again, quick, ceaseless. "All right. Even call it sixty dollars. But you just sent me ten."

"Yes. I sent you the difference." He looked at her, perfectly still. "Between that mule and what you owed Hait."

"What I owed—"

"For getting them five mules onto the tr—"

"Hush!" he cried. (261–62)

Mannie's impertinent insinuations break her bought silence of ten years. They earn her Snopes's literal as well as figurative regard: he sees her for the first time. In the spaces of their broken sentences and interruptions, plenty gets said. Their elliptical dialogue measures the force of economic, social, and gender antagonism. Syntactical and structural disarrangements embody the social disarrangements not far behind. In these shortened stories, new subjectivities, new voices, new sentences may find partial expression.

NOTES

My essay has benefited from comments and suggestions by James Carothers, William Carroll, James Hinkle, Cheryl Lester, Patrick O'Donnell, and Philip Weinstein.

1. Letter from Faulkner to his agent, Morton Goldman, probably late spring 1934, *Selected Letters of William Faulkner*, ed. Joseph Blotner (New York: Random House, 1977), 80.

2. Frederick R. Karl, *William Faulkner: An American Writer* (New York: Weidenfeld & Nicolson, 1989), 401.

3. William Faulkner, "An Introduction to *The Sound and the Fury*," ed. James B. Meriwether, *The Southern Review* (N.S., 1972): 710.

4. Christopher P. Wilson discusses some of the broader features of the fictional and nonfictional material that editors of cheap magazines encouraged during this period in "The Rhetoric of Consumption: Mass-Market Magazines and the Demise of the Gentle Reader, 1880-1920," in *The Culture of Consumption: Critical Essays in American History, 1880–1980*, ed. Richard Wightman Fox and T. J. Jackson Lears (New York: Pantheon, 1983): 40–64. Wilson notes especially the emergence of an ethos of realism—from the direct, personal editorial voice framing each number, through stories devoted to the

advance of modern American business and technology, to a house style inspired by the brisk streamlines of journalism and advertising copy.

James L. W. West III identifies the magazine short story formula as dictating dialogue or action at the outset to catch the reader's attention, rigid plotting moving toward an "artificial climax," and simplistic often "saccharine" conclusions. West's chapter on the magazine market in his *American Authors and the Literary Marketplace Since 1900* (Philadelphia: University of Pennsylvania Press, 1988) contains some useful information, though it avoids generalization in favor of anecdotal illustration.

Susan Donaldson has examined Faulkner's conception of his short story readership and its effect on at least one of his story projects in "Dismantling the *Saturday Evening Post* Reader: *The Unvanquished* and Changing 'Horizons of Expectations'," in *Faulkner and Popular Culture*, ed. Doreen Fowler and Ann J. Abadie (Jackson: University Press of Mississippi, 1990), 179–95.

5. Frank Luther Mott, *A History of American Magazines*, vol. 4: *1885-1905* (Cambridge, Mass.: Belknap Press, 1968), 702.

6. Quoted in Karl, *William Faulkner*, 403.

7. Faulkner instructs Ben Wasson about one story, "Don't try it on Mencken save as a last resort; he only pays me $150.00 for stories" (*SL* 63). Faulkner's reluctance at foregoing the more prestigious *Scribner's* for the higher-paying *Post* comes through in the following suggestion to Morton Goldman: "I would like for Dashiell at Scribner's to see this, but they wont pay much. I dont know what to say about it, since we may get $1000. from the Post. Suppose you ask him if he would like to see it and make an offer; then see what the Post will pay, and wire me" (*SL* 77).

8. Mott's five-volume work gives a panoramic overview of the development of magazines in the United States. Volume 4 (1885–1905) describes the emergence of the conditions of magazine publication that still prevailed in the 1920s: the innovations of reduced price, expanded circulation, major reliance on advertising, aggressive editorship, and technological advances (especially in the reproduction of graphic material). This volume concludes with sketches of the magazines that dominated the period, including *Scribner's* and the *Post*. Volume 5 (1905–1930), left incomplete at the time of Mott's death, comprises only the sketches, among them the *American Mercury.*

Theodore Peterson provides a more synthetic account of the modern American magazine in *Magazines in the Twentieth Century* (Urbana: University of Illinois Press, 1964). I have drawn especially on Peterson's description of the interest in magazines taken by national businesses in the postbellum United States, and in the deployment of print advertising. Richard Ohmann has written two important essays on this topic. The first, "Where Did Mass Culture Come From?," argues that the cheap magazines contributed to the establishment of mass culture in the American 1880s by serving as an instrument of market formation by national companies, many of them struggling with the country's first crisis of overproduction. In a related piece, "Advertising and Mass Culture," Ohmann analyzes the new style of advertising that emerged in mass magazines, a style that promised an array of psychic and social gratifications in the imagery attached to commodity consumption. Both essays appear in Ohmann's *Politics of Letters* (Middletown, Conn.: Wesleyan University Press, 1987), 135–51 and 152–70, respectively.

T. J. Jackson Lears delineates the grip of modern advertising on a nation's profoundest desires by demonstrating how early advertisers transformed traditional Protestant concerns with personal salvation within the company of believers into an ethos of personal self-revitalization within a society of managed workers and contented consumers. "From Salvation to Self-Realization: Advertising and the Therapuetic Roots of the Consumer Culture, 1880–1930," in *The Culture of Consumption*, 3–38.

9. As quoted in Joseph L. Blotner, *Faulkner: A Biography* (New York: Random House, 1984), 222.

10. Edward J. O'Brien, *The Dance of the Machines: The American Short Story and the Industrial Age* (New York: Macaulay Company, 1929), 15–16.

11. *Liberty* (24 November 1928) 8., as quoted in O'Brien, 150; italics O'Brien's.

12. Karl's is a recent and egregious example: Aunt Jenny's anti-Semitism "carries the weight of the author's approval, and the Yankee Jew becomes an instrument of the new world, a reincarnation of the evil Reconstruction foisted on the South" (421). Such a reading ignores the conflict of behaviors and implied viewpoints in the story, thus misidentifying the author's position with a character's, and it discounts entirely the function of formal and stylistic effects in determining what a work means.

13. William Carlos Williams, *A Beginning on the Short Story: Notes* (Yonkers, N.Y.: Alicat Book Shop Press, 1950), 10–11.

14. Isom is only relatively accurate since the actual distance is under a thousand miles. The road to educational enfranchisement still looms long in the twenties.

15. Peterson, 21. Wilson describes the new breed of entrepreneurial, sales-oriented editor of the cheap magazines.

16. Lears, "From Salvation to Self-Realization," 6.

17. Lewis M. Dabney, *The Indians of Yoknapatawpha* (Baton Rouge: Louisiana State University Press, 1974), 11, n. 15; as quoted in Karl, 419.

18. Wilson describes how "the engineered 'realism' of the topical magazines threatened to deepen the passivity of the reader" (61), in part by presenting knowledge of the world as something to be consumed by the well-informed subscriber.

19. Faulkner recalls seeing a stage production of *Ben Hur* when he was a child—especially memorable because it had live horses and camels in it (*Faulkner in the University: Class Conferences at the University of Virginia, 1957–1958*, ed. Frederick L. Gwynn and Joseph L. Blotner [Charlottesville: University Press of Virginia, 1959], 285. Faulkner also knew the novel on which it was based, a bestseller that Ohmann points to as an example of the earliest successes of organized marketing in book publishing in the 1880s and '90s ("Where Did Mass Culture Come From?," 139).

20. In *Alice Doesn't: Feminism, Semiotics, Cinema* (Bloomington: Indiana University Press, 1984), Teresa De Lauretis develops an argument that female identity according to most social discourses in the West is described as divided or fissured by opposing functions: on the one hand, women seek to establish themselves as human subjectivities; on the other, culture defines them as objects (of exchange, under Lévi-Strauss's account of society's origin in masculine property, and of desire, under Freud's account of the Mother as the primary object of desire). This situation has been screened in the practice of semiotic analysis because semiotics has generally neglected desire as the motor of narrative. De Lauretis wants semiotics to acknowledge that "masculine" and "feminine" functions mark all narrative: the masculine represents the desires to know, to see, "and thus depend on a personal response, an engagement of the spectator's subjectivity, and the possiblity of identification" (136). The feminine is produced as an image of resolution or closure—that which is to be known, to be seen. Given such discursive formations, then, cinema has up until now reinscribed these incommensurate gender positions, blocking an alternative subject relation for the female viewer: "How can the female spectator be entertained as subject of the very movement that places her as its object, that makes her the figure of its own closure?" (141).

21. When he began the manuscript first entitled "Twilight," Faulkner thought it would be "a short story, something that could be done in about two pages, a thousand words, I found out it couldn't" (*Faulkner in the University*, 32). Malcolm Cowley extends this view in his description of the selections he has made for the Viking Portable edition of Faulkner (though he betrays an anthologist's bias): "All the extracts from novels are stories independent in themselves (his novels are most of them composed of stories, which is their greatest structural fault)—except for the story called 'Dilsey,' from 'The Sound and the Fury'" (Malcolm Cowley, *The Faulkner–Cowley File* [New York: Viking Press, 1966], 33).

Faulkner's Short Story Writing and the Oldest Profession

JAMES B. CAROTHERS

"Dear Hal—" Faulkner wrote his publisher, Harrison Smith, early in 1932 while he was working on *Light in August,* "$250.00 will stave me off for the time. Send it on. Sorry to bother you at all right now, when you are cluttered up yourself with overhead instead of revenue. But it's either this, or put the novel aside and go whoring again with short stories. When it's convenient, send me another slug."[1]

Faulkner was by no means the first nor the last writer to select the metaphor of prostitution to describe writing for the mass circulation magazines.[2] His linking of short story writing with whoring, however, raises a number of questions, when we consider the significant and complex role that the writing of short fiction played at various stages in his career, and when we further consider Faulkner's pervasive use of whores, whoring, whorehouses, pimps, madams, and johns as character, subject, and theme throughout the entire range of his fiction. In what ways did Faulkner understand the resemblance between short story writing and prostitution? What was his attitude toward prostitution and its participants, be they victims or beneficiaries? What are we to make of his self-identification as a practitioner of "the oldest profession"? And how, if at all, should this self-identification affect our reading of his short stories on the whole, or in particular?

To begin the search for some answers to these questions, I want first to stipulate some definitions, and to consider two relatively limited sources of evidence: that of the biography, and that of the short stories themselves. Then I want to discuss some aspects of prostitutes and prostitution in the novels, although I will focus my attention on the novels other than *Sanctuary, Requiem for a Nun,* and *The Reivers,* in which prostitution receives extended treatment. Finally, I wish to consider, briefly, Faulkner's treatment of the subject in light of the conclusions of an American social historian who has studied prostitution in America during an important era for Faulkner's fiction, and to return to the metaphoric equivalence of prostitution and short story writing.

By way of definition, let us note the general derivation of the verb from the Latin *pro,* "before," and *statuere,* "to cause to stand, set up, place." But the commercial context is invoked immediately, "to place before, expose publicly, offer for sale," and the *OED*'s first extended definition of the adjectival form is "offered or exposed to lust (as a woman) . . . abandoned to sensual indulgence, licentious." From there it is but the work of our culture's gender assumptions to the noun form: "a woman who is devoted or (usually) who offers her body to indiscriminate sexual intercourse, esp. for hire." And the primary definition of the verb further incorporates the bias: "To offer (oneself, or another) to unlawful, esp. indiscriminate, sexual intercourse, usually for hire; to devote or expose to lewdness. (Chiefly *refl.* of a woman.)" Although we must also be cognizant of the more generalized definition, "one who debases himself for the sake of gain, a base hireling, a corrupt and venal politician," in what follows, I shall be especially concerned with prostitutes and prostitution in their female, sexual, and commercial senses. So, we may ask, what do prostitutes and short story writers have in common? As a working hypothesis, let us consider that both undertake to trade pleasure for money, though the pleasure is seldom theirs, though most of the money is almost invariably skimmed off by other (male) agents of the industry, and though the consumer may well feel debased by the failure of the illusion, as the provider almost invariably does.

We must, of course, leave to the biographers the task of documenting Faulkner's own experience in brothels. Certainly there is sufficient evidence to show that the young Faulkner spent a good deal of time in what he called "the equivocal purlieus of Memphis" (*US* 26), and that he was familiar with the opportunities for commercial sex in New Orleans as well. But, according to what evidence I have been able to find, Faulkner was more the observer and conversationalist than the patron when he accompanied his friends to brothels. This was, at least, the assessment of Joseph Blotner, who concludes: "Apparently he never went upstairs himself, but he was a familiar visitor on good terms with the madams and their girls."[3] This is consistent with Faulkner's assertion to Meta Carpenter: "I know whores. I wrote *Sanctuary* out of what whores in Memphis told me. They were friends, but I don't bed down with whores. Not here, not in Oxford, not anywhere."[4] Whether this assertion should be accepted at face value in its totality seems to me to be questionable, just as so many of Faulkner's other statements about what he had or had not done, or why he had or had not done something are similarly suspect.[5] Faulkner sometimes enjoyed telling stories about himself, such as that he told Jean Stein:

> . . . the best job that was ever offered to me was to become landlord in a brothel. In my opinion it's the perfect milieu for an artist to work in. It gives him perfect economic freedom; he's free of fear and hunger; he has a roof over his head and nothing whatever to do except keep a few simple accounts and to go once every month and pay off the police. The place is quiet during the morning hours which is the best time of the day to work. There's enough social life in the evening, if he wishes to participate, to keep him from being bored; it gives him a certain standing in his society; he has nothing to do because the madam keeps the books; all the inmates of the house are females and would defer to him and call him "Sir." All the bootleggers in the neighborhood would call him "Sir." And he could call the police by their first names.[6]

Faulkner later repeated a variant of this story in *The Mansion*, where Reba Rivers makes a similar offer to Montgomery Ward

Snopes (78). But the direct evidence that Faulkner ever or "actively"—in Ratliff's sense—patronized brothels is conspicuously lacking.

Faulkner depicts a number of male characters who go to brothels for something other than sex. Horace Benbow, in *Sanctuary,* for example, goes to Miss Reba's place in an effort to secure Temple Drake's evidence to clear his client, Lee Goodwin. Fonzo and Virgil, in the same novel, rent a room at Miss Reba's under the mistaken impression that it will be a satisfactory rooming house while they attend barber college. In *Pylon* Roger and Laverne Shumann rent a room in an Amboise Street crib, while they await the payoff from Roger's unexpected success on the first day of the air meet, "because in the Amboise streets you can sleep tonight and pay tomorrow because a whore will leave a kid sleep on credit. . . . so they left the kid asleep on the madam's sofa" (70). In *The Mansion* Montgomery Ward Snopes goes to Miss Reba's to secure help in sending money to his kinsman, Mink Snopes, whom Montgomery Ward has contracted to betray into attempting to escape from the penitentiary at Parchman. And, finally, in *The Reivers,* Lucius Priest goes with Boon Hogganbeck to Miss Reba's in a general quest for "nonvirtue," but without sexual desire or sexual knowledge. Such incidents suggest that the brothel was more than simply the locus of commercial assignation; it was the point of interface between the respectable and the disreputable for a variety of transactions.

Faulkner's relatively infrequent treatment of prostitutes and prostitution in his own short stories should not surprise us. He was most usually writing short stories for a national market that sometimes balked at references to outhouses, to say nothing of "cathouses."[7] In fact, of the 120 or so texts that we may conveniently label as short stories, only a handful feature prostitutes as named characters, or concern themselves significantly with prostitution as subject or theme. One thinks immediately, of course, of Nancy of "That Evening Sun," who sells herself to Mr. Stovall.

He was the cashier in the bank and a deacon in the Baptist church, and Nancy began to say:

"When you going to pay me, white man? When you going to pay me, white man? It's been three times now since you paid me a cent—" Mr Stovall knocked her down, but she kept on saying, "When you going to pay me, white man? It's been three times now since—" until Mr Stovall kicked her in the mouth with his heel and the marshal caught Mr Stovall back, and Nancy lying in the street laughing. She turned her head and spat out some blood and teeth, and said, "It's been three times now since he paid me a cent." (CS 291)

Of the many things we might say about this passage, we should note especially that Nancy is poor, female, black, and outlaw. She is the victim of Mr. Stovall, paragon of white male respectability, himself buttressed by the power of the bank and the church and protected by the law. We should note that Mr. Stovall becomes violent, that Nancy laughs at him—surely the laugh of Sisyphus, that the incident is narrated by Quentin, thus inviting comparison with a number of elements of *The Sound and the Fury*, and that Nancy's story was adapted, *mutatis mutandis*, as the story of Nancy Mannigoe in *Requiem for a Nun*, twenty years after Faulkner, following considerable editorial wrangling with H. L. Mencken, first published the short story in the *American Mercury*.[8] This incident, as Quentin recalls it, is but one of several that contribute to the image of Nancy as doomed victim of the racial, sexual, and economic matrices by which she is defined. The more or less respectable judgment of Nancy is offered by Quentin's father, who gives only bland reassurance in the face of what Nancy considers her imminent death: "There's nothing for you to be afraid of now. And if you'd just let white men alone." That Nancy is powerless against men, white or black, is implicit in Caddy's response, "How let them alone?" (CS 295). Nancy's servicing Mr. Stovall differs little from her washing of the Compson laundry. It is one of the few bleak choices the Jefferson economy affords her.

Another prostitute who plays a significant role in a Faulkner short story is the unnamed Memphis woman who marries Willy

Christian in the 1935 story "Uncle Willy." Uncle Willy is first a cocaine addict; then, apparently "reformed" by the good women and Christians of Jefferson, he finds solace in the more pedestrian pleasures of alcohol and prostitution. Uncle Willy has the temerity to bring his Memphis whore to town, as his new wife, "a woman twice as big as Uncle Willy, in a red hat and a pink dress and a dirty white fur coat . . . with hair the color of a brand new brass hydrant bib and her cheeks streaked with mascara and caked powder where she had sweated" (CS 236). "It was worse than if he had started dope again," the unnamed narrator recalls. "You would have thought he had brought smallpox to town" (236). That, at least, is the reaction of the women and the church, although she is appreciated by at least some of the townsmen:

> . . . she come down town the next day to shop, in a black hat now and a red-and-white striped dress so that she looked like a great big stick of candy and three times as big as Uncle Willy now, walking along the street with men popping out of the stores like she was stepping on a line of spring triggers and both sides of her behind kind of pumping up and down inside the dress until somebody hollered, threw back his head and squalled: "YIPPEEE!" like that and she kind of twitched her behind without even stopping and then they hollered sure enough. (CS 237)

The forces of moral order, however, quickly separate the new Mrs. Christian from the illusion that she attained respectability and economic solvency through her marriage, telling her that Uncle Willy is bankrupt. The prostitute, making the immediate best of a bad bargain, manages to pry a thousand-dollar payoff from Uncle Willy's rich sister, and her parting shot to the same crowd that had appreciated her the previous day shows that she has the same kind of contempt for the town that it has shown for her. "Come on up to Manuel Street and see me some time," she tells them, "and I will show you hicks what you and this town can do to yourselves and one another" (CS 238).

"Uncle Willy" is by no means one of Faulkner's best or best-known short stories. It has been criticized for its failure of style, and for its failure to resolve the tension between the pernicious influence of Uncle Willy on the children on the one hand, the hypocritical and repressive behavior of his opponents on the other, but it has also been suggested that the story, an autobiographical fantasy, perhaps represents Faulkner's contempt for his own community.[9]

The Faulkner short story, or, rather, the short Faulkner story, that most directly and extensively develops the subject and theme of prostitution is "Peter," a sketch Faulkner may have written for possible newspaper publication in New Orleans in 1925. The sketch was not published during Faulkner's lifetime, however, and has been generally available only since the publication of the *Uncollected Stories* in 1979.

"Peter" contains an arresting combination of images of art, nature, civilization, innocence, and debasement. "Here was spring in a paved street, between walls," the sketch begins, "and here was Peter sitting on a stoop, kicking his short legs in brief serge, banging his heels rhythmically against a wooden step. Behind him an arching spacious passageway swam back between walls of an ineffable azure into which one passed as into sleep, sweeping back into light again and a shabby littered court and something green and infernal against a far wall" (*US* 489).

The action of the story is very slight, and of very brief duration. The narrator—whom I shall call "Faulkner"—and his friend Spratling have come to the Negro district of New Orleans, so that Spratling can sketch. There they encounter the boy named Peter, who serves as a lookout for his mother, a prostitute. While Peter talks with Spratling and Faulkner, various men come and go from his mother's room. Peter, at Spratling's request, agrees to pose for the artist's sketch, but he is self-conscious and uncomfortable in attempting to hold his pose. Nevertheless, he cries when his mother appears and takes him up to their room. Spratling finishes his sketch, and Peter bids him farewell from a window.

Faulkner manages to compress a number of moving juxtapositions into a relatively brief space and time. First there is the juxtaposition of created nature and man-made civilization: "Here was spring in a paved street, between walls." Then, there is the boyish innocence of Peter's interest in learning to spin a top and his streetwise conversations with and about his mother's customers, who themselves represent a variety of racial or ethnic types. Next, there is the contrast between the painter Spratling, who has come to sketch, and finds Peter an unsatisfactory model—"Stop wiggling so much! Stand as if God was looking at you" (492)—and the writer Faulkner, who sees Peter's motion as natural and inevitable. Faulkner, too, has something of an artist's eye. "The sunlight was immaculate as a virgin: hanging washed garments were planes of light and a washing line took the golden moon like a tight-rope dancer" (492).

This story is uncompromising in its rendering of the dialogue of the prostitutes, no doubt explaining why the story was not published.

> The victrola again broke into a tortured syncopation. Here were dark trees, and stars on an unknown water—all the despairs of time and breath.
>
> A voice—Baby!
> Another voice—Break dem springs, if you can.
> Peter—That's Euphrosy: she got more sense than any of these gals, mamma says. (US 491)

Peter talks knowledgeably of his role and of his mother's business.

> "I have to sit here and tell 'em when mamma's busy talking to some body. And the others, too. I got to watch out for 'em."
> "Watch out for what?"
> "I don't know. Just watch out for 'em. They are nice folks here. Baptis' says we got the nicest girls in town here." (490–91)

At one juncture, Peter asks Spratling, "You aint going up to mamma's room, are you? . . . she's busy talking to that Chink that just went in. She dont like to be bothered while she's talking to some one" (491). But it is also clear that Peter is essentially innocent. "What does he see?" Faulkner wonders, "thinking of him as an identical coin minted between the severed yet similar despairs of two races" (490). Peter's mother finally appears, "languorous as a handled magnolia petal," "languorous as a decayed lily," "like a languorous damaged lily" (493). She looks at Faulkner and Spratling for a moment with "her dark eyes in which was all the despair of a subject race and a thinned blood become sterile except in the knowledge of the ancient sorrows of white and black" (493).

In essence, I would suggest, Peter's mother is simply a working mother who has come to retrieve her child at the end of her labors. To be sure, Faulkner does nothing to minimize the dangers and the degradations of her profession, but neither does he do anything to sensationalize them. One of the customers is a Chinese, "his face rife with sex." Her current lover is "Eagle Beak." As Peter explains, "He's the one that sleeps with mamma. He works on Dock 5. He can move more cargo than anybody on Dock 5" (490). "Negroes brushed by us: black and tan and yellow faces wrung to an imminence of physical satisfaction" (491), the narrator notes. Later, he adds, "Steps thundered on the stairs, washed clothing flopped in a faint breeze. Negroes came, flushed and gray with sex, negroes went, languorous with repletion" (492).

But if the apparent text of "Peter" is a prose equivalent to Spratling's sketch, the subtext concerns the differences between drawing and writing. Faulkner's story begins before Spratling's sketch, and it continues after Spratling has finished. Peter's natural impulse to motion is rendered with precision and variety in the story, as opposed to the drawing, and Faulkner's vision comprehends them all:

> While Spratling finished his sketch I watched the noon become the afternoon, the sunlight change from silver to gold (if I slept and waked, I think I could know afternoon from morning by the color of

the sunlight) in spite of art and vice and everything else which makes a world; hearing the broken phrases of a race answering quickly to the compulsions of the flesh and then going away, temporarily freed from the body, to sweat and labor and sing; doomed again to repair to a temporary satisfaction; fleeting, that cannot last. (493–94)

In addition to significant characterizations of prostitutes in "That Evening Sun," "Uncle Willy," and "Peter," the short stories yield a variety of incidental allusions to prostitutes and prostitution. "Victory," for example, tells the story of Alec Gray, a Scottish shipwright's son, who after serving with fierce personal pride and with eventual distinction as an enlisted man in France in World War I, "goes for an officer" against his father's wishes. Thus he becomes a cadet, in the sense of "one who enlists in a regiment . . . to acquire military skill and to obtain a commission." After the war, Gray refuses to return home, attempting rather to live like a gentleman: "With one correct bag he went to France. But he did not bear eastward at once. He went to the Riviera; for a week he lived like a gentleman, spending his money like a gentleman, lonely, alone in that bright aviary of the svelte kept women of all Europe" (CS 456). But in postwar London, his funds dwindling and then exhausted, and too proud to accept work as a shipwright, Alec Gray is reduced to employment as a kind of pimp: "with his waxed moustaches and his correct clothes he revealed the flesh-pots of the West End to Birmingham and Leeds. It was temporary" (CS 457). Although I will not insist that Faulkner was aware that one term for Alec Gray's temporary occupation was "cadet," one who steers or guides prospective customers to brothels, I find it convenient to suggest that he may have understood that Alec Gray moved from being one kind of cadet to another.

A more extensive brothel allusion in another World War I story occurs in "Ad Astra." On the evening of 11 November 1918 an unlikely group of RAF officers, including the unnamed narrator, the Irishman Comyn, the Americans Bland, Sartoris, and Monaghan, along with an Indian subadar and a captured and head-bandaged German officer set out to celebrate the Armistice. After a great deal of drinking, a skirmish with the military police, and an inevitable barroom brawl, Comyn and Monaghan propose to continue their celebration at a brothel, and to take the captured German with them.

A distinction is made between Comyn and Monaghan on the one hand, and the remainder of the group on the other, expressed in Comyn's challenge: "What fool would rather fight than fush? All men are brothers, and all their wives are sisters. So come along, yez midnight fusileers" (CS 426). After another near-fight, Comyn and Monaghan take the German away with them.

> We watched them come into silhouette in the mouth of an alley where a light was. There was an arch there, and the faint cold pale light on the arch and on the walls so that it was like a gate and they entering the gate, holding the German up between them.
>   "What will they do with him?" Bland said. "Prop him in the corner and turn the light off? Or do French brothels have he-beds too?"
>   "Who the hell's business is that?" I said.[10] (426–27)

This facet of "Ad Astra" is interesting in that it shows again that some men are naturally drawn to the pleasures of the brothel— one thinks here of the sculptor Gordon at the conclusion of *Mosquitoes*, the young Mink Snopes recollected in *The Mansion*, and Boon Hogganbeck in *The Reivers*—and that some men, just as naturally, decline the commercial sexual gambit, as Faulkner himself apparently did.[11] Similarly, there are some men who decline the opportunity for sex with women to whom they are not married, as Gavin Stevens declines Eula Varner Snopes in *The Town* and Linda Snopes Kohl in *The Mansion*. The architectural imagery of "Victory" also recalls "Peter," and it is clear that Faulkner took pains to describe the physical passage into the whorehouses in *Sanctuary* and *The Reivers*, perhaps as a metaphoric exploration of the container for the thing contained.

Another ascetic in Faulkner's short stories is Henry Stribling, the "Hawkshaw" of both "Hair" and "Dry September." Hawkshaw, the Jefferson barber, loses his fiancée, Sophy Starnes, and quietly takes on the responsibility of caring for her aging mother, and, eventually, of paying the taxes and mortgage on the Starnes property. In the meantime, he becomes smitten with the young Jefferson girl, Susan Reed, "a thin little girl then, with big scared eyes and this straight, soft hair not blond and not brunette" (CS 131). The other barbers, barbershop regulars, and townspeople are quick to impute base motives to Hawkshaw, particularly when he begins giving Susan presents, from a doll to a wristwatch. The unnamed narrator of the story articulates the town's assumptions and values:

> She got grown fast. Too fast. That was the trouble. Some said it was being an orphan and all. . . .
> It's not that she was bad. There's not any such thing as a woman born bad, because they are all born bad, born with the badness in them. The thing is, to get them married before badness comes to a natural head. But we try to make them conform to a system that says a women can't be married until she reaches a certain age. And nature don't pay any attention to systems, let alone women paying any attention to them, or to anything. She just grew up too fast. She reached the point where the badness came to a head before the system said it was time for her to. I think they can't help it. (CS 133)

I quote this passage neither to demonstrate nor to attempt to rationalize Faulkner's supposed misogyny, but to show his understanding of the depth and pervasiveness of the overwhelmingly negative community attitude toward female sexual desire. Faulkner delineated this problem frequently and variously among his women characters: Caddy Compson, Charlotte Rittenmeyer of *The Wild Palms*, and Eula Varner come to mind from the novels, while from the short stories Miss Emily Grierson of "A Rose for Emily," Miss Minnie Cooper of "Dry September," and the title characters of "Elly" and "Miss Zilphia Gant" are all driven to perverse or violent rebellion against the prevailing community standard.

Hawkshaw, too, is a victim of this standard, which maintains that an unmarried man—and some married men as well—will inevitably seek sexual fulfillment by exchanging money or goods for sexual favors.

> "He bought her a wrist watch two years ago," Matt Fox said. "Paid sixty dollars for it."
> Maxey was shaving a customer. He stopped, the razor in his hand, the blade loaded with lather. "Well, I'll be durned," he said. "Then he must—You reckon he was the first one, the one that—"
> Matt hadn't looked around. "He aint give it to her yet," he said.
> "Well durn his tight-fisted time," Maxey said. "Any old man that will fool with a young girl, he's pretty bad. But a fellow that will trick one and then not even pay her nothing—" (CS 136)

When Matt Fox explains that Hawkshaw has refrained from giving Susan the watch because he believes that "she is too young to receive jewelry from anybody that aint kin to her," Hawkshaw is condemned as foolish for being ignorant of Susan's reputation. As for Hawkshaw himself, the townspeople assign him to a conventional bachelor's sexual behavior pattern.

> He boarded at Mrs Cowan's and he had joined the church and he spent no money at all. He didn't even smoke. So Maxey and Matt and I reckon everybody else in Jefferson thought that he had saved up steam for a year and was now bound on one of those private sabbaticals among the fleshpots of Memphis. (CS 142)

To the town, Hawkshaw's behavior is explicable in a limited number of ways: he has surely seduced Susan Reed, so he is either paying for her favors or simply taking them. If he has not been intimate with her, he is a fool for having a romantic attachment to a fallen girl/woman. At the least, if he is a man like other men, he consorts with prostitutes at regular intervals. But Hawkshaw here, as differently in "Dry September," reveals that he is not a man like other men, for, with the Starnes mortgage paid in full, and Susan now having reached "a certain age," he marries her.

"Hair" ends abruptly on this note leaving the narrator and, presumably, the reader to face some radical revisions of the facts, speculations, and inferences that they have made previously about both Susan Reed and Hawkshaw. Hawkshaw's persistent fidelity to the memory of Sophy Starnes and to the honor of Susan Reed—whether it existed or not—serves to redeem a supposedly fallen woman, and their story serves as a corrective to those who, like Maxey, the narrator, Matt Fox, and just about everybody else in Jefferson who are so quick to assume the worst about both men and women.

Another variety of prostitution, or at least commercial seduction, is treated in "Wash," when Thomas Sutpen rewards Wash's granddaughter, Milly, with ribbons and a dress. When Milly becomes pregnant, Wash knows that the Sutpen Negroes are saying that he has engineered a trap for Sutpen. "I know what they say to one another," he thought. "I can almost hyear them: *Wash Jones has fixed old Sutpen at last. Hit taken him twenty years, but he has done hit at last* (*CS* 542). Wash, however, has been faithful to his own misplaced confidence in Sutpen's honor, telling Sutpen, "If you was ara other man . . . I wouldn't let her keep that dress nor nothing else that came from your hand. But you are different" (*CS* 541). Wash is convinced that Sutpen will "make hit right" with Milly, but when Milly bears Sutpen's child and Sutpen shows casually brutal indifference to her, Wash murders Sutpen, Milly, and the child, and makes a suicidal charge against the men of Sutpen's own kind who have come to restore order. The message of "Wash"—which differs from that of the corresponding materials of *Absalom, Absalom!*—is twofold. First, Wash learns that it is dangerous to assume the divinity or innate superiority of a man such as Sutpen, and second, it is a fatal mistake for Sutpen to assume that Wash Jones will be subservient without principle, especially in a matter of honor concerning the women of his family.

Although prostitutes and prostitution are treated relatively briefly and infrequently in Faulkner's short stories, they are, of course, treated frequently and extensively in his novels. In addition to the minor treatments in *Mosquitoes* and *Pylon*, previously mentioned, additional allusions occur in *Absalom, Absalom!*, in which Miss Rosa Coldfield recounts that she once heard that Wash Jones's daughter died in a Memphis brothel, and in *A Fable*. More significant to my purposes are *The Sound and the Fury*, *Light in August*, and the Snopes trilogy, to say nothing of *Sanctuary*, *Requiem for a Nun*, and *The Reivers*, this last a selection of novels that Michael Millgate once proposed to call Faulkner's "cathouse trilogy."[12]

Nowhere in Faulkner's fiction is the sexual double standard more vividly realized than in the character of Jason Compson in *The Sound and the Fury*. Aware that his sister Caddy is a prostitute, he lords it over her and condemns the source of her earnings, but he also uses that knowledge to extort money from her. Further, he embezzles from her earnings to deny money to Caddy's daughter, and he commits forgery to hoard Caddy's money for himself, in large part so that he can keep a prostitute of his own. Through perfect hypocrisy towards Caddy, Quentin, and Lorraine, Jason conforms precisely to the code of male behavior that Jefferson assumes to govern Hawkshaw in "Hair."

Although much has been said about the sexual education of Joe Christmas, I want to concentrate on the relations between Joe and the waitress-prostitute Bobbie Allen in chapter 8 of *Light in August*. Joe is, ironically, brought into Bobbie's proximity by his puritanical stepfather, McEachern, when he is seventeen. The two take a hurried luncheon in "a small, dingy back street restaurant" in the railroad town to which MacEachern has come on business. Bobbie is described at some length, though Joe notices her but briefly: "the waitress with her demure and downlooking face and her big, too big, hands setting the plates and cups, her head rising from beyond the counter at about the height of a tall child" (*LIA* 193). Afterwards, MacEachern tells Joe: "I'll have you remember that place. There are places in this world where a man may go but a boy, a youth of your age, may not. That is one of them. Maybe you should never have gone there. But you must see such so you will know what to avoid and shun" (192–93).

Six months later, monetarily free of his stepfather, and with a dime in his pocket now, Joe goes straight to the restaurant. Ordering pie and coffee, he is chagrined when Bobbie tells him that pie alone is ten cents and she covers his gaffe by taking the coffee away, telling Max that she "misunderstood" (199). Later, with half a dollar in his pocket, he returns in an attempt to pay Bobbie the nickel for the coffee. Thus begins a halting, inarticulate romance, in the course of which Joe undergoes a rake's progress from virginal courtship through effective rape to proprietary whoring. In this chapter, Joe makes a number of shocking discoveries about female sexuality and the commerce in it: "he began to steal, to take money from the hoard. It is very possible that the women did not suggest it to him, never mentioned money to him. It is possible that he did not even know that he was paying with money for pleasure" (210). Bobbie is criticized by her employer, Max Confrey, for consorting with "John Jacob Astor from the cowshed," and when Bobbie defends herself by saying, "Maybe I like him" (211), Max and Mame the Madam are contemptuous. "Get this," Max says. "She says maybe she likes him best. It's Romeo and Juliet. For sweet Jesus"; and when Mame finds that Joe pays Bobbie, she says to Bobbie, "Coming all the way down here from Memphis. Bringing it all the way down here to give it away" (212). In spite of this unpromising context, Joe proceeds with his rough and barely articulate courtship with Bobbie, adding smoking, drinking, and dancing to his accomplishments.

But Bobbie's past and especially the economic exigencies of her association with Max and Mame, as well as the problematic sexual, religious, and racial heritage of Joe Christmas lead "Romeo and Juliet" to disaster. When MacEachern surprises him at a dance, Joe strikes him, perhaps fatally, and when he returns for Bobbie with money Mrs. MacEachern has given him to marry her, she repudiates him with the alleged fact of his mixed blood. Rejected and beaten, not knowing whether he is a murderer, Joe enters the street that will run for fifteen years.

Prostitution is referred to occasionally in *The Hamlet,* and becomes prominent as metaphor and subject in *The Town* and *The Mansion.* In *The Hamlet* the schoolmaster Labove joins his university classmates in a postcommencement trip to Memphis. "He knew what that meant: drinking in a hotel room and then, for some of them at least, a brothel." As soon as the group left the train, he refused to go with his companions to register at the hotel but instead asked for directions to a brothel. "He went alone to the address given him. He knocked firmly at the equivocal door. This would not help him either. He did not expect it to." Labove's problem of course, is his infatuation with Eula Varner. "At least it wont be my virginity she is going to scorn, he told himself" (117).

Jack Houston, the man of action, in contrast to Labove, takes his first wife from a Galveston brothel. "They lived together for seven years. . . . he was mentally and spiritually, and with only an occasional aberration, physically faithful to her who in her turn was loyal, discreet, undemanding, and thrifty with his money" (211).

When he thinks of marrying her it is because of "the impact of the West which was still young enough then to put a premium on individuality, softened and at last abolished his inherited southern-provincial-Protestant fanaticism regarding marriage and female purity, the biblical Magdalene" (212).

Mink Snopes too takes a wife who is a kind of prostitute-in-residence in the lumber camp where he works, perhaps not so much a prostitute as an avid and talented amateur, treating the men in the lumber camp, where Mink sees her "not as a nympholept but the confident lord of a harem" (237).

> He entered not the hot and quenchless bed of a barren and lecherous woman, but the fierce simple cave of a lioness—a tumescence which surrendered nothing and asked no quarter, and which made a monogamist of him forever, as opium and homicide do of those whom they once accept. (238)

Mink's wife, then, abandons promiscuity, if not nympholepsy, for the arduous and brutalizing lot of a tenant farmer's wife. She remains loyal to Mink even though she is threatened and outraged by his murderous feud with Houston. After Mink murders Houston, she prostitutes herself to secure money for Mink's escape, but Mink spurns the money. "Did you sell Will something for it," he asks her scornfully, "or did you just take it out of his pants when he was asleep? Or was it Jody?" (240). Even after his rejection, and after Mink threatens to beat her with a stick, she remains loyal. While Mink bides his time in jail, waiting for Flem to return, his wife boards with Ratliff:

> Her job was in a . . . boarding house with an equivocal reputation, named the Savoy Hotel. Her work began at daybreak and ended sometime after dark, sometimes well after dark. She swept and made the beds and did some of the cooking. . . . She had her meals there and received three dollars a week. "Only she's going to keep her heels blistered running barefooted in and out of them horse-traders' and petty juries' and agents for nigger insurance's rooms all night long," a town wit said. But that was her affair. Ratliff knew nothing about that and cared less and, to his credit, believed even still less than that. (260)

For Mink Snopes's wife, prostitution becomes an expedient of desperate economic necessity. Like Ruby Lamar in *Sanctuary*, she does the best she can with what she has and what she knows, in service to the man who spurns her wages of sin.

In *The Town* prostitution becomes a controlling metaphor for Flem Snopes's manipulation of Eula's affair with Manfred de Spain. As Ratliff explains: "Not catching his wife with Manfred de Spain yet is like that twenty-dollar gold piece pinned to your undershirt on your first maiden trip to what you hope is going to be a Memphis whorehouse. He dont need to unpin it yet" (29). While the simile is superficially witty, even cute, it nevertheless suggests some grim thoughts. Flem, himself sexually incapable, is "going to the whorehouse," first de Spain's bank, and then to de Spain's mansion through his knowledge of, and his ability to manipulate, his wife's frustrated romantic and sexual desires, and those of de Spain as well. And the town tolerates it.

Charley Mallison, the father in one of the few whole and conventionally wholesome families in all of Faulkner's fiction, professes to be immune to Eula's physical attractions, and when his wife, Maggie, laments that her husband is therefore "a mole . . . a Mammoth Cave fish." Charley responds, "That's what you want, is it? A husband that will spend every Saturday night in Memphis chasing back and forth between Gayoso and Mulberry Street——" (48). And Maggie, herself the subject of prostitution after her brother, Gavin Stevens, has been thrashed by de Spain, screams, "You fool! You fool! They dont deserve you! They aren't good enough for you! None of them are, no matter how much they look and act like a—like a—like a god damn whorehouse! None of them! None of them!" (77).[13]

A more substantive reference to prostitution begins when Gavin Stevens reveals that Montgomery Ward has been a whoremonger in France. Beginning with a regular "canteen" dispensing "candy bars and sody pop and hand-knitted socks," Ratliff explains to Chick Mallison, "it got so popular that finally your cousin went his-self and looked at it and found that Montgomery Ward had . . . fixed it up as a new fresh entertainment room with a door in the back and a young French lady he happened to know in it, so that any time a soldier got tired of jest buying socks and chocolate bars he could buy a ticket from Montgomery Ward and go around through the backdoor and get his-self entertained" (114). The French, Ratliff speculates,

> "probably thought the kind of canteen Montgomery Ward was running this time [in Paris] was just about the most solvent and economical and . . . self-perpetuating kind he could a picked out . . . in jest strict entertainment there aint no destructive consumption at all that's got to be replenished at a definite production labor costs: only a normal natural general overall depreciation which would have took place anyhow." (115)

Returning to Jefferson, Montgomery Ward opens a "photographic studio," which proves to be popular at night, at first leading Ratliff and Stevens to speculate that Montgomery Ward is running a whorehouse in Jefferson, but eventually it is revealed that Montgomery Ward is running a "magic lantern," a "peep show," in which the good men of Jefferson can ogle "French postcards." "It's Kodak pictures of men and women together," Ratliff explains to Chick, "without no clothes on much" (162).

Today, of course, Montgomery Ward would be running a fantasy telephone service or an x-rated video store, but for Jefferson of the 1920s, he was outrageous enough. It is only by the most direct action Flem Snopes ever apparently takes that he is able to divert the charge against Montgomery Ward from sending pornography through the mails to simple possession of bootleg alcohol, and it is not until *The Mansion* that we find out why Flem wants his kinsman in the state penitentiary in Parchman rather than in Leavenworth.

And finally there is Eula, whose adultery with de Spain, Flem eventually reveals in order to dispossess Manfred de Spain of his bank. Unpinning his gold piece, Flem drives de Spain from Jefferson and Eula to suicide, " in order to leave her child a mere suicide for a mother instead of a whore" (340).

In *The Mansion* prostitution is treated even more explicitly, in large part because Mink Snopes is headed for Memphis to buy a pistol with which to kill Flem. Mink remembers a trip to Jefferson to buy buckshot shells to kill Jack Houston, and his visit in the train station, "full of the men and boys come down to see the train pass, that were there the three times he had got off of it, looking at him also like he had come from a heap further than a Memphis whorehouse" (35). Memphis is also the milieu of Senator Clarence Egglestone Snopes, "the apostolic venereal ambassador from Gayoso Avenue to the entire north Mississippi banloo" (62). The story of Fonzo and Virgil from *Sanctuary* is retold (71ff), and Montgomery Ward Snopes appears; declining Miss Reba's offer to make him "landlord," he arranges for money to be sent to Mink in Parchman (78).

In Memphis, Mink remembers his own youthful expeditions to

the brothel: "Three times . . . he had wrenched, wrung enough money from the otherwise unpaid labor he did on the tenant farm of the kinsman who had raised him from orphanhood, to visit the Memphis brothels" (282). In 1946

> he knew exactly where he was; by merely turning his head (which he did not) he could have seen the street, the actual housefront (he didn't know it of course and probably wouldn't have recognised her either, but his younger daughter was the madam of it) which he had entered with his mentor that night forty-seven years ago, where waited the glittering arms of women not only shaped like Helen and Eve and Lilith, not only functional like Helen and Eve and Lilith, but colored white like them too, where he had said No not just to all the hard savage years of his hard and barren life, but to Death too in the bed of a public prostitute. (290)

If making love, even in the bed of a commercial prostitute, is saying No to Death, so is making art a way of saying no to death, even in the apparently ephemeral text of a short story in a mass circulation magazine.[14] Faulkner's attitude toward the writing of short stories, I think, was as richly ambivalent as his attitude toward women, be they Madonnas, Magdalenes, or the myriad possibilities in between. He could be lyrical and idealistic about women, and he could express his need for a woman as for "a physical spittoon."[15] "A short story," Faulkner wrote to Joan Williams, "is a crystallised instant, arbitrarily selected, in which character conflicts with character or environment or itself. We both agreed long since that, next to poetry, it is the hardest art form" (SL 345). Faulkner's short stories are, among other things, crystallized instants, often arbitrarily selected, showing Faulkner and his characters in conflict with one another, with their environment, or with themselves. They were also the tricks that he turned. By saving them, transforming and re-forming them, he made "honest women" out of them in his novels, but he was matter-of-fact about the compelling necessities of his own financial situation, writing his agent, Morton Goldman, in 1934, "I have too goddamn many demands on me requiring and necessitating orthodox prostitution to have time to give it away save it can be taken from me while I sleep, you might say" (*SL* 85).

In her study of prostitution in America from 1900 to 1918, Ruth Rosen notes, "Some contemporary feminists, like their Progressive counterparts, regard prostitution as the quintessential exploitation of women in a patriarchal society."[16] But, Rosen contends, women of this era (contemporaries of Caddy Compson, Ruby Lamar, Nancy Mannigoe, and Everbe Corinthia) made choices—bleak though those choices may have been: they could sell their bodies in loveless marriages contracted solely for economic protection, or they could sell their bodies for starvation wages as unskilled workers, or they could sell their bodies as sporting women. Most women who chose to enter prostitution, Rosen concludes, did so because they perceived prostitution as a means of fulfilling particular economic, social, and psychological needs (137). Though I have no desire whatsoever to reopen the old argument about whether Faulkner does or should conform to some canons of sociological and historical realism, it seems to me that the prostitutes in Faulkner's fiction enter their trade for some combination of the reasons Rosen identifies for the women of this period: economic factors, including fragile family economics, the need for supplemental income, the lack of other occupational options, or contempt for other occupational factors, and rising economic expectations. Social and personal problems also contribute, including emotional deprivation, generational conflict, and the double standard of sexual conduct.

But surely these same causes—fragile family economics, the need for additional income, and lack of other occupational options, or contempt for them—drove Faulkner to writing short stories for the national magazines, as the same exigencies on numerous and extended occasions drove him to attempting to write for the movies.[17] And surely emotional deprivation, generational conflict, and the sexual double standard were as much a part of his life as they were a part of the lives of his characters.

If the short stories were Faulkner's tricks, and if writing short stories made Faulkner the whore, then his agent was the pimp, and his publisher was the madam. Our role as readers, in this casting, becomes alarmingly clear, and those who would be critics of the short stories must identify themselves with the impotent and perverse Popeye, panting and drooling in fascination and envy above an act of degradation in which he cannot otherwise participate. But if we take a more charitable view of Faulkner, of his short story writing, of his short stories, and of ourselves, we may, perhaps, achieve some crystallized moments of our own.

NOTES

1. *Selected Letters of William Faulkner*, ed. Joseph Blotner (New York: Random House, 1965), 59. Hereafter cited as *SL*. Citations from Faulkner, noted parenthetically in the text, are to the following editions: *Collected Stories* (New York: Random House, 1950), cited as *CS*; *The Hamlet* (New York: Random, House, 1940); *Light in August*, The Corrected Text (New York: Vintage, 1987); *The Mansion* (New York: Random House, 1959); *Pylon*, The Corrected Text (New York: Vintage, 1987), *The Reivers* (New York: Random House, 1962); *The Town* (New York: Random House, 1957); *Uncollected Stories of William Faulkner*, ed. Joseph Blotner (New York: Random House, 1979), cited as *US*.

2. The typical attitude of the time was well expressed by Hemingway in his recollection of an early conversation with Fitzgerald:

I thought of him as a much older writer. I thought he wrote *Saturday Evening Post* stories that had been readable three years before but I never thought of him as a serious writer. He had told me at the Closerie de Lilas how he wrote what he thought were good stories, and which really were good stories for the *Post*, and then changed them for submission, knowing exactly how he must make the twists that made them into salable magazine stories. I had been shocked at this and I said I thought it was whoring. He said that it was whoring but that he had to do it as he made his money from the magazines to have money ahead to write decent books. I said that I did not believe anyone could write any way except the very best he could write without destroying his talent (*A Moveable Feast* [New York: Scribner's, 1964], 155–56).

3. *Faulkner: A Biography* (New York: Random House, 1984), 100–101.

4. Meta Carpenter Wilde and Orin Borsten, *A Loving Gentleman: The Love Story of William Faulkner and Meta Carpenter* (New York: Simon and Schuster, 1976), 52.

5. His comment about whores to Meta Carpenter, as she recalls it, immediately follows his assertion that he did not sleep with Estelle Faulkner after the birth of their daughter, Jill. But Faulkner also told Meta the fabulous story of the silver plate in his skull, a story he had told other women in the course of appeals for sympathy or intimacy. See *A Loving Gentleman*, 46–47.

6. *Lion in the Garden: Interview with William Faulkner, 1926–1962*, ed. James B. Meriwether and Michael Millgate (New York: Random House, 1968), 239.

7. See Faulkner's letter to Harold Ober early in 1942 anticipating the *Saturday Evening Post*'s possible objection to "My Grandmother Millard and General Bedford

Forrest and the Battle of Harrykin Creek": "They may throw it out because of the can motif" (*SL* 150). For whatever reason, the *Post* refused the story, which was eventually published (for a token price) by *Story* magazine for March-April 1943.

8. For Temple Drake's recounting of this episode, see *Requiem for a Nun* (New York: Random House, 1951), 121. For Faulkner's negotiations with Mencken, see *SL*, 48–49, Blotner, *Faulkner: A Biography*, 267, and Hans H. Skei, *William Faulkner: The Short Story Career* (Oslo: Universitetsforlaget, 1981), 65.

9. On the style of the story see Hans Skei, "Inadequacies of Style in Some of William Faulkner's Short Stories," in *Faulkner's Discourse: An International Symposium*, Lothar Hönnighausen, ed. (Tübigen: Max Niemeyer Verlag, 1989), 234–41. On the moral ambiguity of "Uncle Willy," see Noel Polk, "Faulkner and Respectability," *Fifty Years of Yoknapatawpha*, Doreen Fowler and Ann J. Abadie, eds. (Jackson: University Press of Mississippi, 1980), esp. 114–19. On the possible autobiographical significance of "Uncle Willy," see Barry Hannah, "Faulkner and the Small Man," in *Faulkner and Humor*, Doreen Fowler and Ann J. Abadie, eds. (Jackson: University Press of Mississippi, 1986), 191–94.

10. Bland's question and the narrator's answer subtly but unmistakenly raise the issue of the narrator's sexual preference.

11. The contrast between Faulkner and Hemingway on this point is, as usual, instructive. In the immediate aftermath of the success of *Sanctuary*, Hemingway gave Faulkner one of his typical backhanded compliments:

> My operatives tell me that through the fine work of Mr. William Faulkner publishers will now publish anything rather than trying to get you to delete the better portions of your works, and I look forward to writing of those days of my youth which were spent in the finest whorehouses in the land amid the most brilliant society there found.
>
> *Old lady:* Has this Mr. Faulkner written well of these places?
>
> Splendidly, Madame. Mr. Faulkner writes admirably of them. He writes the best of them of any writer I have read for many years.
>
> *Old lady:* I must buy his works.
>
> Madame, you can't go wrong on Faulkner. He's prolific too. By the time you get them ordered there'll be new ones out.
>
> *Old lady:* If they are as you say there cannot be too many.
>
> Madame, you voice my own opinion.
> (*Death in the Afternoon* [New York: Scribner's, 1932], 173)

12. "Faulkner's First Trilogy: *Sartoris, Sanctuary*, and *Requiem for a Nun*," in *Fifty Years of Yoknapatawpha*, 90–109; see esp. 103–104.

13. Maggie's choice of words here is curious. Surely she is thinking of Eula Snopes, and "they" makes the threat to Gavin both anonymous and multiple, but why the metonymic "whore*house*"?

14. See Robert W. Hamblin, "'Saying No to Death': Toward William Faulkner's Theory of Fiction," in "*A Cosmos of My Own": Faulkner and Yoknapatawpha, 1980*, ed. Doreen Fowler and Ann J. Abadie (Jackson: University Press of Mississippi, 1981), 3-35.

15. See *A Loving Gentleman*, 244.

16. *The Lost Sisterhood: Prostitution in America, 1900–1918* (Baltimore: Johns Hopkins University Press, 1982), xvii.

17. Too, we should remember the avidity with which Faulkner sought the national magazine market in the late 1920s and early 1930s. "If they do not please you," Faulkner wrote of his short stories to the *Post* in 1927, "the Post does not know its own children." "And hark in your ear," he concludes, "I am a coming man, so take warning." James B. Meriwether, "Faulkner's Correspondence With *The Saturday Evening Post*," *Mississippi Quarterly* 30 (Summer 1977): 465.

Beyond Genre?
Existential Experience in Faulkner's
Short Fiction

HANS H. SKEI

William Faulkner's contribution to the short story genre has been described as slight or of minor importance by some critics. He has accordingly been read and analyzed as a born storyteller who had few other concerns than to get his stories told, so that the readers were allowed to listen to old tales and talking and to the best of gossip, presented as directly and simply as possible.[1] By and large, the art of Faulkner's short fiction is not much different from that found in a strong American tradition, and literary scholarship has thus only had to analyze form and style and narrative technique in order to interpret his short fiction. And since the stories relate so significantly to so many of the author's great novels, the stories have often been used to help in the analysis of a novel, and only a few stories have been extensively discussed in their own right. It is of course no surprise that Faulkner's shorter narratives have been regarded as inferior to his longer works, if only tacitly or implicitly; in this respect his short fiction shares the fate of the short story form itself in literary history and scholarship.

A decade ago it was probably still correct to maintain that Faulkner's short fiction had not received the attention it deserved; today I do not think we should hide behind such commonplaces. Yet even if his short fiction has been taken more and more seriously, one may well feel that this has occurred mainly because of the interesting and intriguing interdependency of novel and story. The study of this relationship is a valid and important one in itself, but it also tends to blur significant distinctions between two related but very different forms of narrative: the novel and the short story.

It is also possible to maintain that generic concepts are of little interest in a study of Faulkner's short fiction, not because of the uneven quality of the stories or the relatively few experiments in the short narrative Faulkner made, but because his use and reuse of material in novel and short story form in a sense implies the upheaval of the borderlines between long and short narrative. In Faulkner's work, the German critic Ruth Kilchenmann says, "Unterscheidungen nach Genres [haben] keine Bedeutung."[2] But to see in the dense intertextuality of Faulkner's work a transcendence of the traditional boundaries between types of literature, so that generic concepts are of little interest, is perhaps to rely too heavily on the obvious and superficial.[3] The reuse of material, the reappearance of characters, the echoing of phrases and the propensity for talking and for proverbial wisdom, the linking of episodes in order to create loosely connected novels or cycles of stories, the final impact of which may well be that of a novel, can in my understanding not be called to go "beyond genre." It is to make use of a keen understanding of the functions of literature, so that the individuality of a single short story can be reused with a totally different function in a new context.

The alleged small contribution to the short story as form and the liberty Faulkner took to move freely between short and long fiction, both seem to indicate that generic studies are of little value in any assessment of his short story achievement. I do not agree. In my opinion, a discussion of generic observations, as well as of the instances where Faulkner in any meaningful or significant sense can be said to have transcended the short story form, is needed if the study of his short fiction is to make improvements. If this seems contradictory, let me give only a brief explanation at this point: Modern generic studies are descriptive and seem to recommend a position somewhere between, on one side, Croce, who wanted to do away with all generic divisions, and, on the other side, the many rigid taxonomies where all texts can be pigeonholed once and for all. We should focus on the function of literature, *not* on the borderlines between texts; which is of course also what modern text theory insists on.[4] All the same, we cannot rid ourselves of the idea of forms of literature. It remains a fact that generic concepts have a strong influence in literary studies, and it would not be wise to underestimate their role in most of our interpretive work.

In accordance with this, *my* reason for asking if Faulkner's stories may be said to go beyond genre has nothing to do with his use of the same stories in short and long narratives, nor does it imply that distinctions between types of literature are no longer valid. After all, to know when a story transcends the type or class of literature it belongs to, one has to have a fairly clear understanding of the *differentiae specificae* of that class. What I want to discuss is whether it is reasonable to find in Faulkner's best stories a special kind of interest and a specific narrative mode, which set them apart from most of his own stories and from the average of most stories. If this is so, we could say that the art of his short fiction transcends the limits of the traditional short story, even most of his own stories, and I think this is true for the stories in which an existential experience is described and reflected upon. Since I shall have to modify this statement later on, let me make it perfectly clear that most of Faulkner's stories still must be seen as a novelist's short stories, and that they remain firmly placed within a story telling tradition in which action and plot are key components.[5] Yet Faulkner's best stories, three or four, perhaps a dozen on a generous day, go beyond the short story as it is commonly described and defined, and they do so thematically as well as formally, since the formal aspects are thematized. They present experience, episodes, critical situations, which are not of the everyday type, which are not controlled and tempered by society, rules, and conventions, which somehow elude us in normal daily life, but which may be seen as more basic, more primitive, and perhaps more *genuine* than the experience relayed in stories of action and event in a society of men and women, at a given time and in a specific place, from which the stories never take off. I have called this "existential" experience; I might have used terms such as experience of the mythic, religious, or sacred, or perhaps of the uncanny. The strength of Faulkner's best short stories is their combination of the realistic, detailed everyday world, *and* the sudden, at times epiphanic, experience of the self in a much larger context, often implying a choice of values which through symbolic language and imagery may be interpreted as more general than the individual's experience of the crisis which led up to it. Very often we may find that the momentary insights die quickly, or that they only have a vague feeling which escapes the protagonists, an *epiphany manquée*, as in a number of the early sketches and story attempts, or a foreboding of knowledge which will be obtainable only later, as in the stories with Quentin Compson as child protagonist.[6]

Now, some of you may feel that this description of the stories in which Faulkner presents existential experience places them very much within the genre, not beyond or outside it. Although I feel that the literary short story's most prominent feature is its particular emphasis on existential problems—aloneness, meaninglessness, anxiety, emptiness, freedom, choice—I cannot exclude nine-tenths of the short story canon in order to reach a new definition which suits my purpose. Even if it complicates my argument, Charles E. May's fine essay on "The Nature of Knowledge in Short Fiction,"[7] should be mentioned here, not because it insists on the absolute difference between long and short narratives, which it does, but because it describes aspects of the modern short story which are clearly present in Faulkner's best stories.

"The short story is the most adquate form to confront us with reality as we perceive it in our most profound moments,"[8] according to Charles May. "Our most profound moments" may here well be used to indicate just the kind of existential experience which I find in Faulkner's best short fiction, and the quotation obviously also supports the notion of a close link between the short story form and the special kind of experience presented in it. In comparison with the narrative long form—the novel—with its broader perspective and wider range, the brief narrative seems to be much more subtly adjusted to present our encounters with something beyond ourselves and everyday life; it is admirably suited to present existential experience and thus function as exemplary. The modern short story reflects a modern experience and conscience, an experience of loss and pain, of something broken and not mended, of strings and attachments gone, of uncertainties as to one's place in the world and in society.

This should help to give an indication of the close affinity between existential experience and much although certainly not *all* short fiction. Heide Ziegler's very competent study, *Existentielles Erleben und kurzes Erzählen*,[9] investigates this affinity by looking at the comic, tragic, grotesque, and mythic in Faulkner's short fiction. And Charles May's short story theory is based upon the alleged different experience and knowledge in the brief narrative. Yet contrary to Ziegler, who stresses that the combination existential experience / short fiction cannot be understood as a necessary constituent of the genre,[10] May insists that "short fiction, by its very length, demands both a subject matter and a set of artistic conventions that derive from and establish the primacy of 'an experience' directly and emotionally created and encountered."[11] As mentioned, I am reluctant to define short fiction as narrowly as I find this to be, yet willing to insist upon the short story's unique ability to present a different reality in which we experience disruptions and dangers which we normally avoid in our protected lives. And since all short story definitions have stressed the intensity of vision and the focus on the climax of a situation, it is perhaps not very radical to claim that the short story is particularly suitable for presenting existential experience. If a choice involving an ethical value is at the center of the story, the text is free to make use of only the absolutely necessary story elements to establish the crisis and the choice. Accordingly the very subject matter and the thematic interest become responsible for the narrative strategy, resulting in the brevity of the story.

Many of Faulkner's brief narratives are of the kind that give confirmation, comfort, and safety, albeit that hyperbolic humor or a very generous irony may be needed to abate some of the hardships and pains. In some texts tensions remain unresolved; characters are torn between conflicting forces and interests; oppressed and poor and weak, they fight to convince at least themselves that they exist, that they have a choice, or that some day they shall know more and be better off. Faulkner's best short stories very often become a vehicle for expressing not only the protagonist's vague or misunderstood feeling of bereavement, but they include a description of and a reflection about the very moment when opposing forces struggle for command of soul and body. That Faulkner's narrative principle for presenting such central scenes is the "frozen moment" seems to be generally accepted by Faulkner scholars today,[12] but one should bear in mind that to capture and isolate a split second from the everlasting flow of time, freezing it, halting time, and showing man in his ageless struggle, before sending him off again, is more than technique or habit. It shows man's plight in an unappeasable temporality, and in the final analysis the effectiveness of the frozen moments, of the tableaux, depends not on the tableaux themselves—that is, the story components—but on the reflections which are transmitted in a voice coming from a different place than the point of view and which often implies questions of historicity and temporality. So perhaps, after all, Faulkner's "time novels" have their equivalents in his best short stories, if we look beneath the obvious surface meaning. It is also significant to be aware that man is in motion, despite the key rhetorical device, and it may be more correct to describe the frozen moment as dialectic of nature; we always encounter stasis *and* change, immobility *and* motion, sound *and* silence.

Independent of our interpretation of the "frozen moment," its central function in Faulkner's narrative strategy cannot be doubted, and it is furthermore possible to suggest a close connection between this technical device and the special thematic concern which I have called existential. Man is viewed in midstride, and stopped for a moment, on his way to some new foolishness or deviltry, but man is also subjected to inevitable choices. The choices are often of the kind that can only be made by individual man, in situations where he is left completely alone, and in fictional accounts of these crisis situations they often appear as ephiphanic moments of clarity or possible insight. Whatever the outcome of the confrontation with oneself, some sort of basic value, a personal ethos, is revealed if not reached. The created and narrativized existential crisis situation may easily be seen as exemplary because of its apparent universality. When or if *conditio humana* is depicted in Faulkner's short stories, we are inclined to interpret such texts less in relation to a particular situation for one human being, as in relation to the common plight of mankind. This tendency to generalize in humanistic terms is, I think, not so much a part of the inheritance from the New Critics as it is something inherent in the short story form itself, when explored and exploited to its fullest.[13]

From these remarks on generic problems in general and on the significance of the existential mode of experience in short fiction, it is time to become more pragmatic. But let me present a few more observations about the nature of the short story, before I resist all theory.

The short story at its most characteristic is placed in a world different from the social world with its civilized life in most novels, and it seems to put our accepted knowledge of the world and our fellow men in jeopardy. The short story, as Frank O'Connor says, "remains . . . remote from the community" and gives "an intense awareness of human loneliness." In William Faulkner's short story world we find a number of "outlawed figures wandering about the fringes of society,"[14] but we also find numerous lonely, estranged, lost souls in the midst of organized life in a community of men.

Although we may discuss the lonely outsiders in stories such as "The Hill," "Barn Burning," "That Evening Sun," "Red Leaves," and "A Justice," the strange but not so surprising fact is that existential crisis situations occur more frequently in Faulkner's "Middle Ground" stories;[15] that is, in the short stories in which "mainstream America" and middle class values, rules, and regulations are presented and scrutinized through the fate of an outsider: "Uncle Willy," "There Was a Queen," "Golden Land." The loneliest figures in Faulkner's short fiction are lonely in the company of men, and because they try to keep their integrity and some pride and self-esteem in the midst of a deterioration of all values, their estrangement is the result of a society which has forgotten all the important values, those values Faulkner's narrators refer to as the old verities of the heart. These truths are compassionately defended in some of the short stories from World War I, notably in "All the Dead Pilots," and they are preached as if they were the gospel in the World War II stories, notably in "The Tall Men" and "Shall Not Perish." These sentiments seem to have been an inevitable and almost inadvertent part of the rhetoric in stories about a collective crisis, and are of little interest here. More important are the "Beyond" stories, which present man as essentially alone in critical situations, and which also have a philosophy of life to discuss, in some cases even with comments on the artist's special kind of lonely life in the never-ending struggle with elusive words.

The existential mode of experience is not found in Faulkner's short fiction all through his career. As he grew older and perhaps even wiser, more and more stories were located in the countryside regions of Yoknapatawpha, and the loyal and courageous and hardworking people there were used to *demonstrate* ways of being which other characters in earlier stories fought hard to achieve. As readers we are left uncertain in the early open-ended stories.[16] The potential for freedom, even to choose one's own ethical value, in a world apparently devoid of meaning, requires open texts, and it demands a technique which allows the hero to reflect. Hence the frozen moment's significance in these stories, and the use of narrated monologues which somehow gives access to the consciousness of the protagonist and the existential situation he experiences. Faulkner's "old verities" may perhaps, in relation to the particular experience one character has, be seen as an unchanging anthropologic value, a universal ideal, towards which the existential experience and a discovery of a personal ethos may lead the character.

If we look at a few Faulkner stories in which "the existential," meaning questions regarding choice, freedom, suffering, anxiety, absurdity, death, but also meaning the struggle to create oneself, to become, to come into being, we may begin with a text from the period when the author himself suffered through all sorts of crises and when his art was extremely self-reflective: the apprenticeship years. I have selected "The Hill"[17] as my example, and it is such an obvious choice that the text does not really need much comment. This is the case also because the nameless protagonist in the sketch only is on the border of experiencing something which may change the direction of his life. The solitary dreamer leaves behind him "a world of endless toil and troubled slumber,"[18] but returns to it, a little shaken, but hardly with any new insights except that he shall have to live in a sordid but social and organized world, and the idealized world of beauty and dreams is not to become his.

The feeling of alienation seems to set in only when the hill-climber vaguely feels that there is a better way to live, but the failure to comprehend is complete. Yet the abstract character of the sketch, its poetic language, and the hill-valley motif may be seen as indicative of a self-awareness which would later include reflections on the very self, identity, and being: in short, existential problems.

In contrast to the tieless casual of "The Hill" most of Faulkner's characters carry with them the burden and the blessing of a living past, be it the Civil War, family matters, lost pride, guilt, or remorse. They have to adjust this past and their own self to the present in order to have some degree of freedom in the future, or to have a future life at all. The wounded war veteran on his way home in "Mountain Victory"[19] is an example of this, and in this slowly unfolding but carefully structured story important ethical values are tested. The story ends violently and conclusively, yet the problematic motivation behind the protagonist's decision not to negotiate for his life lingers on in the reader's mind as in an open story. The existential conflict is perhaps not central enough to show how all textual elements derive from this key situation and contribute to it. Yet the story is among the best Faulkner ever wrote, and I shall discuss it at some length.

"Mountain Victory" has been given only cursory treatment by scholars and critics. I find this to be very strange, since the most important elements in the story clearly transcend the interpretive level where the Civil War and its effects on people is emphasized. On a superficial level the conflict in the story is that between a Confederate officer and a Union soldier, and the action is in a sense the aftermath of the great conflict. Moreover, racial attitudes are at stake, and the racism is also fuelled by a strong class hatred. But the local and private conflicts are transferred onto a different level, so that more basic and universal problems pervade the text, and we experience a struggle with personal and existential problems on the part of more characters than the protagonist himself.

All through "Mountain Victory" there is a sense of irrevocable tragedy, of unappeasable destiny, and we watch a conflict unfold from what should have been a normal encounter between strangers. Although the text gives external motivation for the conflict, this chance encounter seems to become a force stronger than the individuals and their part in it, and their very existence is threatened with a ruthlessness that seems inevitable.

The skeleton of this story in eleven parts is very simple, almost anecdotic in its brevity. Major Saucier Weddel, on his way home to his plantation in Mississippi after four years of fighting in Virginia, halts at a cabin in the Tennessee mountains and asks for shelter for himself, his Negro servant, and their horses. In the poor white family of five the elder son, Vatch, has also been to the war. He hates his enemies with uncontrolled violence, and no one can stop him when he smells rebel blood again, although the others do not want any more killing. When leaving early on the following morning, Saucier Weddel and the young boy, Hule, who has tried to persuade Weddel to take him and his sister away with him but who never seems to have really made up his mind whether to help the Major to escape or to help his father and brother in preparing the ambush, are shot and killed, and the Negro must then die because he has seen it all.

The most interesting interpretive questions have to be concerned with the deeper reasons for the conflict between Weddel and Vatch and why Weddel did not try to escape, and with the young boy's and his sister's interest in Weddel. The story is very subtle in its ethical implications, and the reader has to balance his reactions to a text which mostly consists of dialogue but also has a rather detached, omniscient narrator to present setting and character from the outside.

Weddel and Vatch have both been to the war: Weddel is tired of war, and he is defeated. Vatch is one of the victors, and has lost all decency and respect for people. Weddel feels nothing, whereas Vatch feels a mad hatred. Weddel, having fought and lost, has learned a lesson in humility; Vatch has learned nothing. Given his background, Weddel's arrogance and cynicism only slowly give way to more life-giving forces, which, ironically, prove to be fatal.

Weddel contemplates his situation—having lost a war and being trapped on his way home to what must be ruins—and inadvertently he sums up some of the things that make life so important—and so difficult:

> He lay rigid on his back in the cold darkness, thinking of home. "Contalmaison. Our lives are summed up in sounds and made significant. Victory. Defeat. Peace. Home. That's why we must do so much to invent meanings for the sounds, so damned much. Especially if you

are unfortunate enough to be victorious: so damned much. It's nice to be whipped; quiet to be whipped. To be whipped and to lie under a broken roof, thinking of home." (CS 766)

Weddel's experience during the war has changed him, but he still acts within character and consistently. He is afraid that he has forgotten to be afraid, but when he leaves in "the thick cold dawn," he realizes that he is still *alive*, in a deeper sense of the word:

> "And so I am running away," Weddel said. "When I get home I shall not be very proud of this. Yes, I will. It means that I am still alive. Still alive, since I still know fear and desire. Since life is an affirmation of the past and a promise to the future. So I am still alive—Ah." (CS 772–73)

Weddel is then killed, also because he could not possibly trade with his new-won insights, with the humility and humanism that seem to be internalized in his character, and which the brief encounter on the Tennessee hill-top puts into relief. But since I can only give a few examples and arguments here, I can only hope that they indicate the overriding value standpoints in the story and the validity of interpreting the text in this direction.

There are other elements in the story which add to the existential mode of experience in it: The girl in the family and her youngest brother share a dream of a less barren, less harsh world than the one they are doomed to live in—a better world in which girls even wear shoes. The dream, and the desperate attempts to use Weddel to make it come true, adds a moving touch of human frailty, loneliness, and desire to the story. The youths are lost, helpless and pitiable creatures, and when it ultimately becomes Weddel's choice to *save* them or not, we can see how the emotional poverty and the pathetic dreams of these characters add to the conflict and become instrumental in the ensuing tragedy.

In the ruthless and sublime inevitability of "Mountain Victory" Faulkner created a drama in which conflicts far beyond those immediately related to the encounter and the action are described. In my opinion there is thus every reason to compare this story with, for example, "Barn Burning" or even with "Red Leaves," because of the obvious intertextual relationship and because of the treatment of a particular existential experience which transcends the limits of the story elements in the text.

Major Saucier Weddel, a company commander in Jackson's Army of the Valley, is completely *alone* and *lost* and *defeated*, but he has something which sets him apart from numerous other estranged and alienated figures in Faulkner's short fiction: He has a set of ethical norms to guide him, and having had them put to a final test, he knows that they are still valid. Other characters go through experiences where their very existence is threatened, in order to reach an uncertain value, which they may later try out, and have confirmed. I can only refer you to a number of the stories that accompany "Mountain Victory" in the collection *Doctor Martino and Other Stories,* and to a number of stories describing the uncertain experiences or memories of them in a child narrator's voice; for example, "Uncle Willy" and "A Justice." Rootless and homeless characters in extreme situations are found also in the "Beyond" stories, as when Don and I in the story "Mistral,"[20] two Americans in Europe and outsiders to everything and everybody around them, feel the wind and the cold in their bones. But the desperate sense of helplessness and frustration they feel stems from their inexperience and now being subjected to forces beyond their grasp:

> It was like being at the bottom of a dead volcano filled with that lost savage green wind dead in its own motion and full of its own driving and unsleeping dust. (*CS* 860)

The narrator reflects later on in the story that perhaps, in "any natural exaggerated situation—wind, rain, drouth—man is always alone" (*CS* 864). In a different but as real sense the unnamed poet of "Carcassonne" is also alone in deep agony and despair, brought about by the dreams and hardships of artistic creation, and here the final solution to a crisis that may well become existential, death's quietude and solitude, is discussed in a body-soul conflict which runs through the whole story, and it also finds expression in the fabulations and reflections of the poet which in fact make up the whole text.

The struggle for survival combines with the struggle for individuality, for being, for asserting one's place in the world. Characters are often so degraded and poor that they fight hard to convince themselves that they *are*, repeating insistently to themselves *I am, I exist,* but they have to prove this, through their existence. Perhaps we as readers are so accustomed to subtleties and high tragedy that we do not see the existential experience of such characters as very important, because it happens on a small scale, in familiar settings, and with few of the overtones modernistic literature has prepared us to look for.

Yet the struggle for a personal ethical value and a recognition of self, in the eyes of oneself and the world, is at the center of the existential experience in Faulkner's short fiction, although I would not say that it is in the foreground of most stories. The values are often so traditional and basic that they may escape our attention, but they are also so basic that without them life would not be worth living. Numerous narrators and characters lend their voices to statements of this sort, or we may say that they express one of the proverbial truths that are echoed so often in Faulkner's stories that we are tempted to ascribe them to a different voice, a voice above, behind, or beyond the narrators and characters. It is a troubled voice, yet always in good faith, characteristic of the author's most prominent quality: his generous acceptance of man's folly and man's greatness.

It is perhaps not necessary, by way of conclusion, to return to generic questions, and to test the validity of the alleged close affinity between the short story as a form of narrative literature and existential experience. There can be little doubt that the short story form lends itself admirably to descriptions of existential crisis situations, and it may well be that the combination of the two often results in short stories better than the average. In Faulkner's case I think this is true; also because most of his stories are of a different kind, even when they imply important choices on the part of their protagonists.

Having discussed existential experience in Faulkner's short fiction and related it to the problematics of generic concepts, one may wonder if the ethics of reading Faulkner's short fiction, or the *ethicity* of it as Hillis Miller would have said,[21] should not have been included. But perhaps that is exactly what I have been talking about all the time.

NOTES

1. When answering questions at the University of Virginia and in other interviews, Faulkner himself contributed to such an understanding of his short story achievement. See *Faulkner in the University* (Charlottesville: University Press of Virginia, 1959). For a negative evaluation of Faulkner's short stories, see, e.g., Dorothy Tuck, *Crowell's Handbook of Faulkner* (New York: Thomas Y. Crowell, 1964). See also the introductory chapter to my *William Faulkner: The Novelist as Short Story Writer* (Oslo: Universitetsforlaget, 1985).

2. Ruth Kilchenmann, *Die Kurzqeschichte, Formen und Entwicklung* (Stuttgart, Berlin, Köln, Mainz, 1967), 149.

3. Related problems are discussed briefly in Hans-Wolfgang Schaller's dissertation, "Kompositionsformen im Erzählwerk, William Faulkners: Entwicklunqszüqe von der Kurzprosa zum Roman" (Göttingen, 1973); see in particular chapter 4, 1.

4. Very sensible discussions of genre theory, based on a study of the most important genre discussions in the last decades, can be found in Paul Hernadi, *Beyond Genre: New Directions in Literary Classification* (Ithaca: Cornell University Press, 1972).

5. This is of course my central argument in *William Faulkner: The Novelist as Short Story Writer.* Faulkner seems to have used very inclusive and wide-ranging material for his short stories, material that in a sense would have lent itself more readily to a novel.

6. It is important to note that I distinguish between a subgroup of short stories and the short story genre here, so that Faulkner's *best* or most competent stories to me appear to belong to the subgroup which most often deals with existential experience. Charles May (cf. note 7 and further in the text) insists that the short story genre should be defined on the basis of the special kind of knowledge found in the stories, and which he finds to be closely related to the question of *length.*

7. See Charles E. May, "The Nature of Knowledge in Short Fiction," *Studies in Short Fiction* 21 (1984): 327–38.

8. Ibid., 338.

9. Heide Ziegler, *Existentielles Erleben und kurzes Erzählen. Das Komische, Traqische, Groteske und Mythische in William Faulkners "Short Stories"* (Stuttgart: Metzler, 1977).

10. See Ziegler, *Existentielle Erleben und kurzes Erzählen,* 167.

11. See May, "The Nature of Knowledge in Short Fiction," 328.

12. Heide Ziegler centers her study on the "frozen moment" as the agent for bringing about existential experience, but is also aware of the problems in using such a term when *growth and maturation* often are key thematic components of the text.

13. Ziegler's arguments also tend to go in this direction: what she calls the *exemplary* nature of the existential experience is related to its inherent universality. May would probably prefer terms such as "basic" or "more original," rather than anthropological or universal.

14. Quotations from Frank O'Connor, *The Lonely Voice* (Cleveland: World Publishing Company, 1963), 19–21. May uses some of the same quotations on page 333 of his essay on "The Nature of Knowledge in Short Fiction."

15. The designations "The Middle Ground" stories, the "Beyond" stories, etc., refer to Faulkner's own section titles in *Collected Stories*.

16. It is dangerous to present a theory of different attitudes and different interests in certain phases of Faulkner's career; e.g., from the "outrage of a potential believer" in his early years, to a much more balanced acceptance of man's capacities in his post-Nobel Prize years. A number of interesting discussions of trends in the late career can be found in Michel Gresset and Kenzaburo Ohashi, eds., *Faulkner: After the Nobel Prize* (Kyoto: Yamaguchi, 1987).

17. "The Hill" is most readily available in Carvel Collins, ed., *Early Prose and Poetry* (Boston: Little, Brown, 1962).

18. *Early Prose and Poetry*, 92.

19. "Mountain Victory" in *Collected Stories*, 745–77. The versions before the story's inclusion in the collection *Doctor Martino and Other Stories* (1934) are all titled "A Mountain Victory."

20. See *Collected Stories*, 843–76.

21. J. Hillis Miller, *The Ethics of Reading* (New York: Columbia University Press, 1987).

"Carcassonne," "Wash," and the Voices of Faulkner's Fiction

DAVID MINTER

Compared with most of his famous contemporaries, William Faulkner went through a long apprenticeship. F. Scott Fitzgerald, Faulkner's senior by one year, published his third novel, *The Great Gatsby* (1925), one year before Faulkner published his first, *Soldiers' Pay* (1926), by which time Fitzgerald had also published three volumes of short stories. John Dos Passos, who was also a year Faulkner's senior, published three novels, including *Manhattan Transfer* (1925), before Faulkner published one. Compared with Fitzgerald and Dos Passos, Ernest Hemingway was a slow starter, but compared with Faulkner, his senior by one year, he was a sprinter. Like *Soldiers' Pay*, *The Sun Also Rises* was published in 1926. It was Hemingway's fourth book, and his second major book, *In Our Time* having been published in 1925.[1]

Slow starts are, of course, not always fatal in literature. Wallace Stevens, perhaps America's greatest lyric poet of the twentieth century, published his first book, *Harmonium* (1923) when he was forty-four, by which age Hart Crane had been dead eleven years and T. S. Eliot had published at least seven books. Still, especially for a writer of fiction, Faulkner was a conspicuously slow starter. His was in fact a career in which almost everything truly memorable happened in the middle, between *Sartoris* and *The Sound and the Fury* in 1929 and *Go Down, Moses* in 1942. Good cases have, of course, been made for the significance of the earlier and later writings. But even the strongest of these revolve around the great fiction that he wrote between 1929 and 1942. Having stated this as an observation, let me state it as a challenge. To what extent are we prepared to have Faulkner's early writings—his poems, his poem sequences, his dream-play, and his prose sketches and stories—challenge assumptions shaped by our reading of the great fiction that drew us to him in the first place?

Marginalized texts, as we continue to learn, frequently possess the power to be unsettling. This is true of works written by lost or forgotten writers—Kate Chopin (1851–1904) and Zora Neale Hurston (ca. 1901–1960), for example—within a country that decides to reclaim them. In a nation like our own, which is so powerful that it can declare other nations "third-world countries," the shelf of marginalized texts is likely to include most if not all the work of writers who happen to have been born in that other, so-called "third" world. In thinking about Faulkner's ties to "third-world" authors, furthermore, and his considerable appeal to them, it is important to remember that in 1950, when he received the Nobel Prize for 1949, he remained so marginal that the New York *Times* felt free to disavow completely his "picture of American life."[2]

It is, of course, not always clear whether we marginalize texts because they are unsettling or make them more unsettling by marginalizing them. Similarly, it is at least possible that we lose as well as gain from the process by which we turn puzzling texts into established classics. For a part of the work of cultural assimilation, which is one of the social functions of literary criticism, is the domestication of the strange, the taming of the wild, the co-opting of the *other.* It is at least possible, therefore, that "minor" works of "major" writers, simply because they remain relatively neglected, possess the potential to challenge us, provided we control our inclination to domesticate their exoticism and tame their wildness.

We can, I think, find instructive examples of both good and bad readings of strange, disconcerting texts in *Absalom, Absalom!,* after Mr. Compson introduces Charles Bon's letter, which tells its own story and has, as you may recall, a history: it has been given by Judith Sutpen to Mr. Compson's mother, a week after Judith has buried Charles Bon. Once Mr. Compson finds himself holding the letter in his hands, however, he finds himself wanting what most of us want some of the time and some of us want all of the time: he wants closure with regard to its origin, purpose, and meaning. He wants to become or to find a final, authoritative reader capable of providing a final, authoritative reading. What Bon's letter triggers in *Absalom, Absalom!*, however, is an opening up of new possibilities through readings and rereadings, some of which at least appear to be misreadings, since they appear to be contradictory of one another. Perspectives not only multiply— Bon's, Judith's, Henry's, Mr. Compson's, Quentin's, Shreve's; they overlap and overcross, so that we get, for example, both Mr. Compson's sense of Judith's reading and his critique of his own reading: "It just does not explain," he says. Time and again Faulkner teases us into and out of thought by the sense that everything is about to fall into place, about to fit into some explanatory pattern, about to become clear and distinct. But this promised moment of certitude remains elusive, just out of reach, "almost now, now, now," as Faulkner puts it at one point, but never quite.[3]

Through the puzzled, resonating voices of his fiction, Faulkner makes the act of writing a form of reading, and he makes the act of reading a form of writing. Though never identical, these acts are so closely related that each always suggests as well as assumes the other. Many of the difficulties that Faulkner creates for his characters, like many of those he creates for his readers, derive from the special form that his generosity as an author takes: his willingness to share his tasks and even his prerogatives as a writer with his characters and his readers. Like many gifts, however, this one imposes obligations, which is one of the main reasons that it took Faulkner's fiction so long to teach us how to read it. In the listening, remembering, and talking of Miss Rosa, Mr. Compson, Quentin, and Shreve, and in their inventions, which include not only characters and events but also large interpretive schemes, we locate versions of Faulkner's labor as an artist; in their willingness to listen endlessly, to try for a total recall, to speculate and surmise, to arrange and rearrange, to repeat, condense, elaborate, and invent, we locate versions of what Faulkner as writer is doing and what we as readers must do if we are to become his readers. In some of his works—in *Go Down, Moses* and *Light in August*, for example—one story leads to another; in others—in *As I Lay Dying* and *The Sound and the Fury*, for example, one version of a story leads to another version; and in others, notably *Absalom, Absalom!* but also *Go Down, Moses*—both of these processes—the one by which stories lead to stories and the one by which versions of stories lead to more versions—go on simultaneously.

Such interplay yields many things—"such mixed motion and such imagery," to borrow a line from Wallace Stevens's poem, "The Rock," that even seeming "barrenness becomes a thousand things/And so exists no more."[4] What it does not yield—in fact positively resists and even defies—is closure. We do not move from tentative stories, or provisional versions of stories, to final, complete, authoritative ones. Faulkner goes on and on, strewing difficulties in our path, which is why we often find ourselves moving back and forth between fascination and frustration, engagement and resistance, insight and bafflement. Partial, filtered scenes, shadowy, elusive characters, tentative, provisional stories are frequently all we have. Finally, however, the remarkable inadequacies of the elements that we possess do nothing so much as justify the remarkable repetitions and proliferations that we encounter.

The ways in which the vacancies and deficits of the elements of Faulkner's fiction not only match but justify his extravagancies of style can, I think, tell us something about Faulkner's sense of the occasion and purpose of art. Let me try to get at this by pairing quotes from two very different thinkers. "If we *had* life," Richard Wagner once remarked, "we should have no need of art." "The very disintegration and inadequacy of the world," Gyorgy Lukacs tells us, in *The Theory of the Novel*, "is the precondition for the existence of art and its becoming conscious."[5] Faulkner not only seems to assume these things; he also discovers them, time and again, always with a sense of surprise that constitutes both an affront and a gift, an occasion for dismay and an occasion for joy. Within his great novels, art takes its deeper logic from what Wagner calls *life* and Lukacs calls *the world*. For Faulkner it is nothing so much as the inadequacy and the possible disintegration of individual works of art—or individual versions of stories— that provide the precondition and the justification of more art. Yes, and if we *had* art—that is, fully and finally possessed it—he seems to add to Wagner's statement, we should have no need of more art. Just as loss leads to invention—Miss Rosa's loss of hope as well as not-husband, for example; or the South's loss of the War; or Sutpen's loss of his design; or America's loss of its innocence— so also does the failure of one invention lead to another, as flawed words lead to stubborn sounds in Wallace Stevens's "The Poems of Our Climate."

> The imperfect is our paradise.
> Note that, in this bitterness, delight,
> Since the imperfect is so hot in us,
> Lies in flawed words and stubborn sounds.[6]
>   (Wallace Stevens, "The Poems of Our Climate")

Faulkner goes on inventing, and permitting his characters to invent, and inviting his readers to invent, not only in order to celebrate imagination and invention as the novelist's and the novel's strength, nor merely in order to incorporate imagination and invention as subjects of his novels, but also in order to define them as deeply human capacities born of deeply human needs.[7] A sense of community, like the sense of beginnings and endings, is everywhere felt in Faulkner's fiction, but it is everywhere felt as imperiled. Like beginnings and endings, the sense of community is a human creation, a fabrication, and like them, it exists only as it is being recreated. We go on, then, as Faulkner's readers just as

Judith goes on as Sutpen's daughter, half convinced that "it cant matter" but knowing, too, that "it must."[8]

Given our desire for closure, which is, of course, also a need, one temptation we face as Faulkner's readers lies in this: that, in seeking to recover the core event or the original utterance in their intrinsic meaning—like some archaeologist seeking in old ruins the lost city where culture began; or as some primatologist seeking in sounds emitted by nonhuman primates, the lost beginnings of language itself—we will resort to fitful grasping of events and their meanings that are already simplifications and reductions. This, I think, is Mr. Compson's failing. Another risk, matching the first, but set as it were to a different tune, is this: that given our desire, which is also a need, to avoid simplification and reduction, especially of the documents that mean most to us, we will resort to deferral, avoidance, or evasion.[9] These two risks, motions of the soul known to most of us, lead in different ways to the same place: to knowing that stops short of being and imagining that stops short of at-onement.

We can, however, recognize in our predicament, caught between these two unsatisfactory alternatives, a third possibility: that of recognizing in Faulkner's great fiction texts so replete with meanings that they seem not to withhold or defer meaning so much as to bequeath it by giving us approximations, or models of approximations, that are probably true enough, which is to say approximations that suffice, and so come to constitute what Robert Frost called momentary stays against confusion.[10] Since philosophy must also work with language, and since language is a locus of confusion, error, and deception as well as truth, it may well be that philosophy, too, must talk around experience, must proceed, not by directly mapping truth but by formulating and presenting approximations of it. But two things seem clear: that literature fulfills itself in dialogue, not assertion; and that Faulkner's fiction not only exemplifies but dramatizes this. As a result, its motion is always double. On one side, it yields approximations; and on the other, it holds in reserve further approximations, additional to those that, with care, skill, diligence, and luck, we have discerned. It holds this plenitude of approximations, furthermore, not in some impossible sacred grove but in a community of human discourse. *Absalom, Absalom!* establishes such a community, I think. And it is a community in which faith (what Judith Sutpen calls the "it must" of meaning and purpose) becomes a form of doubt (what she calls the "it cant" of meaning and purpose), and doubt becomes a form of faith, so that, like her, we are always, in saying one of these, already saying the other.[11]

2

But what has any of this to do with "Carcassonne" and "Wash," or "the voices of Faulkner's fiction"? "Carcassonne" was first published in *These 13* (1931) which included such famous stories as "A Rose for Emily" and "Dry September." Yet in both *These 13* and later in his *Collected Stories* (1950), Faulkner gave this strange, early poetic sketch or prose poem a special place of honor, as the last story in both books. It held, we may fairly assume, a special place in his memory: "that's a piece I've always liked," he remarked, at the University of Virginia, "because there was the poet again. I wanted to be a poet, and I think of myself now as a failed poet, not as a novelist at all but a failed poet who had to take up what he could do."[12]

During most of his long apprenticeship, Faulkner devoted himself primarily to writing poems and poem sequences. Many of the prose sketches, including "The Hill" and "Nympholepsy" as well as "Carcassonne," that seem likely to belong to the period between 1920 and 1925 are written in lush, poetic prose, and are as much prose poems, or poetic sketches, as short stories. Like the poems and poem sequences—*The Marble Faun, The Lilacs,* and *Vision in Spring*—that Faulkner wrote and revised between 1920 and 1925, and like his dream play, *The Marionettes,* and his chivalric tale, *Mayday,* his sketches are full of echoes of other writers—Byron, Shelley, Keats, Robert Browning, Tennyson, Swinburne, Housman, and Eliot, to name a few prominent examples.[13] Like Melville, Faulkner was troubled by the thought that writers are always inheritors and descendants, yet like Melville he went on borrowing shamelessly. Like Emerson, he began early to feel that further imitation might mean suicide, but like Emerson he had a hard time knowing when to stop. In his early writings the web of associations in which he was moving as a young man is felt everywhere. Fiction, of course, played a large part in his early education, particularly works of the great nineteenth-century "realists" of England, France, and Russia. So, too, did Hawthorne, Poe, Melville, Mark Twain, and Conrad as well as the unavoidable William Shakespeare. But the long tradition of literary romanticism, stretching from the late eighteenth century to the early twentieth, dominated, instilling a high regard for inspiration and genius and a certain kind of sincerity, both as concepts and as values.

In the early '20s, however, and after his fashion, which meant for the most part alone, in his room or in the woods, Faulkner also began using both his writing and his reading to school himself in the works of a group of writers, of France as well as England, who were giving late romanticism a new tilt.[14] With Arthur Symons's *The Symbolist Movement in Literature* (1919) as his guide and older, more advanced contemporaries, like Eliot and Conrad Aiken, as models, Faulkner began reading Laforgue, Mallarmé, and Verlaine, as well as Walter Pater and Oscar Wilde. If, like Yeats, it was in part from Pater that he learned to write lush, extravagant, poetic prose,[15] it was from the French poets, and from Aiken and Eliot, that he acquired his affinity for that French master of the mask, Pierrot, both as a playful, amoral, Harlequin and as a sincere, confused, and doomed Hamlet.[16]

Examination of both of these parts of Faulkner's literary heritage might well be extended, particularly by focusing on their interplay in Faulkner's own writings. But it is on two of his early prose sketches that I want to focus, first, in order to get at some of Faulkner's own divided impulses and allegiances as a writer, and second, in order to locate several things that he needed to free himself from before he could become a great writer, including certain parts of his conception of poetry and poets.

Faulkner's early, recurring explorations of the role of the creative imagination and the plight of the artist have received considerable attention, in part because Faulkner continued to call attention to them. We've already glimpsed his doing this in response to a query about "Carcassonne," which he characterized as a failed poet's dream-song about a heroic but doomed dreamer. But this kind of thing came up repeatedly. We have, for example, only to picture Faulkner, sitting in the small, sparsely furnished rooms in which he preferred to work, wondering, as he did in 1931, whether he had created the world of his fictions, filled with "shady but ingenious shapes," or "it had invented me,"[17] to be reminded of several resemblances, including one to Balzac's description of the exiled Dante in *The Proscribed:* "he closed himself in his room, lit his lamp of inspiration, and surrendered himself to the terrible demon of work, calling forth words from silence, and ideas from the night."[18]

Before it veered toward his sense of himself as a failed poet, however, Faulkner's response to the question about "Carcassonne" followed a more mundane line—"I was still writing about a young man in conflict with his environment."[19] The temptation to wrap the isolated, besieged young man of imagination in sympathy, and side with him against his environment, presented itself to Faulkner time and again, and is, I think, one of the central temptations acted out in his poetry. Poetry was, in Faulkner's practice of it, overwhelmingly "literary." It tilted him toward what Henry James called the *romantic*—"the things that . . . we never *can* directly know"—"things that reach us only through the beautiful circuit and subterfuge of our thought and our desire." As a result, it also tilted him toward the timeless. For Faulkner, the lyric often began with a move toward the poet's interior or consciousness, only to reverse itself to move up and out of time itself, as though in an effort to bring the internal thought and desire of the poet, and by extension the reader, into harmony with the music of the spheres, or at least with the timeless world of "great" poems and "noble" thoughts which together formed some "supreme" or "absolute" song that had begun when time began. Even in moments when Faulkner's sense of poetry's enterprise seemed pagan, it remained so imagination-dominated as to seem ethereal. In the process, it tended to leave out, or transmute beyond recognition, what James called the real: all "the things we cannot possibly *not* know sooner or later in one way or another," the quotidian world of regional folkways, scenes, voices, and stories, of which Faulkner, like James Joyce, learned to create fiction once he had stopped trying to write poetry.[20] Poetry impoverished Faulkner, as it had Joyce, precisely because it tilted him too much toward the timeless, the pure, the universal, leaving him with little more than his own more obvious emotions and the words of other poets as resources.

Before examining the ways in which what we might call "the real" breaks into "Carcassonne" with all its matter-of-factness, I want briefly to glance at the prose sketch or story called "Nympholepsy," which was probably written in 1925. Here Faulkner presents the travail of a nameless male protagonist whose days are filled with labor and whose nights are filled with food, sleep, and "perhaps a girl" wearing "blue gingham." Suddenly, however, on an evening that begins like every other evening of his life, with a walk from the field where he labors to the village where he eats and sleeps, Faulkner's protagonist glimpses "at a distance" an almost apparitionlike figure, a nymph, "a woman or a girl," whom he pursues, enraptured. Since the desires awakened in him by this part flesh and part dreamlike creature include sexual longings as well as cosmic yearnings, they soon transport him into a state of near-rapture in which striving and being still, living and dying, individual identity and oceanic merging are almost reconciled. But this state of rapture quickly dissolves into confusion, and then into disappointment. For the nymph is a "troubling Presence"— and that's "Presence" with a capital P. She is resistive as well as enticing, threatening as well as inspiring, even before she fades away, leaving Faulkner's protagonist alone with nothing but days of monotonous labor stretching out behind him as the stuff of his actual history, and before him as the sum and substance of all that he will ever directly know.

Like Faulkner's early poetry, "Nympholepsy" is full of echoes— Byron, Shelley, Keats, Browning, and Swinburne all put in appearances. What gives "Nympholepsy" its rhythm and its significance, however, is the intrusion of the "troubling Presence" of the nymph—as a creature both born and possessed of imagination— into the everyday world of the laborer, where she disrupts more than she bequeaths, heightening his discontent. Faulkner repeats several crucial phrases from his first two paragraphs in his last three paragraphs, describing the monotonous labor that lies behind and before his protagonist, as though to emphasize the degree to which reality tames dreams. Although dream and reality seem to gain meaning from one another, and though the deficiencies and inadequacies of reality provide the need and occasion of the dream, reality has the first and last word, and it remains unaltered.[21]

Like "Nympholepsy," "Carcassonne" is full of echoes and allusions, including several to Faulkner's own poetry. Its first paragraph—

> And me on a buckskin pony *with eyes like blue electricity and a mane like tangled fire, galloping up the hill and right off into the high heaven of the world*

which ends, or rather stops, without punctuation, turns out to be an ending as well as a beginning.[22] But not even these strange lines prepare us for the rest of Faulkner's nonstory about a horseman-poet-dreamer who lives in a port town called Rincon. In Spanish *rincon* means "corner" and conveys a sense of a space that is lost or neglected or wasted.[23] Within Faulkner's wasted town, his protagonist lives in a dark rat-infested garret above a tavern run by a man named Luis but owned by the Standard Oil Company, which, together with Mrs Widdrington,[24] "the Standard Oil Company's wife," in fact owns everything, even "the darkness" in which Faulkner's protagonist sleeps, and the silence in which the rats, "shadowy and huge as cats," move on "fairy feet."

With ownership, as it turns out, goes power not only over space, including the world's dark, lost corners, but also over class, caste, vocations, and even ordinary words, including those of would-be poets. In league with her spouse, the Standard Oil Company, Mrs Widdrington stands astride her world like some colossal wife and mother. She would "make a poet of you . . . if you did not work anywhere," Faulkner writes, because "she believed that, if a reason for breathing were not acceptable to her, it was no reason. With her, if you were white and did not work, you were either a tramp or a poet." Of all Mrs Widdrington's possessions, only the rats justify their existence simply by being what they are and doing what they do. They are not even expected "to pay for using her darkness and silence by writing poetry." Faulkner's protagonist, on the other hand, jumps from the requirement that he become something useful to a larger, unspecified ambition conceived as an act of defiance that remains shrouded in mystery: "I would like to perform something," he says, "shaping his lips soundlessly in the darkness."

What ensues can best be described as a brief double action. In one motion, Faulkner's protagonist begins a dialogue with his troublesome skeleton, introduced in the sketch's second paragraph, who insists "that the end of life is lying still." Jerked out of his retreat by this notion, Faulkner's poet-rider imagines his own body lying "on the rippled floor" of the sea, "tumbling peacefully to the wavering echoes of the tides," whereupon he recalls his defiant ambition and begins to fill it out: "I want to perform something bold and tragical and austere," he repeats, "shaping the soundless words in the pattering silence *me on a buckskin pony with eyes like electricity and a mane like tangled fire, galloping up the hill and right off into the high heaven of the world*," away from "the dark and tragic figure of the Earth, his mother."

These two actions, one of easy surrender to the real, the other of failed yet grand defiance, are not, I think, resolved in "Carcassonne," which is why two very careful readers—Cleanth Brooks and Noel Polk—have come to opposite conclusions about what this sketch does. For Brooks it reflects Faulkner's fascination with artists who dream of grand, unattainable things. It has "to do with failure, but failure made certain by the magnitude of the ambition," which is to say, the kind of splendid failure Faulkner admired. For Polk, on the other hand, Faulkner's protagonist-dreamer is so afraid of life that he lacks both the courage and the resolve to create anything except empty dreams. His failure, Polk concludes, is pathetic, not splendid, and his life ends, like "one of Eliot's Hollow Men," not with a bang but a whimper.[25]

Forced to choose between these two readings, I'm not sure where I would come down. Brooks is better on the sketch's last paragraph; Polk is better on the two or three before that. But what does this tell us if not that in 1925, the probable date of the composition of "Carcassonne," Faulkner remained either uninterested in or incapable of resolution. In "Nympholepsy" Faulkner begins and ends with the "real" world of day-to-day labor, only to interrupt it with the "troubling Presence" of a nymphlike creature full of promises and threats. In "Carcassonne" he begins and ends with a wild-eyed rider who actually lives in a lost corner of the world, presided over by the Standard Oil Company and a woman "so wise" she knows how to live and prosper "unconfused by reality, impervious to it." What we have in "Nympholepsy" is a world of normalcy interrupted by a dream-nightmare that opens what Michel Foucault describes as "a void, a moment of silence, a question without answer" that in turn calls everything about the laborer's day-to-day world into question. What we have in "Carcassonne" is an oscillation, a going back and forth, between particulars of the real and visions-dreams-nightmares of the bizarre, that poses the same kind of question and then leaves it unresolved. In "Carcassonne," furthermore, this going back and forth is not only between heaven and earth, imagination and reality, art and life, nor merely between grand gestures of empty dreams and deeds done. It is also between Faulkner's own divided response to the evocations of the far and the strange and the presence of the near and the familiar. In this layered process, Faulkner imaginatively explores a conception of life, a conception of art, and a conception of art in its relation to life. He examines, as it were, the modern sense that in life as we experience and know it—that is, in life institutionally and experientially as well as conceptually—there is a gap between the private and the public, the psychological and the social, the poetic and the political, or put another way, between individual selves with their needs and longings and historical societies with their political economies. In addition, he examines the modern sense, which arose in response to this sense of life, that art in general and literature in particular always go contrary, always go against the grain, and are, therefore, basically adversarial and oppositional to history and its societies, the final power of which is felt in their ability, which is to say, culture's ability, to socialize the antisocial, to assimilate the anticultural, to co-opt or even legitimate the subversive—to tame the wildness and madness of art.

Imbedded in my description of what Faulkner explores in "Nympholepsy" and "Carcassonne" is, of course, the seemingly inescapable desire for clear demarcations and systematic organization of everything in life, from work and play and love to consciousness itself—a desire that depends upon and perpetuates the boundary-making urge which makes itself felt, on one side, in our careful atomizing and analyzing of objects and roles, and on the other, in our elaborate, totalizing schemes of explanation. In short, what we might call our own habits of heart and mind—the poetics as well as the politics of our lives—reinforce and reassert what Faulkner was trying to work his way through in order to be free. Faulkner was slow to develop as an artist for several reasons, but a big one was this: that he had to learn by going where he wanted to go precisely because it was the freedom of play more than the satisfactions of resolution that as an artist he most needed and desired. If in "Nympholepsy" one form of failure—the too easy acceptance of the force of the real—is in the ascendancy, in "Carcassonne" another—the too easy alternative of flight—almost dominates. But in neither is resolution achieved.

What Faulkner signals in these sketches is, I think, first, his gradual ongoing discovery of himself as a writer governed by a rich passion for extremes, and second, his emerging determination to try for everything by honoring that passion. Even when, as in "Carcassonne," his romantic fascination with the artist as demon-driven creature doomed to pursue some grand unattainable end remains strong, it is balanced by a matching fascination with the quotidian historical world that began and ended for him in a certain form of captivity: with the families, institutions, traditions, and history—the voices, the tales, and the talking; the scenes and the hills, the dust and the heat—of North Mississippi.[26] For him, furthermore, that entangled, implicated, and conditioned world constituted an historical force that entangled, implicated, and conditioned every creature born into it, including its greatest artists.

Faulkner's discovery of himself as an artist, worked out in and through sketches like "Nympholepsy" and "Carcassonne," turned not only on his discovery of North Mississippi as the place he knew but also on the realization that in fiction he could commit himself to what James called *the real* and *the romance*, making interplay his mode and his goal, and resolution a thing to be deferred rather than forced. To become prolific, he needed the sense of being able to commit himself to opposing possibilities that projected themselves for him in endless interplay.[27] Within a few years, certainly by 1928–1929, with this large lesson learned, he was prepared to begin the work that made him famous because by then he knew that for an artist knowing a place and its people—knowing its history and delusions, its dreams and evasions, its forbidden secrets—means neither copying what is known nor fleeing from what is there to be known, but acting upon these things so as to give them spaces and voices that were theirs as well as his, his as well as theirs. His storytelling thus became a mode of knowledge no less than a mode of creative response. It became a way of searching out his origins, in a dialectic of surrender and resistance, of tenderness and fear, of love and hatred that resulted in his constructing something like what Jean Piaget has called a "system of transformations" on the world he had inherited. In the great period between 1929 and 1942, he made various forms of discontinuous narratives his own, as though to signal the degree to which recalcitrance tamed his desire for form. In work after work he found ways to give space to the noises, conflicts, and anomalies of the quotidian, historical world around him, signs of the marginal, the neglected, the forbidden, and the repressed. His was an ongoing struggle of observing against dreaming and dreaming against observing; and it was also a struggle of remembering against forgetting and forgetting against remembering, waged in recognition that the gifts of culture are inseparable from its restraining and constraining forms.[28]

3

"Wash" was first published in *Harper's* magazine in February 1934. Later that same year it appeared in *Doctor Martino and Other Stories*. Later still, Faulkner included it in *Collected Stories* (1950). In the meantime, however, he had incorporated it in chapter 7 of *Absalom, Absalom!* (1936). As a story, "Wash" begins in "early sunlight," shortly after the birth of the child of Milly Jones, granddaughter of Wash Jones. Seeing the child, Thomas Sutpen, its father, rejects it because, as a girl, it is not an acceptable inheritor of his dream and design. "Well, Milly," Sutpen says, "too bad you're not a mare. Then I could give you a decent stall in the stable."[29]

In a long middle section of "Wash," we enter the world of Sutpen's Hundred in the aftermath of the Civil War. It is a world once undergirded by property not only as land but as slaves, and now crippled by loss, not only of property but almost of hope. It is a world of class and caste in which race and gender loom large as shaping forces, though not always in completely predictable ways, since neither Wash Jones nor the slaves nor the former slaves can ever quite be sure which of them is lower and which, higher. Only Sutpen's status seems assured. "If God Himself was to come down and ride the natural earth," Wash says, "that's what He would aim to look like," Thomas Sutpen galloping on his black thoroughbred stallion, Rob Roy. In fact, however, by the time "Wash" begins, Sutpen has slipped. Once a proud landowner who could ride "ten miles across his own fertile land," and later a gallant soldier decorated by General Lee himself, he has become a storekeeper, haggling for dimes and quarters. Only in Wash Jones's mind's eye and Sutpen's flagging dream does he remain undiminished: "Well, Kernel," Wash says, "They kilt us but they ain't whupped us yet, air they?" "We ain't whupped yit, air we? Me and you kin do hit."[30]

This alliance between Sutpen and Wash is supported in part by Wash—not only his limitless admiration but also his loneliness and his need to feel the pride and satisfaction of knowing Sutpen. But it is also supported by Sutpen's loneliness and by his need of someone to take care of him when, driven "by impotent and furious undefeat," he drinks himself into delirium. In addition, their relation has a clear sociological basis. In "Wash" we sense what in *Absalom, Absalom!* we learn: that Sutpen's own family were poor, shiftless people without property or status, like Wash Jones. And in "Wash" we learn that both Wash Jones and Sutpen are conscious of two big facts: that neither of them is black and neither of them is female. "Women. Hit's a mystry to me," Wash says, speaking of his granddaughter and remembering his wife. "Hit's a mystry to me. To ara man."[31]

Yet it is this alliance that the action of the story destroys, or more specifically that Sutpen's remark destroys. "I kain't have heard what I thought I heard," Wash thinks quietly. "I know I kain't." But he knows that he has. "You said," he finally says to

Sutpen, standing before him, armed with Sutpen's own scythe and speaking in a flat voice, "like a deaf man's": "You said if she was a mare, you could give her a good stall in the stable." "Stand back. . . . Don't touch me," Sutpen replies, assuming that his world is still governed by social inequality and status pride. "I'm going to tech you, Kernel," Wash replies, before cutting him down, like the grim reaper himself. Soon after, Wash feels the gathering presence of "men of Sutpen's own kind," come to put him in his place for daring to rise up against one of their own. These are the men, he thinks, who set "the order and the rule of living," and whose decrees include this one: that they alone possess the power of turning insult, injury, and rage into revenge, which in killing Sutpen Jones has claimed for himself. Knowing what is about to happen, Jones kills both Milly and her daughter, sets fire to the cabin, and then lifts the scythe with which he has killed Sutpen and walks out to die, "without any cry, any sound."[32]

As a story "Wash" is grim, taut, and powerful. Only Faulkner's refusal directly to present its several deaths saves it from becoming horrific. Yet the prevailing context of the story is more social and historical than psychological. Its characters—Milly no less than Wash and Sutpen—want to be set free of the conditions and circumstances that limit and oppress them. They want to be able to forget who and what they are—how old, what gender, what class, how poor, or how lonely. They want, in short, what the protagonist of "Carcassonne" wants, what people have always wanted, to change the past, to be able once and for all to rive themselves forever free of its tracks and its chains. Yet their story culminates when Wash surrenders this dream of freedom by refusing to try to escape or to let Milly and her child try to escape, out of the conviction that there is no place on earth for them to go: that "men of Sutpen's own kind" control "the order and the rule of living," and that in running away, he and his kind "would merely be fleeing one set of bragging and evil shadows for another just like them."

In *Absalom, Absalom!* Faulkner expands and enlarges the basic elements of "Wash" in at least five ways. First, he presents Thomas Sutpen not only as an ancient varicose and aging Faustus who is about to die, but also as a young "amazed and desperate child," offended and affronted by a black servant who denies him entrance to the white door of the large plantation house where he has been sent on an errand. We thus see Sutpen as a vulnerable young boy who transforms himself, in his own mind's eye, into a "boy symbol," for whom he then determines to build a plantation and mansion as shelter. Second, we see him become a man set on avenging the poor people who have lived, suffered affronts, and died in order to make him. Third, we see him as one determined to know that he has "riven forever free from brutehood," as well as history's chance and circumstance, all those descendants who would come after him, even if they never so much as hear his name. Fourth, we see that, for reasons strange almost beyond understanding, it has been his fate to live not his dream of power, revenge, and vindication but a nightmare of impotence as repetition in which he moves from affront to affront, insulting those he set out to champion. Even as we see Sutpen edging near his insult of Milly—his last save the condescension implicit in a line like "Stand back, Wash, Don't you touch me"—we are told that three years earlier, driven by the desperate sense that time is running out on him, he had turned Miss Rosa Coldfield into a not-bride by withdrawing his proposal of marriage and substituting for it a crude proposition: "that they try it first and if it was a boy and lived, they would be married." Sutpen's more generous desires, both his desire to redeem the long line of dispossessed ancestors who have made him and his desire to secure a future for his descendants, are simply overwhelmed by his determination to replicate himself, which we see not only in the name *Sutpen's Hundred* and in the children who resemble him but also in his rejection of Charles Bon as an acceptable son and in his assumption that only a son can be a proper heir. His own ruthless, patriarchal urges deprive him of his chance to establish both a genealogical memory and a legacy of hope and promise, leaving him intensely isolated. Finally, Faulkner places the story in a larger interpretive framework by presenting it as a tale that has been told by others to Mr. Compson, then by Mr. Compson and Miss Rosa to Quentin, and then by Quentin to Shreve. Near the end of the chapter, after the retelling of "Wash," we hear Sutpen's plaintive cry ("You see, all I wanted was just a son. Which seems to me, when I look about at my contemporary scene, no exorbitant gift from nature or circumstance to demand—"), and then we hear again the voice of Shreve, addressing Quentin, as he retells the story, "*Will you wait?*," and of Quentin in response, as they begin yet another round of trying to get the elements of Sutpen's story to behave.[33]

"Carcassonne," as I have noted, limns an unresolved tension between unity born of surrender and isolation born of defiance. In Faulkner's later fiction, including *Absalom*, this tension is amplified. Though it remains personal, it becomes cultural by being made a part of the ceaseless opposition between centrifugal forces that keep things apart and the centripetal forces that bring them together and make them cohere. In the telling and hearing of stories, as in the writing and reading of them, we see this tension enacted and reenacted. And though the centrifugal forces that work toward disunity remain powerful in the language as well as the culture of Faulkner's South, the centripetal forces keep on keeping on, refusing to quit, so that they come through even in individual human voices, like Quentin's, that feel beseiged by isolation, division, and uncertainty.[34]

Faulkner's great novels, like *Absalom, Absalom!*, lift his narrative art to a higher level of play by gathering characters who collect the rag-tag and bob-ends of old tales and talking and then shape them into new, changing patterns that in turn trigger a new round of change and exchange. Faulkner thus made his fiction a celebration of the whole range of passive and active articulation. Having moved beyond lyric poems and poetic sketches, he retained his commitment to the scene and moment of human utterance. In distinguishing lyric poetry from dramatic literature and narrative fiction, Barbara Herrnstein-Smith observes that while "a lyric may be dramatic or narrative in certain respects, what distinguishes it from a versified play or novel is the fact that it is the representation, not of an action or the chronicle of an action, but of an utterance."[35] Yet novels like *Flags in the Dust* and *Absalom, Absalom!* remain lyrical in the sense of being, among other things, representations of an ongoing series of utterances. Long before we can claim to have the narrative elements of Faulkner's works sorted out, we begin to recognize voices and to locate identities in and through utterances. For Faulkner's characters exist in and through words become actions and actions become words, not as stable presences but as such presences might have been or might yet be. Here are four brief passages, two from *Flags* and two from *Absalom:*[36]

As usual old man Falls had brought John Sartoris into the room with him. Freed as he was of time, he was a far more definite presence in the room than the two . . . [men] cemented by deafness to a dead time and drawn thin by the slow attenuation of days. He seemed to stand above them, all around them, with his bearded, hawklike face and the bold glamour of his dream.

She [Virginia Du Pre/Miss Jenny] had told the story [of Bayard Sartoris' death] many times . . . and as she grew older the tale itself grew richer and richer . . . until what had been a hair-brained prank of two heedless and reckless boys wild with their own youth, was become a gallant and finely tragical focal-point to which the history of the race had been raised from out the old miasmic swamps of spiritual sloth by two angels valiantly and glamorously fallen and strayed, altering the course of human events and purging the souls of men.

[Miss Rosa Coldfield was] talking in that grim haggard amazed voice until at last listening would renege and hearing-sense self-confound and the long-dead object of her impotent yet indomitable frustration would appear, as though by outraged recapitulation evoked. . . . Her voice would not cease, it would just vanish. . . . Out of the quiet thunderclap he would abrupt (man-horse demon) . . . then in long unamaze Quentin *seemed* to watch. . . .

But you were not listening, because you knew it all already, had learned, absorbed it already without the medium of speech somehow from having been born and living beside it, with it, as children will and do; so that what your father was saying did not tell you anything so much as it struck, word by word, the resonant strings of remembering. You had been here before, seen these graves more than once . . . just as you had seen the old house too, been familiar with how it would look before you even saw it, . . . No, you were not listening; you didn't have to. . . .

These passages present voices engaged in acts of evocation, celebration, and revision. Such triumphs as their speakers experience originate in their ability to make language responsive not only to their sense of loss and exile, nor merely to their entanglements in a community and its history, but also to their desire to defy and transcend these things. Their voices originate in separation and loss, which is to say the advent of consciousness, signs and traces of which are found everywhere in the faint letters and graved words of their voices as they rise and fall. Faulkner's characters remain deeply divided, torn between the longing for union and the longing for separation; the desire for immersion and the desire for flight; the pursuit of marriage and community and the pursuit of loneliness and isolation; the urge to disclose and the urge to withhold. The motions of their bodies, like the motions of their minds, are at odds with one another. Yet their lives lie and their humanity resides not in the resolution of these tensions but in the play of them through words.

For Faulkner as for Nietzsche, memory is always for something as well as of something: it goes back into the past in the name of some present need, often hidden. There is, therefore, an inescapable historicity to both the activities and the motives of memory, which frequently include, among other things, a desire to change the past. As Faulkner moved from poetry to fiction, however, his voice began to multiply and divide. The violent divisions within his characters constitute responses to violences from without, and they find expression in a thousand ways,[37] including the violences they practice on ordinary speech. Although Faulkner wrote ten or twelve masterful short stories, the novel was his proper form because it is of all forms the most commodious. His novels devoured his short stories and sketches, as *Absalom, Absalom!* devoured "Wash." But they also ingested myth and drama and lyric utterances, in the name of providing us, as he puts it in *Absalom, Absalom!,* "something like peace, like quiet in the raging and incredulous recounting (which enable men to bear living) of that feather's balance between victory and disaster." [38]

The voices that speak to us in his fictions are characteristically born of needs that arise from losses as they come to bear on people, places, and events. For old man Falls, it is the loss of energy and vitality, even the loss of substance ("Drawn thin by a slow attenuation of days") and of sound ("cemented by deafness to a dead time"). For Miss Jenny, it is loss of the world she knew and the life she possessed before the war: "This was Virginia Du Pre, who came to them, two years a wife and seven years a widow at thirty. . . . It was she who told them of the manner of Bayard Sartoris' death prior to the second battle of Manassas. She had told the story many times since." For Miss Rosa it is loss that has left her sitting like a crucified child in her too-tall chair dressed in her eternal black: loss of mother, father, sister, niece, nephew, and not-husband; or loss, as she puts it in another passage, of her summer of wistaria: "Once, there was—Do you mark how the wistaria, sun-impacted on this wall here, distills and penetrates this room *as though.* . . . That is the substance of remembering . . . no more, no less: and its resultant sum is usually incorrect and false and worthy only of the name of dream. . . . Once there was . . . a summer of wistaria. It was a pervading everywhere of wistaria (I was fourteen then) and though of all springs yet to capitulate condensed into one spring, one summer . . . That was the miscast summer of my barren youth." [39] For Quentin, it is the burden of having heard so many voices and stories that, as a boy and young man, he has become "a barracks filled with stubborn back-looking ghosts," and even more, has begun to sense that in the stories of those ghosts lie clues to understanding his own life.

What is striking, however, in addition to the fact that Faulkner's characters carry needs and purposes from their present into their active remembering of their pasts, is this: that no familiar typology, including Nietzsche's and Foucault's, can do justice to the motions of their memories.[40] Old man Falls is more antiquarian and escapist; he is even more purely evocative. Miss Jenny is more monumental and celebratory, as she searches for and tries to create heroes fit to instruct, inspire, or edify the present. But neither of these voices speaks simply in one mode, and it is probably not too much to say that Miss Rosa moves in all of these and more—that she wants and tries for everything: she evokes ("Until at last . . . the long dead object of her . . . frustration would appear"); she judges and celebrates ("man-horse-demon"; "the up-palm immobile and pontific, creating the Sutpen's Hundred, the Be *Stupen's Hundred* like the oldentime Be Light."); and she revises and recreates in the name of "that might-have-been," "the single rock we cling to above the maelstrom of unbearable reality" which she offers as some compensatory supplement to the fleeting spring and lost summer of wistaria.[41]

To the rendering of these and other voices, Faulkner brings irony and playfulness as well as commitment and devotion. He endows them with a rhythm and idiom, an authenticity, of their own. Even when the discrete voices of which he often makes his novels give way to a less specific voice, as they do repeatedly and increasingly in *Absalom*, for example, or in both the fourth section and the Appendix of *The Sound and the Fury*, it is not so much Faulkner's own voice that we hear as it is a medleyed voice created out of a particular imaginative context. To some extent in *The Sound and the Fury* and to a greater extent in *Absalom, Absalom!*, Faulkner's medleyed voices acquire considerable authoritative force, so much so that they seem almost preemptive and overwhelming. But gaps remain in the stories they tell; even in *Absalom, Absalom!*, the voice Faulkner creates continues to echo prior voices, as Shreve's echoes Mr. Compson's (see p. 207). As a result, it continues to ally itself with process more than with formal closure. Even in its most assertive moments, it continues the narrative's plea that other resonating voices join and extend its community of interpretation. Like Faulkner's medleyed voices, moreover, the discrete voices that precede them are often multiple rather than singular. Imbedded in both Miss Rosa's voice and in Quentin's is a submerged, implicit dialogue. Our task, therefore, is often double: we must attend the dialogues we hear, mindful of the tensions within as well as between the voices of which they are constituted. Among other things, this helps to explain why we often seem to be entering the middle of conversations, or to be immersed in scenes structured as dialogues yet executed as monologues.

There are, of course, many ways to describe the tensions we encounter in the voices of Faulkner's fiction, and there is considerable danger in trying to generalize about them, though it does seem to me remarkable how often Faulkner's created voices disclose both a skeptical urge and a visionary one, both a critical, judgmental impulse and an imaginative, reconciling one. But it is not his own voice that Faulkner takes us toward; it is his own needs and purposes. In sharing the voices that sang to him, he also shares his tasks, directly with his characters and indirectly with his readers. His fictions come to us like the headstones Quentin discovers in the Sutpen cemetery, "in light more dark than gray even," sometimes "leaning a little awry" and sometimes "cracked," "the faint lettering, the graved words," obscure at times yet "decipherable too."[42]

In the end, it is the remarkable incompletenesses and inadequacies of the tales his voices relate that justify their proliferation. Similarly, it is their remarkable commonalities, stretching across their distinctive qualities, that justify their mergings. Just as loss leads to invention in Faulkner's fiction (Miss Rosa's of almost everything, Quentin's of Caddy, and Benjy's), so does the incompleteness and imperfection of each act of mind and voice lead

to another, as flawed words to stubborn sounds. Faulkner's characters begin to speak out of a sense of hope as well as need; they
continue to speak not only out of a lingering sense of hope and a
renewed sense of need, but also out of an acute sense of the
incompletenesses of what they have said.[43]

The mood of Faulkner's fiction remains so deeply provisional
because its voices remain so deeply circumstanced.

> The boy would just wait and then listen and Sam would begin, talking
> about the old days and the People whom he had not had time even to
> know and so could not remember (he did not remember ever having
> seen his father's face). . . .
>
> And as he talked about those old times and those dead and van-
> ished men of another race from either that the boy knew, gradually to
> the boy those old times would cease to be old times and would
> become a part of the boy's present, not only *as if* they had happened
> yesterday but *as if* they were still happening, the men who walked
> through them actually walking in breath and air and casting an actual
> shadow on the earth they had not quitted. And more: *as if* some of
> them had not happened yet but would occur tomorrow, *until at last it*
> *would seem* to the boy that he himself had not come into existence
> yet, that none of his race nor the other subject race which his people
> had brought with them into the land had come here yet; that although
> it had been his grandfather's and then his father's and uncle's and was
> now his cousin's and someday would be his own land . . . their hold
> upon it actually was as trivial and without reality as the now faded and
> archaic script in the chancery book in Jefferson which allocated it to
> them. . . .[44]

Like many passages in Faulkner's fiction, this passage comes to us
as a quest for origins that is in part a search for sources that can in
turn become resources, or for past moments that invite reap-
praisals. Faulkner knew almost as much as Shakespeare about the
possibilities and necessities of such acts of mind and imagination.
But his quests for origins were also quests for a sense of the world
prior to division and loss. Sam and the boy at once instance such a
quest and approximate its completion. Their tilt toward the past

becomes a preparation for living a life that both is and is also always about to be.

In addition, Sam and the boy engage in a critique of such social institutions as property and law as well as a celebration and a critique of language. Here language becomes an instrument of society as well as an instrument of the imagination. It is our analytic and imperial tool as well as our poetic tool. Precisely because it is so deeply human, it is an instrument by which people stake claims, create confusion, and commit errors or even atrocities. Insofar as it is saved, it is saved by its own self-examination and self-criticism, its own articulations of its betrayals and its corruptions. In its limited victories, it acknowledges its defeats. Between Sam and the boy lies a distance, and behind them lies a succession of terrible divisions and losses. Both the waiting and listening of the boy and the remembering and speaking of the man are born of loss—loss of the old days and the old people; and of divisions—including those between parents and children, men and women, rich and poor, landed-gentry and landless laborers, and among three human races. The power Faulkner attributes to resonating words is at one with the power his own words display: "And as he talked *about* those old times and those dead and vanished men of another race . . . [they] would cease to be old times and would become. . . ." As Faulkner renders Sam's resonating voice, he celebrates it. Sam sings his world, and in singing not only makes but bequeaths it. He thus becomes another of the remarkable range of characters in Faulkner's fiction who discover both the necessity and the joy of invention through language. Through him Faulkner includes invention and imagination among the subjects of his story.[45] But even as Faulkner celebrates Sam's voice, rendering its power in the plenitude it adds, he reminds us of anterior plenitudes, prior to loss and division, that are the occasion of Sam's speaking; and he insists as well on reminding us that Sam's song is a fiction by forcing us to see its achievement under the aspect of the phrase he thrice repeats: *as if.* Seeking the thing itself, Sam finds the apparent thing itself: it was "as if . . .

until at last it would seem." Insofar as Sam's voice fills the voids of his world, it is *as if* it fills them.

Faulkner came to the particulars of his world through words and so learned with words to enable us to see and experience those particulars. But for all the allure of flight and the appeal of the unattainable, and all the tentativeness loaded into the *as ifs* of his fiction, he wanted to keep his art human. Fiction gave him what through his fictions he gives us: a workable confidence that the ordinary particulars of our own unmapped worlds are in their own way extraordinary. The life he exposes to view is often unseemly, or unspeakably grim and ugly, or ridiculously inflated and deluded. But he holds these things together, under the aspect of the human, determined to make us see them whole, until we see that, in defiance of simplifying divisions, they are fit and proper as well as unseemly, ineffably beautiful as well as grim and ugly, grand and necessary as well as inflated and deluded. Like his simplest turns of speech, his extravagances serve the larger end not of mere invention and disclosure but of reconciliation, perhaps because he believed, as he put it in "Monk," a crude story in *Knight's Gambit*, that "the paradoxical and even mutually negativing anecdotes in the history of the human heart can be juxtaposed and annealed by art into verisimilitude and credibility," and because, as he suggests in *Absalom, Absalom!*, he also believed that mere approximations, including his own "raging and incredulous recounting[s]," could yield "something like peace."[46]

NOTES

1. Fitzgerald's earlier novels were *This Side of Paradise* (1920) and *The Beautiful and Damned* (1922), and his short story collections were *Flappers and Philosophers* (1920), *Tales of the Jazz Age* (1922), and *All the Sad Young Men* (1926). Dos Passos's other novels were *One Man's Initiation* (1920) and *Three Soldiers* (1921). Hemingway's other books were *Three Stories and Ten Poems* (1923) and *Torrents of Spring* (1926). Faulkner's only published work before *Soldiers' Pay* was *The Marble Faun*, which was written in 1920, revised ca. 1923–1924, and published in 1924.

2. Quoted in the introduction to Robert Penn Warren, ed., *Faulkner: A Collection of Critical Essays* (Englewood Cliffs, N.J., 1966), 9.

3. See *Absalom, Absalom!* (New York, 1972), 100–101 and 313; compare 129–132 and

377. See also David Krause's fine essay, "Reading Bon's Letter and Faulkner's *Absalom, Absalom!*," *PMLA* 99 (March 1984): 225–41.

4. See Wallace Stevens, "The Rock," *Collected Poems* (New York, 1964), 527.

5. See Gyorgy Lukacs, *The Theory of the Novel: A Historico-Philosophical Essay on the Forms of Great Epic Literature*, trans. Anna Bostock (Cambridge, Mass., 1971), 38.

6. See Wallace Stevens, "The Poems of Our Climate," *Collected Poems* (New York, 1964), 194.

7. Compare Alain Robbe-Grillet, "On Several Notions," *For a New Novel: Essays as Fiction*, trans. Richard Howard (New York, 1965), 32.

8. *Absalom, Absalom!*, 127.

9. See Roland Barthes, "From Work to Text," in Josue Harari, ed., *Textual Strategies* (Ithaca, N.Y., 1979), 73–81; and S/Z, trans. Richard Miller (New York, 1974), 4–6 and 216–17.

10. See "The Figure a Poem Makes" [1939] in E. C. Lathem and Lawrence Thompson, eds., *Robert Frost: Poetry and Prose* (New York, 1972), 394.

11. See *Absalom, Absalom!*, 127; and compare Paul Tillich, *The Protestant Era*, trans. James Luther Adams (Chicago, 1957), esp. x–xi.

12. Frederick L. Gwynn and Joseph L. Blotner, *Faulkner in the University* (New York, 1965), 22.

13. *The Lilacs* was written in 1920; *Visions in Spring* was written in 1921, was probably revised in 1923, when Faulkner renamed it *Orpheus and Other Poems*, and was published in 1984; *The Marionettes* was written in 1920 and published in 1975; and *Mayday* was probably written in late 1925 and early 1926 and was published in 1977. See Brooks and Sensibar as cited in n. 14 below.

14. See Cleanth Brooks, *William Faulkner: Toward Yoknapatawpha and Beyond* (New Haven, 1978), especially 1–66; and Judith Sensibar, *The Origins of Faulkner's Art* (Austin, Texas, 1984), especially Parts One and Two.

15. See Brooks, *William Faulkner: Toward Yoknapatawpha and Beyond*, 32.

16. Among Faulkner scholars, Cleanth Brooks has done most to elucidate the "depth and quality of Faulkner's romanticism," and Judith Sensibar the most to elucidate his varied appropriations of "the quintessential masker himself, Pierrot, the darling of the Symbolists and Modernists alike." See Brooks and Sensibar as cited in n. 14 above. See also Sensibar's introduction to *Visions in Spring* (Austin, Texas, 1984), xvi–xix.

17. See the published version of an untitled manuscript in the Beinecke Rare Book and Manuscript Library, Yale University, in Joseph Blotner, "William Faulkner's Essay on the Composition of *Sartoris*," *Yale University Library Gazette* 47 (January 1973): 121–24.

18. See Peter Brooks, "The Melodramatic Imagination: The Example of Balzac and James," in David Thorburn and Geoffrey Hartman, eds., *Romanticism: Vistas, Instances, Continuities* (Ithaca, 1973), 220.

19. See *Faulkner and the University*, 22.

20. Henry James, "Preface to *The American*," in R. P. Blackmur, ed., *The Art of the Novel: Critical Prefaces* (New York, 1962), 31.

21. See "Nympholepsy," in Joseph Blotner, ed., *Uncollected Stories of William Faulkner* (New York, 1981), 331–37. Compare especially 331 and 336–37.

22. See "Carcassonne," in *Collected Stories of William Faulkner* [1950] (New York, 1977), 895–900, esp. 895.

23. I am indebted to my friend and colleague Ricardo Gutierrez-Mouat of Emory University for help with the word *rincon*.

24. I have followed Faulkner's omission of a period following Mrs in deference to his care in such matters.

25. Compare Brooks as cited in n. 14 above, pp. 60–66 and Noel Polk, "William Faulkner's 'Carcassonne,'" *Studies in American Fiction* 12 (1984): 29–43, esp. 41–42.

26. See "Carcassonne" as cited in n. 22 above, esp. 895 and 899–900.

27. With regard to Faulkner's preference for open-endedness, compare one of the

"Carcassonne," "Wash," and Voices of Faulkner's Fiction 107

themes in Ezra Pound's *Cantos*, especially "The Pisan Cantos": "And if I see her not, no sight is worth the beauty of my thought."

28. See Jean Piaget, *Genetic Epistemology*, trans. E. Duckworth (New York, 1970), 15.

29. "Wash" in *Collected Stories*, 535; cf. 544–45.

30. Ibid., 538–39 and 540.

31. Ibid., 546.

32. Ibid., 544–45. See Hans H. Skei, *William Faulkner: The Novelist as Short Story Writer* (Oslo, 1985), 212, 214, and 216–18; and compare Clifford Geertz, *The Interpretation of Culture* (New York, 1973), 334–35.

33. See *Absalom, Absalom!*, 217–92.

34. See Michael Holquist's splendid introduction to M. M. Bakhtin's *The Dialogic Imagination: Four Essays*, trans. Caryl Emerson and Michael Holquist (Austin, Texas, 1981), xviii–xxi.

35. Barbara Herrnstein-Smith, *Poetic Closure: A Study of How Poems End* (Chicago, 1968), 122.

36. See *Flags in the Dust* (New York, 1973), 5 and 12; and *Absalom, Absalom!*, 7–8 and 212–13.

37. See Wallace Stevens as cited in n. 4 above.

38. *Absalom, Absalom!*, 161.

39. Ibid., 143–44.

40. See Friedrich Nietzsche, *The Use and Abuse of History*, trans. Adrian Collins (Indianapolis, 1957); and Michel Foucault, *The Archaeology of Knowledge*, trans. A. M. Sheridan Smith (New York, 1972). Compare Walter Benjamin, "Theses on the Philosophy of History," in Hannah Arendt, ed., *Illuminations*, trans. Harry Zahn (New York, 1968), 253–67.

41. *Absalom, Absalom!*, 8–9, 143–44, and 149–50.

42. Ibid., 187–88, 190–91.

43. "It remains, then, for us to *speak*," Jacques Derrida says, "to make our voices *resonate* throughout the corridors in order to make up for [*suppleer*] the breakup of presence. . . . Rising toward the sun of presence, it is the way of Icarus." Faulkner honors the human mind as it remembers, now in evocation and celebration, then in revision, just as he honors the human voice that speaks, now in a mood skeptical, critical, judgmental, then in a mood visionary and imaginative. Finally, however, Faulkner shares his prerogatives, even his predicament as a writer, as well as his needs and tasks. There "is a fatal necessity," Derrida also notes, "that the substitute makes one forget the vicariousness of its own function. . . . But the supplement supplements . . . if it fills, it is as if one fills a void." See Jacques Derrida, *Speech and Phenomena: And Other Essays on Husserl's Theory of Signs*, trans. David B. Allison (Evanston, 1973), 88–104, and *Of Grammatology*, trans. Gayatri Spivak (Baltimore, 1976), 280.

44. *Go Down, Moses* (New York, 1955), 171.

45. See Robbe-Grillet as cited in n. 7 above.

46. See "Monk," *Knight's Gambit* (New York, 1949), 49–50, 39; and *Absalom, Absalom!*, 161.

"Ad Astra" through New Haven: Some Biographical Sources of Faulkner's War Fiction

CARVEL COLLINS

Lawrence Wells, author and owner of Yoknapatawpha Press in Oxford, Mississippi, presented the following eulogy before reading the essay Carvel Collins wrote for delivery at the 1990 Faulkner and Yoknapatawpha Conference.

It is an honor to represent Carvel Collins at the seventeenth Faulkner and Yoknapatawpha Conference. I know how much he was looking forward to being here. Carvel died unexpectedly this past April of a cerebral hemorrhage, at age seventy-seven. It was his custom in papers and articles presented here or at the Modern Language Association or other conferences to reveal some previously unpublished fact about William Faulkner. As you are about to see, his paper which I will read today—entitled "'Ad Astra' through New Haven: Some Biographical Sources of Faulkner's War Fiction"—is no exception.

Anyone with even a casual acquaintance with Faulkner scholarship knows that Carvel Collins never finished his biography of William Faulkner. For years the academic community waited in vain to see it published. The question everyone asked was *why?*

As Carvel's friend and supporter, I'd like to address that question briefly.

In his spare time Carvel was a builder, a do-it-yourselfer, a man who liked to fiddle with mechanical problems and find solutions. He worked on his car, he did plumbing repairs and carpentry around the house just as Faulkner himself regularly escaped from the typewriter through physical labor—but it went deeper with Carvel. He found satisfaction in figuring out how things functioned. The personal act of discovery, the moment of understanding, was a fulfillment in itself. Whether under the Mercedes' grease-pan or in the dusty confines of his basement or in a library carrel, Collins wanted answers. With all his highly developed literary sensibilities he remained at heart a pragmatic man.

I think that, apart from the wonders of Faulkner's fiction, what attracted Carvel to a lifelong pursuit of biographical fact was the gauntlet that Faulkner seemed to throw at his feet: *Understand me if you can.* Here was the world's most private man, seemingly inscrutable, who kept his own counsel, dressed in different costumes, assumed various personas, even laid false trails by telling a lie when it suited him. I would hazard a guess that it was one of those little white lies that hooked Carvel, just under the jawbone neatly and irrevocably, and for the rest of his life he was to be driven by a single passion: how to figure William Faulkner.

Collins started working seriously on a biography of Faulkner sometime in the mid-fifties. He approached the author for permission to write a biography and Faulkner asked him to hold off, in effect saying that his work should stand alone, to let the epitaph read, "He wrote the books and he died." As hard as it must have been, Carvel accepted this request. He respected Faulkner too much to do otherwise. In the meantime, Faulkner went to the University of Virginia to be writer-in-residence. Joseph Blotner was assigned to serve as his liaison.

When Faulkner died, his wife Estelle authorized Blotner to write the biography. Collins later remarked, "In most cases the authorized biographer has a terrific inside track. . . . If I did go ahead the author of that book would have mine to draw on. I decided to wait until his was out."

Here is a builder patiently laying the foundation of his house, setting each joist with care and precision, when the sound of rapid hammering echoes across the valley. He turns in mild curiosity to see another house, more or less of the same design, rising before his very eyes—foundation, flooring, wall frames—going up like an Amish barn-raising, like an octopus with nine hammers, like Collins's worst nightmare, and no way to stop it short of murder.

Carvel must have suffered, at that moment, the kind of mortal disappointment which can sidetrack a career. He had a clear choice. He could forge ahead and complete his house at his own pace and allow Faulkner readers to enter, to see how well it was crafted and out of what materials and how it would weather. Or he could begin building a fence around his uncompleted house, which is the course he took. As the years went by, we could hear him sawing and hammering in there and even whistling to himself, but we didn't know what he was building. Some suspected that he was just stacking wood, fussing over his foundations, planning and revising and considering adjustments. In the meantime, other houses were going up across the valley, whole subdivisions in the making. Carvel kept hammering in private, conceding occasionally to stop and bore a hole in his fence and allow us a peek, a fact at a time.

What he gave us instead of the mammoth two-volume biography we expected was a host of innumerable articles and papers, expertly edited books, insightful introductions, advice and counsel on such important projects as the television documentary *A Life On Paper*. He was always ready to help answer questions, to serve as a bulwark against error, and he left behind an invaluable collection of records—twenty-four filing cabinets filled with transcripts of interviews and correspondences, news clippings, rare photos, and notations, which have been bequeathed to the Humanities Research Center at the University of Texas.

Carvel once told me he had prepared a manuscript for Farrar, Straus and Giroux to publish. Then he changed his mind and sent back their advance, promising that when and if he was ready to publish a revised draft, they would still be his publisher. We can only hope that the scholar or team of scholars who unravel the riddle that was Carvel Collins's legacy will do it justice, preserve his judgment, his measured cadence, his humility and sense of humor. The biography which evolves from his materials should bear his distinctive mark, perhaps even his style and voice.

Yet Carvel Collins's many friends are still hoping that somewhere among those filing cabinets is a manuscript box weighing nine pounds and bearing the inscription: "W. Faulkner: *This is it.*"

"Ad Astra" has seemed to many readers the best of William Faulkner's short fiction set in the Great War. Taking its ironic title from the Royal Air Force motto *"per ardua ad astra"*—usually translated as "through difficulty to the stars"—Faulkner first published the story in *American Caravan IV*, March 1931, and later that year put a revised version into *These 13*, his first short story volume. Today it is most available in the paperback edition of his *Collected Stories.*

Sometimes, like many writers, Faulkner conceived works of fiction long before he published them and he may have done so with "Ad Astra." At least, he referred briefly in *Flags in the Dust*—which he is thought to have begun by 1926—to the central physical event of "Ad Astra," the fight at the Cloche-Clos café. But, as might be expected, he apparently finished the first published version of the story in 1930, the year he recorded submitting to the *American Mercury* a typescript with that title, for the story's fictional narrator states that in recounting what he had observed in 1918 his mind is going back twelve years. And Faulkner probably did not write "Ad Astra" as we know it until after he had read the 1929 English translation of Remarque's *All Quiet on the Western Front*, because what appear to me to be parallels between the two works are more numerous than those ordinarily common to fictional treatments of the Great War.

Like his imaginary narrator of "Ad Astra," Faulkner also was recalling events personally observed twelve years earlier. Though he had not gone overseas in 1918, having been still in RAF ground school at Toronto when the Armistice was signed, his "Ad Astra" seemed to many readers so authentic that they assumed without question its author had been at the Front. That authenticity comes, of course, primarily from Faulkner's narrative genius, but it also owes much, I believe, to his observation of a cluster of people and events he encountered far from the combat zone—at New Haven, Connecticut, during ten weeks in April, May, and June of 1918. This biographical essay looks at that encounter and some of its effects on Faulkner's fictional treatment of the great War, in "Ad Astra" and beyond.

In 1918 Phil Stone, Faulkner's Oxford, Mississippi, friend, was at New Haven as a Yale law student when Estelle Oldham of Oxford, with whom Faulkner had taken out a wedding license, decided to marry another man instead. Stone, concerned for Faulkner's welfare, persuaded him to come to New Haven and apply for a job at the Winchester Repeating Arms Company, which was hiring all comers to meet enormous armament orders for the fighting in Europe. Stone said several times in our many conversations that he had had three reasons for urging Faulkner to come to Connecticut: He assumed Faulkner would feel especially miserable if he had to be in Oxford on the wedding day of Estelle Oldham. He feared that if Faulkner remained in Mississippi he and she, whom Stone considered not suited to each other, might elope before her planned wedding. Third, he thought Faulkner talented and likely to profit from some experience of a larger world than Oxford.

Faulkner did profit from going to New Haven. For one thing, he discovered there that a number of his new acquaintances considered writing a legitimate occupation. His experience of Connecticut in 1918 seemed to him so rewarding that three years later he returned for another period, not described in his biographies, saying in 1921 that he preferred New Haven to New York. He found New Haven memorable enough that it supplied material for more of his fiction than "Ad Astra." As just one example, in *The Sound and the Fury*, partly set at a fictional Harvard, he drew not on any acquaintance with Cambridge, Massachusetts, but instead on his experience at New Haven for the atmosphere around a New England university, for many details of the novel such as the black man in the parade which Quentin Compson watches, and—most important—for Quentin's general condition of despair over his loss, by marriage, of the girl he loves back home in Mississippi, a sad real condition which was Faulkner's own at New Haven in 1918 while Estelle Oldham was marrying in Oxford.

"Ad Astra" begins with conversation among Allied officers near the Western Front on what we later learn is the evening of 11 November 1918, the day which ended the largest and most destructive armed conflict our species had yet accomplished. Four officers of the Royal Air Force—an Irishman named Comyn and three Americans, Sartoris, Bland, and the unnamed narrator—are drinking heavily to inaugurate the new period of peace, almost unbelievable after the years of combat. With them and doing much of the talking but none of the drinking is a subadar, officer of Indian forces fighting under the British. As they drive to the Cloche-Clos café in Amiens, another American, Monaghan, joins them accompanied by his prisoner, a German pilot with bandaged head whom he has been leading about while planning drunkenly to take him to live in the United States.

At the crowded Cloche-Clos, whose French patrons are outraged by the German's presence, the talk among the officers increases, with the turbaned subadar and the turban-bandaged prisoner the chief speakers along with Monaghan. The café brawl, violent but brief, begins when the French no longer contain their hatred of the German and ends when Sartoris breaks the light with a chair. Near a fountain in a quiet street while band music sounds far off, the talk resumes, with Bland concerned about the German's additional physical damage from the café patrons, Monaghan eager to go back to the café to punish them for inflicting it, and Sartoris silently carrying water from the fountain to help the briefly unconscious German.

After the narrator promises he will write to the German's wife in Beyreuth, Comyn and Monaghan drunkenly depart half carrying

the German between them, and the story ends with narrator,
subadar, Sartoris, and Bland talking by the fountain, the distant
band intermittent and forlorn. At New Orleans in the mid-twen-
ties Faulkner had spoken vigorously with Harold Dempsey in
support of a belief which he seems to have followed in writing "Ad
Astra": Plot, he had said, is such an unpleasant element in fiction
that authors should keep it to a minimum.

For "Ad Astra"—as well as for *The Sound and the Fury,* published three years earlier—Faulkner obviously drew on an officer
he had come to know at New Haven in 1918. The officer was
recuperating there because combat had left him, in the termi-
nology of that day, "shell-shocked." Information about how that
officer's psychic war wounding manifested itself I have not been
able to exhume, but his name was Bland and he was considered
handsome. For *The Sound and the Fury* he supplied Faulkner
with the appearance and name of the fictional student Bland, who
before the war, in the imaginary 1910 of Quentin Compson's
monologue, is the handsome, supercilious young man with whom
Quentin fights shortly before drowning himself. Later, in the
imaginary 1918 of "Ad Astra," the fictional Bland, eight years older
and now an RAF pilot, still is handsome, supercilious, and said by
the narrator to be better liked by women than by men. But just as
he is closer to the real officer whom Faulkner had met in Connecticut by both his age and his experience of war, so is he closer
because of his psychic wounding: Though his fellow RAF pilots in
"Ad Astra" know him to be unmarried, he makes frequent and
pathetic references to a nonexistent wife. This aberration, like his
minimal combativeness as a fighter pilot with no bullet hole in his
plane during five months of flying at the Front, presumably is
attributable to limited "shell shock" from the ground combat
which the story points out had wounded him before his transfer to
the RAF.

There were innumerable aberrations from which Faulkner
could have selected one which would make readers of "Ad Astra"
immediately realize that the fictional officer Bland is psychologi-

cally damaged, but because Faulkner was basing much of the story on recollections of his weeks at New Haven in 1918 it is easy to see one reason why he chose to present Bland as sorrowing over a wife he does not have. Faulkner ("Poor kid," said Katrina Carter, his and Estelle Oldham's mutual friend) had felt at New Haven very real, not fictional, emotional distress for the wife he had expected to have but did not. In addition, Faulkner's situation a dozen or so years later at the time he was putting "Ad Astra" down on paper, possibly early in 1930 or near the end of 1929, must have contributed to that choice: Estelle who, to what Faulkner had called his "heartbreak," had married Cornell Franklin in 1918, divorced him in April 1929. Two months later, years after Faulkner had gone to New Haven to be out of Oxford during her wedding, he himself married her. Recollections told me by his acquaintances—for example, Mrs. Martin Shepherd, a next-door neighbor on the Gulf Coast where Faulkner and his bride spent the summer of 1929—and contemporary letters by Faulkner now in the Alderman Library make clear that he then was very kind to Estelle. Yet information from those same sources also reveals that Faulkner, worried about her distraught emotional condition, was obviously in a much different situation with her than he idealistically had imagined at New Haven in 1918 he would be if she then had carried out her agreement to marry him.

This conclusion receives considerable additional support from what Faulkner in 1929 reported to his friend and publisher, Harrison Smith, when he asked for an unusual advance of $500. He explained he needed the money because he both wanted to marry and had to marry. Dispelling the conventional assumption that the problem was pregnancy and explaining why pregnancy would not move him to marriage, he reported that he had to marry because of his guilty feeling of responsibility for the extraordinary distress of his bride-to-be, which he considered life-threatening. He explained that he believed her distress was genuine because he and she had known each other too long for him to be taken in by pretense. Writing later that year or possibly at the start of the next, given his present painful circumstances combined with his memories of pain at New Haven in 1918, Faulkner must have found it personally meaningful to end "Ad Astra" with the rattled Blanc standing "there, mopping at his face, crying hard . . . 'My poor little wife,' he said. 'My poor little wife.'"

The most indispensable character in "Ad Astra," the German prisoner, also derives from a real person Faulkner spent time with in 1918 at New Haven. He was an American citizen born in the western United States who had been in Europe when the invasion of Belgium began in August 1914. Having studied at a school in Germany he immediately had joined the German army, sharing its euphoric expectation of winning victory within weeks. After he had been wounded he had returned to the United States, American citizenship still intact. Faulkner's association with that man's bizarre veteran status in wartime Connecticut contributed two elements fundamental in "Ad Astra."

One became part of the basis for the major feature of the story, the captured German aviator's peaceful fraternization—during the evening of the first day of the Armistice—with Allied fighter pilots who had been his deadly enemies until the cease-fire at eleven o'clock that morning. This illustration of the instant displacement of war's hostility by brotherhood is a major contribution to the compression of "Ad Astra" toward epiphany. Several thousand miles from the Front in 1918, Faulkner at New Haven saw a similar fraternization, less dramatic and less compressed in time, between the veteran of German front line service and a few Allied officers, including a Canadian who also had been wounded in action and was convalescing in Connecticut. Phil Stone, recalling Faulkner's New Haven sojourn, volunteered decades later in some of our conversations that Faulkner in 1918 obviously had been struck by the amicable association between men who earlier had been under orders to kill each other—in a war which was still going on and to which the Canadian, after being declared again physically fit, soon returned.

The other useful element for "Ad Astra" from Faulkner's Connecticut association with the American veteran of the German army was the counterpart of the first, presumably contributing to the story's café brawl caused by the French patrons' hatred of the German prisoner. Connecticut in 1918 was sharing with the other forty-seven states a prolonged wave of anti-German hysteria. Nationwide, German measles and sauerkraut were renamed liberty measles and liberty cabbage, dachshunds were kicked about, and mobs harassed fellow citizens who had Germanic names. In New Haven, a few days after Faulkner arrived, an automobile dragged a figure of the Kaiser through the city and a newspaper reported that street sweepers would be busy clearing away the "bricks, rocks, bottles and even rotten eggs that were hurled at the effigy." Given such an atmosphere it is no wonder that, according to the recollections of Faulkner's New Haven friends, some of the Connecticut citizenry were resentful when Faulkner and his companions, sitting around drinking beer, would encourage the veteran of the Kaiser's army to sing German songs. Though there was no physical explosion by the angry Connecticut observers, Faulkner's imagination would not have had to strain to build on this personal experience for his story's account of the attack by the French patrons of the Cloche-Clos in resentment of the German and his Allied drinking companions.

"Ad Astra" significantly foreshadows Faulkner's most ambitious fictional treatment of the Great War, *A Fable* (1954), which for some time he euphorically but inaccurately considered to be his greatest novel and perhaps even the greatest of his time. The focus of the more than four hundred pages of *A Fable* is the fraternization of opposed combatants within war's hatred, a phenomenon Faulkner had observed in a mild form at New Haven while in the presence of the American veteran from the German army and later intensified and encapsulated in the café scene of the twenty-three-page "Ad Astra." For information about such fraternization—but on a very large scale—Faulkner also had found at New Haven a useful source: the conversation of his acquaintance William Aspenwall Bradley.

Bradley had published two books of poetry and a literary
biography by the time Faulkner met him at New Haven in 1918.
Soon he settled in France and in addition to continuing to write
became for many years an important expediter in the exchange of
literary works between that country and the United States.
Bradley's Paris agency later would arrange French publication for
some of Faulkner's writings in a helpful service which the remarkable and effective Jenny Serruys Bradley continued long after her
husband's death in 1939. The year before Faulkner reached Connecticut, Bradley had received a visit from the American poet
Robert Hillyer, a friend back in the United States for a short
respite from the Western Front, to which he promptly returned.
During that visit Hillyer recounted to Bradley what he had observed during the extensive 1917 mutiny in the French army. A
few months after listening to Hillyer, Bradley reported in the
Brick Row Book Shop to Faulkner and some of his friends what
Hillyer had said the previous year about the mutiny and the
fraternization between opposing troops—information then, and
for some time afterward, not conventionally available, censorship
having been rigid to avoid both revealing the weakness of the
French front lines while the mutiny was going on and damaging
the morale of other troops and civilians after it had been vigorously suppressed. One of Faulkner's friends at Connecticut
volunteered to me, well before the publication of A Fable with its
featuring of an invented 1918 mutiny and dramatic fraternization of
combatants, that Faulkner visibly had been much affected by
Bradley's report of the information Hillyer earlier had supplied.[1]

That such a report could impress Faulkner enough to become
the base for a work of fiction was further demonstrated a few years
later by a similarly affecting account which led to another of his
fictional treatments of the Great War. His friend and agent, Ben
Wasson, told me, in conversations before Faulkner received the
Nobel award, that in the very early 1930s he and Faulkner had
heard a man describe during a social evening in New York the
hazardous—essentially suicidal—duty of British Navy crews who

had operated small torpedo boats in the war. Walking home after the party Wasson realized how much that report had impressed and moved Faulkner, who kept repeating phrases such as "Those poor fellows!" Faulkner soon left New York for Mississippi, and before long the mail brought Wasson the typescript of a story focused on the crew of a British torpedo boat. Wasson sold it to the *Saturday Evening Post*, which published it as "Turn About." There was a longer delay between Faulkner's being touched by what he heard from Bradley in 1918 concerning fraternization within the 1917 mutiny and his putting thoughts about fraternization to use in "Ad Astra," and an enormously longer delay before he gave the subject extended treatment in *A Fable*.[2]

Faulkner's sojourn in Connecticut thus contributed that major theme to both "Ad Astra" and *A Fable*, but it also contributed additional elements to "Ad Astra." The story's most vocal character, the subadar from India, also comes out of those ten weeks at New Haven in 1918. While working at Winchester Arms, Faulkner talked often with two Hindus and, according to a friend in Connecticut, was especially interested in his conversations with one of them.[3] The subadar of "Ad Astra," in a statement which functions in the story as both an amplifying illustration of the war's irrationality and a contribution to the story's repeated symbolic use of cold, speaks of Indian troops who were miserable in the low temperatures of the European winter and unable to comprehend their strange situation among the combatants. While describing them in "Ad Astra," the subadar names only one of the men in his command, Das. Faulkner also used that name, earlier and later than "Ad Astra," for a central character in an unpublished short story titled "Love" and a few variously titled attempts at other treatments based on that story.[4] "Love" features Das, said in at least one of the versions to be a native of Malaya, where a significant portion of the population was Hindu. Like the Indian troops serving under the subadar in "Ad Astra," Das here uncomprehendingly suffers in the cold of warring Europe.

Whether from his Hindu acquaintances at New Haven Faulkner learned the name "Das" and anything about the related details which he used in both "Love" and "Ad Astra" I have not been able to learn. Perhaps their chief subject of conversation during the early spring was only how chilly all three of them found Connecticut to be, which, according to Faulkner's friends there, was an important issue with him on his first visit out of the South. But New Haven really was, as Stone had anticipated, an educational experience for Faulkner, and the two Hindus probably were the first he had ever talked to at length, or at all. Because of his lifelong interest in comparing religious and philosophical concepts Faulkner must have learned something from them. Perhaps part of what he heard he fitted into some of the subadar's philosophical statements. The subadar begins the talking in "Ad Astra," and what he says throughout the story is consistent with what one can learn about Hinduism in encyclopedias: The nineteenth and early twentieth centuries saw the development of a westernized elite of Hindus who believed in human equality while retaining the traditional so-called Indian pessimism based on their Hindu view of this life as only an enslavement, a bondage in the physical which ideally would be transcended by movement into the One. Whether Faulkner learned this sort of thing from his Hindu acquaintances at New Haven, from the voluminous and ranging reading he did though too many academic critics still deny it, or simply from an encyclopedia article, he authentically made the fictional subadar one who has lectured at Oxford University, tells the other officers repeatedly that all men are brothers, and agrees when the German prisoner says this life is nothing.

With the subadar of "Ad Astra" Faulkner touched on a theme he would develop extensively in subsequent fiction. As part of the story's treatment of "brotherhood" the subadar says that because he is unwilling to accept what he regards as the unfairly elevated social and economic status to which he was born, he has repudiated his inherited position. Bland calls that repudiation nothing and accuses him of merely abandoning his people to be exploited as usual though by someone else. The subadar replies with a question: Was it not something to have destroyed in one day what had existed for two thousand years? The tone in this passage suggests that the author of the story, though quite aware of the importance of the objection he assigns to Bland, at least agrees with the subadar that the action was not nothing. In later works of fiction and in published statements, Faulkner demonstrated that he had gone on to give considerable thought and refinement to this general theme. He made Ike McCaslin in *Go Down, Moses* repudiate his inherited plantation because of its exploitation of people and land. That repudiation was influenced by Ike's special woodland training, which also made him able to live on, to survive. Because one usually votes for life rather than death, when *Go Down, Moses* was first published Ike seemed so remarkably an affirmative advance over destroyed earlier major characters such as Bayard Sartoris, Quentin Compson, Darl Bundren, and Joe Christmas that it was too easy—at least I then mistakenly found it so—to overlook the inadequacies of Ike's repudiation which were to become more obvious later when Faulkner published *A Fable*, with the Corporal (and ultimately the battalion runner) occupying the most admirable of Faulkner's ranked categories of reaction to the world's evils: not just caring and repudiating like Ike and the subadar but acting in full dedication to reform. Surely that was one of the reasons Faulkner at first gave such euphoric high valuation to *A Fable*. Unfortunately, the Corporal, as a less successful fictional creation than the more humanly fallible subadar and Ike McCaslin, demonstrates the difficulty which curing the world's evils presents not only to life but to art.

Just as voluntary renunciation of power in "Ad Astra" prefigures more extensive treatment of the subject in Faulkner's work, so do the additional subjects discussed in the conversations of "Ad Astra": victory in defeat, the Lost Generation, and a third theme favoring such understandable preferences as love instead of force, justice instead of hierarchy, brotherhood instead of fatherland.

Concerning the first of these additional subjects, Faulkner elsewhere in his fiction showed his awareness of the idea that, as he had arranged for the German and the subadar to say in "Ad Astra," defeat is preferable to victory. When the German, who is a musician, places a narrower emphasis on the concept by saying defeat is good for art, we remember that as an artist living in an area once part of the Confederate States of America Faulkner had considerable awareness of the subject and a personal interest in it. By using that concept in "Ad Astra" Faulkner probably was responding to a literary stimulus as well. W. R. Moses effectively has pointed out that victory in defeat is a theme which Faulkner seems in "Ad Astra" to imitate from Hemingway's *A Farewell to Arms* (1929).[5] Faulkner by then had published four novels, one of them a masterpiece, and we reasonably might assume he was already consciously in competition with Hemingway and felt he too should treat the subject. He did have some affinity for it, as he showed, for example, a year or two later in his review of Remarque's *The Road Back*. Yet Faulkner did not give the major emphasis in his story's talk to the subject of victory in defeat.

The theme of the Lost Generation, a staple of much postwar writing in an alteration and great expansion of the famous remark Gertrude Stein claimed she did not make, was important to Faulkner beyond the subject's having been fashionable. He used it in other writings—his early poem "The Lilacs," *Flags in the Dust*, and his 1930 story "Honor" come at once to mind, the latter two showing combat pilots from "Ad Astra" in Lost Generation situations after the war. He was willing to emphasize this theme not just in the talk but in the setting and atmosphere and the brawl and the desperate drinking of "Ad Astra" even though by the time he wrote the story the Lost Generation was far along its path toward becoming an outdated cliché. An important part of the Lost Generation motif of heavy drinking in "Ad Astra" is Faulkner's effective presentation of the release it brings to the narrator. Concerning whether alcohol was a significant part of the life Faulkner observed during his weeks at New Haven in 1918, one can only say Phil Stone recalled that both he and Faulkner there kept it under firm control. Later that year, while Faulkner was in

Canada for RAF training, that control may have relaxed at times. According to the Canadians who told Michael Millgate their recollections of Faulkner in RAF training, he was usually reserved in the presence of the Canadians whose quarters he shared. But according to recollections about Faulkner's behavior with his closest companions among the cadets—all three of them from the United States—when he went into Toronto off-duty with his American friends he brought to drinking a sophistication which interested the late Ted Tebbetts, who in 1918 had been, he claimed to me, "a callow youth."

The third of these additional subjects which the characters talk about in "Ad Astra" is probably the most generally significant as well as the most personally significant to Faulkner. The subadar begins and maintains the talk about "brotherhood," and the German prisoner contributes importantly to it. They speak with authority, for both of them, because of their belief in equality, voluntarily have given up high status, the prisoner formerly a baron, the subadar formerly a prince. The German prisoner's talk reveals the revolutionary thought so widespread during the war, with the Russian revolution taking place in 1917. The German prisoner's report that his officer brother has been shot dead from his horse by a German soldier in a Berlin street brings into "Ad Astra" the revolutionary ferment of Germany which is generally considered a major reason the high command finally consented to the Armistice. And, as the French Great Mutiny of 1917 and the events which caused it demonstrated, that war, even more than most wars, increased awareness of the inequality between highly placed officers who order attacks and combat troops who die in them. In "Ad Astra" when such matters merge into a discussion of nationalism the German prisoner says:

"I return home; I say to my father, in the University I haf learned it iss not good; baron I will not be. He cannot believe. He talks of Germany, the fatherland; I say to him, It iss there; so. You say fatherland; I, brotherland, I say, the word *father* iss that barbarism which will be first swept away; it iss the symbol of that hierarchy which hass stained the history of man with injustice of arbitrary instead of moral; force instead of love.[6]

Years later, among the many links between the story "Ad Astra" and *A Fable*, the novel would present these same conceptions of "fatherland" and of "father" among its major features, notably in the opposition between the protagonist corporal who sparks the mutiny and the generalissimo who is his father.

That theme is both political and psychological, with the psychological more intensely compelling for Faulkner. He demonstrated throughout his writing career great ability to observe objectively his compulsive feelings though most people keep theirs hidden from themselves. A handy, minor sample is in his first novel, *Soldiers' Pay*, where he shows how fatuous the Cadet is in his yearning for military glory, the same yearning which almost all his life drove Faulkner—in spite of his intellectual awareness of its folly—to make misstatements about his military service in the Great War. A more important example is the extremely direct comment about "the word *father*" just quoted from "Ad Astra."

Though rarely so bluntly presented as in that quoted passage, the common conflict between child and parents appears in many of Faulkner's works. When, beginning in 1948, aspects of that subject in his fiction seemed to me important to present in seminars, conferences, and articles,[7] a few critics agreed.[8] But the most influential popular criticism of that early day did not agree, in part because it assumed Faulkner was ill-read, often naive, and concerned almost solely with a sociological, regionalist "saga." Later, subsequent popular critics somehow decided that Faulkner, still considered naive and ill-read as well as limited in subtlety, had devoted his fiction chiefly to fostering one or more among the ideas of the Nashville agrarians. In recent years, though those popular critical conceptions still have their loyal advocacy, other critics have found their overemphasis and exclusivity unsupportable and have returned to the belief that in much of his work Faulkner is not only quite sophisticated but personally intense about several subjects, important among them the relationship of child and parents.[9] In presenting that subject, however briefly, "Ad Astra" adds one more to the list of recurrent and crucial elements it shares with Faulkner's fiction as a whole.

Naturally enough, "Ad Astra" can be shown to contain materials from its author's observations outside Connecticut. So far they seem to me to be chiefly authenticating details drawn from his 1918 RAF training in Canada after his weeks in New Haven and a statement the fictional Irishman Comyn makes about the King of England which Faulkner heard in 1925 at New Orleans from an Irish sailor off a British battleship. But obviously it was on his weeks at New Haven that Faulkner drew for the base of his story. Enriching it by his exceptional imagination and by elements from his reading, using irony beginning with the title, skillfully applying the craftsmanship which knows what to tell and what not to tell, building the pervading sadness by effective repetition of such elements as the drinking and the cold, presenting varied demonstrations of the difficulty of achieving widespread human decency, and giving all of it intensity by compression, Faulkner made "Ad Astra," among his stories of the Great War, more serious than the popular "Turnabout" despite the enlarging import tacked to that story as its conclusion, more ranging than the effectively claustrophobic "Crevasse," and less quickly outdated than "All the Dead Pilots."

"Ad Astra" has survived as what many readers consider the best of Faulkner's short stories about a now ancient war, as one among the fortunately sizable number of his better short stories in general, and as a powerfully compressed presentation of elements important to such works as *The Sound and the Fury, As I Lay Dying, Absalom, Absalom!, Go Down, Moses,* and *A Fable.* Writing the story in creative expansion of a modest cluster of people and events he had observed briefly at New Haven in 1918, William Faulkner demonstrated the truth of what Henry James called "that odd law which somehow always makes the minimum of valid suggestion serve the man of imagination better than the maximum."[10]

NOTES

1. Robert Hillyer and Faulkner did not meet in 1918. Unfortunately, a brief statement I made in 1966 at a Modern Language Association convention—that at New Haven in 1918 a man had told Faulkner about Hillyer's report of the mutiny—has led so far to confusion in three biographies. A 1974 biography, drawing on but altering that statement without evidence, says that at New Haven, "Billy also met the poet Robert Hillyer and was fascinated by his war experiences." A 1980 biography, taking the misconception from the 1974 biography and expanding it without evidence, says that at New Haven "among the poets Stone knew, the one who interested William most was Robert Hillyer, who could talk of his war experiences as well as poetry." In 1984 a revision of the 1974 biography, repeating the inaccuracy and apparently accepting part of the 1980 unsupported expansion of it, says that at New Haven "there was Robert Hillyer, who not only was already accomplished as a poet, but also had undergone fascinating experiences in the war."

2. Concerning the genesis of A Fable, many commentators understandably have accepted Faulkner's statement at the beginning of the book that he had received the idea for the novel from two California filmmakers he had known in the 1940s. The facts are more complex, however, and Faulkner's receipt of much of the basis for the novel was much earlier. Faulkner told his publishers that one of the two filmmakers had supplied "the germ" of the novel: the suggestion that a film might deal with the identity of the Unknown Soldier of the First World War. Faulkner had accepted money to work with those two men to make such a film, and he was indebted to them for getting him started on the project, which none of them then realized would expand quite as it was to do. Impeccable about such obligations, Faulkner published his acknowledgment, but he hardly had needed suggestions in the 1940s for the novel's emphasis on mutiny and punished fraternization. Nor was his technique of presenting the central character in A Fable as a parallel to Christ dependent on any 1940s suggestion from Hollywood, as has been claimed, or even on the earlier Christ parallel in Humphrey Cobb's novel about a French mutiny, Paths of Glory, which one of Faulkner's friends told me Faulkner found impressive in 1935 and talked about to him then at some length. Faulkner was experienced at Christ parallels on his own, for example having put them in a 1925 New Orleans Times-Picayune sketch, "Out of Nazareth," and in Sartoris and The Sound and the Fury, the novels he published during the year before he first recorded submitting "Ad Astra" to magazines. He even momentarily had suggested the subject in "Ad Astra" when the narrator notices "something of the crucified about Monaghan, too" (Collected Stories, 416). Obvious links between A Fable and the story "Ad Astra," which had appeared almost a quarter-century earlier, and recollections by men who had been Faulkner's friends at New Haven more than thirty-five years earlier suggest that Faulkner probably was telling the truth about the inception of the novel when he talked with one of his foreign publishers at the time A Fable was to appear in print: The publisher reported Faulkner had told him that he had been thinking about the novel since the First World War.

3. Whether that Hindu acquaintance of Faulkner's at New Haven was a military officer I have been unable to learn. A 1974 biography says that among "Stone's other friends . . . was a subadar, the ranking Indian officer under the British Imperial officer," but that minor inaccuracy is based only on a misinterpretation of a recording, by notes or tape, at the Modern Language Association meeting of 1966, where in a paper, "Faulkner's War Service and His Fiction," I mentioned a few aspects of his weeks in New Haven. That Faulkner came to know the Indian through Phil Stone is also a minor, unsupportable elaboration of

that paper's remarks, as is the equally minor false statement that Faulkner's acquaintance who sang German songs in New Haven in spite of the war hysteria was a German.

4. *Uncollected Stories of William Faulkner* (1979) omits "Love" because, according to its editor, no complete typescript of it was thought to have survived. But "Love" is not lost: The Rowan Oak papers contain not only a typed version almost fifty pages long and complete except for the final few words (which are available in the accompanying holograph version) but a slightly improved—because shortened—typed version complete in twenty-nine pages. That inaccurate assumption was lucky for Faulkner's readers because "Love" is of almost as appallingly poor quality as Faulkner's 1936 "Two Dollar Wife," of which for some years only one copy was known to exist, in the Faulkner collection of Carl Petersen, who freely allowed interested scholars to read it, to their unanimous shock.

5. "Victory in Defeat: 'Ad Astra' and *A Farewell to Arms*," *Mississippi Quarterly* 19 (Spring 1966): 85–89.

6. William Faulkner, *Collected Stories of William Faulkner* (New York: Vintage Books, 1977), 417.

7. Some published examples: "The Interior Monologues of *The Sound and the Fury*," paper read to the English Institute, 1952, published in *English Institute Essays, 1952* (New York: Columbia University Press, 1954), 29–56; reprinted, revised, in Irving Malin, ed., *Psychoanalysis and American Fiction* (New York: Dutton, 1965); and in James B. Meriwether, ed., *The Merrill Studies in "The Sound and the Fury"* (Columbus: Charles E. Merrill, 1970). "War and Peace and Mr. Faulkner" (review of William Faulkner, *A Fable*), *The New York Times Book Review* (1 August 1954), 1, 13; a section an editor had cut in error from this review appears in the issue of August 8, p. 8, as though from an interview. "The Pairing of *The Sound and the Fury* and *As I Lay Dying*," *The Princeton University Library Chronicle* 18 (Spring 1957): 114–23. "Faulkner's *Mayday*," paper read at Modern Language Association convention, 1957, published, revised, as "Introduction" to William Faulkner, *Mayday* (Notre Dame: University of Notre Dame Press, 1978), 3–40. "Miss Quentin's Paternity Again," *Texas Studies in Literature and Language* 2 (Autumn 1960): 253–60; reprinted in Meriwether, *The Merrill Studies in "The Sound and the Fury."* "William Faulkner, *The Sound and the Fury*," in Wallace Stegner, ed., *The American Novel . . .* (New York: Basic Books, 1965), 219–28; reprinted in Marc Saporta, ed., Faulkner issue, *L'Arc* (Aix-en-Provence), No. 84/85, 1983. "Faulkner and Mississippi," a lecture at the two Faulkner and Yoknapatawpha Conferences in 1975 at the University of Mississippi, printed 1978 in *The University of Mississippi Studies in English*, University, Mississippi, 139–59.

8. Two early examples: Irving Malin, *William Faulkner: An Interpretation* (Stanford: Stanford University Press, 1957); Richard P. Adams, *Faulkner: Myth and Motion* (Princeton: Princeton University Press, 1968).

9. Recent publications which have taken up the examination of this subject include John T. Irwin, *Doubling and Incest/Repetition and Revenge: A Speculative Reading of Faulkner* (Baltimore: Johns Hopkins University Press, 1975); Judith Bryant Wittenberg, *Faulkner: The Transfiguration of Biography* (Lincoln: University of Nebraska Press, 1979), and David Wyatt, "Faulkner and the Burdens of the Past," in his *Prodigal Sons* (Baltimore: Johns Hopkins University Press, 1980), 72–100.

10. "Preface," *The Aspern Papers . . . ,* in *The Novels and Tales of Henry James* (New York: Charles Scribner's Sons, 1908), 12:vii.

Contending Narratives:
Go Down, Moses and the
Short Story Cycle

Susan V. Donaldson

In a 1942 review of William Faulkner's *Go Down, Moses and Other Stories,* Lionel Trilling noted plaintively that the collection of seven stories resisted easy generic labelling and even the grasp of the most careful of readers. Six of the seven stories, he declared, focused on "a single theme, the relation of the Mississippi McCaslins to the Negroes about them, and they have a coherence strong enough to constitute, if not exactly a novel, then at least a narrative which begins, develops, and concludes." Appearing "alien" and anomalous, though, was the seventh story, "Pantaloon in Black." Faulkner's reasons for including the story among the others, Trilling noted, were "hard to understand, for it diminishes their coherence." But far more puzzling was the effort *Go Down, Moses* required of the reader. "I had to read it twice," Trilling complained, "to get clear not only the finer shades of meaning but the simple primary intentions, and I had to construct an elaborate genealogical table to understand the family connections."[1]

Trilling's complaint about the difficulties of labelling and reading *Go Down, Moses* has been echoed by literary critics for nearly five decades now. Particularly impressive is the legion of terms marshalled to describe the volume. At one time or another *Go Down, Moses* has been pronounced—sometimes confidently and sometimes uneasily—a novel, a collection of short stories, a story-novel, a short-story compound, a short-story composite, and a short story cycle. Also generating considerable commentary is the problem of finding unified patterns of meaning in a collection of seven very different short stories. As Hans Skei pointed out some time ago, readings insisting upon the unity of *Go Down, Moses* nearly always seem to be accompanied by a trail of unsettling odds and ends. "If one insists that *Go Down, Moses* is about Ike McCaslin and his repudiation," Skei remarked, "one is bound to be troubled by the apparent inconsistencies in narrative tone and by the fact that Ike is missing from large parts of the book." But focusing on the problem of race in the text, Skei added, leaves the reader "seriously troubled by the hunting stories and the wilderness theme." [2]

Critical struggles of this sort—between impositions of unity and acknowledgements of disruptions and contradictions—originate, I would argue, in the text itself and serve, perversely enough, as the "central" concern of a volume resisting the very notion of centrality. For if *Go Down, Moses* can be described as a short story cycle, as so many critics have indeed argued, it is one whose tales are bound not by unifying themes and principles but by disunity, discontinuity, and never-ending strife. Indeed, I intend to make a case here for reading this collection as a site of struggle between the seven individual stories and that all-encompassing and all-binding "master narrative" of the McCaslins, which in turn is bound to the narrative of mastery defining Southern history and its rigidly defined categories of race, class, and gender. Such an approach reveals something of Faulkner's modernist suspicions of narrative in general, his yearnings to escape its bonds, and his sad, implicit acknowledgement that those bonds often prove to be unyielding. [3]

Even the publishing history of the individual stories in the volume suggests that a reading of *Go Down, Moses* might profit more by emphasizing the underlying discontinuity of the tales than by pointing to their continuity. Thanks to Joseph Blotner and James Carothers, we know that a good many sections of *Go Down, Moses* were published separately as magazine stories, including

"Lion," "The Old People," "A Point of Law," "Pantaloon in Black," "Go Down, Moses," and "Delta Autumn." *Collier's* published "A Point of Law" and "Go Down, Moses," and other stories appeared in the *Atlantic Monthly, Harper's,* and *Story.* In addition, "The Bear," Carothers tells us, appeared in considerably revised and abridged form in the *Saturday Evening Post* on 9 March 1942, just two days before Random House issued *Go Down, Moses and Other Stories.* The only episode in the book that was not published as a short story before the book itself was issued, Carothers says, turned out to be the opening tale, "Was," but even that story was reprinted eventually as a short story.[4]

So tangled was this history and so complicated were the relationships between the stories in *Go Down, Moses* that even Faulkner himself tended to be contradictory in describing the volume. Originally issued as *Go Down, Moses and Other Stories,* the volume later appeared under the title of simply *Go Down, Moses*—largely at Faulkner's own insistence. "Moses is indeed a novel," he wrote Robert K. Haas at Random House in 1948, when the company was considering reprinting the book. "If you will permit me to say so at this late date," Faulkner added, "nobody but Random House seemed to labor under the impression that GO DOWN, MOSES should be titled 'and other stories.' I remember the shock (mild) I got when I saw the printed title page."[5] Years before, though, when *Go Down, Moses* was still in the planning stages, Faulkner had defined the projected volume as one "similar in method to The Unvanquished," yet another collection of stories published in part in magazines.[6] Faulkner even described the volume that became *Go Down, Moses* as "collected short stories, general theme being relationship between white and negro races here."[7] It was in those same terms that he discussed the book in classes at Ole Miss in 1947. "After reworking," he asserted, "it became seven different facets of one field. It is simply a collection of short stories."[8] By the late 1950s, Faulkner had retreated back to his characterization of the volume as a novel. As he told a group of students at the University of

Virginia, "That novel was—happened to be composed of more or less complete stories, but it was held together by one family, the Negro and the white phase of the same family, same people."[9]

Faulkner's wavering between describing *Go Down, Moses* as a novel and as a short story collection calls to mind recent definitions of the short story cycle, a term, J. Gerald Kennedy notes, that has come into use only in the last twenty years or so.[10] Just as Faulkner's remarks hesitate between two generally accepted fictional forms, so too does the short story cycle, a form, Malcolm Cowley once observed, lying somewhere "between the novel and the mere collection of stories."[11] Kennedy has argued, in fact, that the short story cycle, largely a twentieth-century phenomenon, should be regarded as "a hybrid occupying an odd, indeterminate place within the field of narrative, resembling the novel in its panoramic view of life (often focused upon a particular time and place) yet composed of autonomous stories evoking different characters and problems."[12]

In one of the few theoretical studies available on the short story cycle, Forrest Ingram suggests that this strange hybrid quality is responsible for the peculiar tensions characterizing the form, tensions emerging from "the demands of each short story and the patterning of the whole cycle." In one way or another, he argues, each short story cycle poses the same riddle for its reader: at what stage do the individual stories merge to form a coherent whole and at what stage does the overriding framework of the cycle yield to the individuality of each story? Hence reading a short story cycle, delicately balanced between "the one and the many," he argues, requires particularly agile and flexible reading strategies open to the constant modification and revision required in moving from one story to the next. Indeed, Ingram's definition of the short story cycle in general is closely tied to the reading experience it elicits. "A story cycle," he declares at one stage of his argument, "is a set of stories so linked to one another that the reader's experience of each one is modified by his experience of the others."[13]

Despite the constant reorientation required by those reading strategies, though, Ingram assumes that the short story cycle is marked by what he calls at one stage "unifying strands." Among those strands, he argues, are echoes and repetitive themes, in particular the pattern of what he calls "recurrent development"— that is, recurring characters, motifs, concerns, and settings. Ultimately, these recurring patterns are responsible for creating "the unity of a short story cycle," a unity, moreover, that may not finally emerge until the reading experience of all the stories is completed.[14]

It is quite possible, though, as J. Gerald Kennedy has argued, that critics like Ingram see unity and harmony in the short story cycle where discontinuity and disruption may be just as important.[15] Formalist reading strategies, after all, have taught us all to value unity rather than disunity and fragmentation in the reading experience. But what of the radical breaks and gaps often lying between individual stories in a related sequence? And what are we to make of the interruptions in narrative created by the movement from one story to the next? Or the very different perspectives often emerging in the juxtaposition of individual stories? What happens in the reading experience if we concentrate not on the "unifying strands" but on the breaks, disruptions, and even the very tensions emerging between "the one and the many" in a story cycle? What happens, in short, if we question the very value of unity?

This is the question that Austin Wright recently posed in an essay titled—significantly enough—"Recalcitrance in the Short Story." For as he notes at the beginning of his argument, unity has served as a critical touchstone in writing about the short story ever since the early nineteenth century. From Edgar Allan Poe to James Joyce, short story writers have, in Wright's words, "always stressed the vital functioning of parts in a whole." But it might be more worthwhile, Wright adds, to focus attention on the underlying conflicts and tensions of a short story, in particular, "the force of a shaping form and the resistance of the shaped materials." That

resistance Wright calls "recalcitrance," a quality engaging the
reader "in a struggle between the vision of a potential and eventual unity and the obstructions to that vision." It is a quality,
moreover, that points to the ambiguous benefits of unity itself,
which, as Wright warns, can be "regressive, reactionary, imprisoning, or downright mystifying."[16]

That last comment in turn reminds us of the cold eye that
poststructuralist and feminist critics have lately turned on the
unifying compulsions of narrative in general. For narrative, with
its emphasis on ordered beginnings, middles, and endings implicitly demands a hierarchical ranking of events. Resistant to
gaps, contradictions, and discontinuities, stories in general also
seek, in Hayden White's words, "to produce the effect of having
filled in all the gaps, to put an image of continuity, coherency, and
meaning in place of the fantasies of emptiness, need and frustrated desire that inhabit our nightmares about the destructive
power of time." Such an effect, White adds, requires translating
difference into similarity, colonizing the contradictory and the
anomalous and making them compatible with a picture of unity
and order. Those differences that cannot be assimilated are simply
rejected and shuttled aside, small but uncomfortable reminders
of the price to be paid for achieving order and tidy sequence.
Indeed, White concludes that every full narrative is constructed
on the basis of a set of events "which *might have been included but
were left out.*"[17]

Is it any wonder, then, that narrative has been the target of so
many critics and theorists who value the marginal, the border-
line, and the contradictory? In a postmodern world in which all
truths and origins seem elusive, all sequences ultimately incon-
clusive, the *grands récits* or master narratives of recent history—
what one critic has called "the large explanatory systems, the
ideologies of liberalism, Marxism, nationalism, . . . the self-
foundational narratives of religions"—have all generally lost credibility.[18] Large in scale and all-encompassing in their grasp, these
master narratives have fallen under attack for their putative impe-

rialist designs—their insistence on single truths and their assimilation or rejection of alternative possibilities. Art historian Craig
Owens, for one, describes these master narratives and narrative in
general, for that matter, as "narratives of mastery, of man seeking
his telos in the conquest of nature." And he is not alone when he
angrily demands:

> What function did these narratives play other than to legitimize
> Western man's self-appointed mission of transforming the entire
> planet in his own image? And what form did this mission take if not
> that of man's placing of his stamp on everything that exists—that is,
> the transformation of the world into a representation, with man as its
> object?[19]

This description of narratives of mastery resembles to a startling
degree the history that Lucius Quintus Carothers McCaslin bequeaths to his descendants, white and black, in *Go Down, Moses*.
Indeed, L. Q. C. McCaslin himself is a very type of the ruthless
colonizer determined to transform his surroundings in his own
image. Seemingly self-authored, McCaslin emerges from the
mists of Carolina in early nineteenth-century Mississippi, wres-
tles away a sizeable portion of land from the Native Americans
remaining there, builds a plantation based on slave labor, and
bequeaths to his twin sons not just a profitable plantation but an
intricate system of power relations binding whites and blacks,
men and women, aristocrats and laborers. The stories that Mc-
Caslin generates as well are stories of mastery—his ruthless
conquest of everything before him—land, men, and women, his
disregard of compassion and common humanity even to the extent of impregnating a slave girl who is also his own daughter, and
his careless creation of a cash legacy for the offspring of that brutal
union. For McCaslin is nothing if not the quintessential patriarch,
whose power and authority necessitate the submission of all those
he encounters and a rigid hierarchy of race, class, and gender.
    Everything, in fact, that L. Q. C. McCaslin leaves behind bears
his ruthless and undeniable stamp—the land, the large plantation

house, the blacks bound to the land even in the aftermath of slavery, the whites benefiting from the old man's ruthlessness, the commissary ledgers detailing a legacy of enslavement, exploitation, and incest, and even McCaslin's particular brand of masculinity, premised on the appropriation of power and the exploitation of the weak. In a manner of speaking, the story that McCaslin sets in motion, like narrative in general, translates all difference in its path into similarity, and a hundred years later his descendants are still caught in that web of sameness. The very names of some of them, like Lucas Quintus Carothers McCaslin Beauchamp and Carothers Edmonds, hearken back to the past and the progenitor of McCaslin stories, as do the plots of stories defining the lives of McCaslin descendants—Ike McCaslin's attempt to rectify the sins of the past, for instance, by carrying out the instructions of the old man's will and Roth Edmonds's unwitting repetition of the past in his love affair with a black cousin. Even Lucas Beauchamp, the black grandson of L. Q. C. McCaslin, resembles no one as much as the old man himself, as even white family members sometimes grudgingly acknowledge.

But nowhere is the presence of L. Q. C. McCaslin more acutely felt than in the commissary ledgers, those records of daily transactions on the McCaslin plantation that Ike McCaslin, the old man's white grandson, takes down and reads one icy December night. There Ike discovers in his sixteenth year the brutality underlying the patrimony awaiting him—the building of the McCaslin plantation, the slaves required in that building, and his grandfather's reckless contempt for all, white and black, who stand in his way. In particular, of course, Ike discovers that early act of incest and the ties of blood underlying the intricate network of relationships among the white McCaslins and Edmondses and the black Beauchamps. Above all, though, Ike learns that the story to be found in the ledgers is not just that of his "family's chronicle" but of the South as well—of white proprietorship and power, of black bondage in the form of tenant farming and sharecropping, of rigid definitions of race, class, and gender required for the perpetuation of patriarchal power.[20] Each mark made in the ledgers by Ike's cousin McCaslin Edmonds is a continuation, the narrator tell us, of

> that record which two hundred years had not been enough to complete and another hundred would not be enough to discharge; that chronicle which was a whole land in miniature, which multiplied and compounded was the entire south, twenty-three years after surrender and twenty-four from emancipation—that slow trickle of molasses and meal and meat, of shoes and straw hats and overalls, of plowlines and collars and heel-bolts and buckheads and clevises, which returned each fall as cotton—the two threads frail as truth and impalpable as equators yet cable-strong to bind for life them who made the cotton to the land their sweat fell on. (293–94)

This passage reveals, I would argue, as clear and forceful a picture as any of the binding power of narrative, its ability to establish order and hierarchy, its designation of the positions of whites and blacks in the scheme of things, and its complicity with the economic ties continuing to link the races even after the abolition of slavery. Like the man who starts the tale in motion, the McCaslin narrative is so powerful and so relentless in its momentum that it appears to appropriate all potential obstacles lying in its path. Following the ledgers the old man started are "new ones now and filled rapidly, succeeding one another rapidly and containing more names than old Carothers or even . . . [Ike's] father and Uncle Buddy had ever dreamed of" (292). And as that story expands, so too does an elaborate system of economic and racial hierarchy, described by the narrator of "The Bear" as "that whole edifice intricate and complex and founded upon injustice and erected by ruthless rapacity and carried on even yet with at times downright savagery not only to the human beings but the valuable animals too" (298).

Not for nothing, then, does "The Bear" in particular repeatedly hearken back to that disturbing metaphor of economic and narrative bondage, "two threads frail as truth and impalpable as

equators yet cable-strong." Those bonds represent not just the
endless flow back and forth of farm supplies and harvested cotton
but the ties binding whites and blacks, men and women, ex-
ploiters and exploited to the stories emerging from those commissary ledgers. For in those ledgers, we are explicitly told, lies a
"chronicle which was a whole land in miniature," a master narrative not just of the McCaslins' appropriation of power and
property but of the South as well, as Ike McCaslin himself insists
in that crucial dialogue with McCaslin Edmonds in the fourth
section of "The Bear."

Indeed, in the debate between Ike and McCaslin Edmonds
over the former's repudiation of the family legacy, the McCaslin
narrative and Southern history are very nearly interchangeable.
The wrongs done to the black branch of the McCaslin family are
also the wrongs done to blacks in Southern history, just as the
power and property appropriated by L. Q. C. McCaslin allude to
acquisitions seized by the white South. It is with good reason,
then, that Ike explains his decision to renounce his patrimony by
resorting to a sweeping narrative of southern history. From his
perspective, that history is simply the story of the McCaslins,
white and black, writ large, and is all too easily figured by
the McCaslin ledgers and the iron bonds they have forged, those
"two threads frail as truth and impalpable as equators yet cable-
strong."

So compelling and so imprisoning is this master narrative, for
the McCaslins and the Beauchamps and for Southern history at
large, that it tells the same story over and over again. Beginning
with L. Q. C. McCaslin's act of incest and careless disregard of
parentage, that story concentrates on the establishment and perpetuation of patriarchal power and on white possession based on
black dispossession. The resonance of this ur-narrative is such that
it is seemingly reenacted generation after generation. In "The
Fire and the Hearth," the second story in the cycle, Lucas Beauchamp in a sense experiences that act of dispossession and the
brutality of patriarchy with each new generation of white male

Edmondses, the property and status of each serving as vivid reminders of Lucas's own disinheritance despite his direct line of descent from L. Q. C. McCaslin himself. Similarly, white characters like Roth Edmonds in "The Fire and the Hearth" and Ike McCaslin in "Delta Autumn" unwittingly repeat the same act of appropriation and possession begun so long before by the "first" male McCaslin. As a child, Roth suddenly comes to the knowledge of the power bestowed upon him by race, property, and gender, and he brutally demonstrates this knowledge to the black boy who is his closest friend. Just so does Ike McCaslin, confronted many years later with Roth Edmonds's discarded mistress and child, inadvertently repeat past patterns by offering money, as his grandfather did, as a gesture of dismissal and as an assertion of power.

The result is a master narrative that looms large indeed over all seven stories in *Go Down, Moses* and seemingly resists all attempts at circumscription established by beginnings and endings. In a sense, it is as if the story emerging from the McCaslin ledgers is one that has always been told and always will be, so all-encompassing are the time and space that it spans. Even in the opening words of "Was," the first story in the cycle, we get a glimpse of the power of McCaslin storytelling. The story begins without a beginning—just a fragmentary description without capitalization or punctuation of Uncle Ike McCaslin, who strictly speaking plays no role at all in the tale:

> not something he had participated in or even remembered except from the hearing, the listening, come to him through and from his cousin McCaslin born in 1850 and sixteen years his senior and hence, his own father being near seventy when Isaac, an only child was born, rather his brother than cousin and rather his father than either, out of the old time, the old days. (4)

Similarly, the fourth section of "The Bear" begins and ends in a headlong rush of words also lacking capitalization and punctuation, and the result, as Dirk Kuyk, Jr., has pointed out, is a sense of "tuning in on a continuous narrative."[21] Neither beginning nor ending, that narrative seemingly spans the length and breadth of the seven stories making up *Go Down, Moses*, and so far-ranging is its reach that figures like Ike McCaslin himself more often than not suggest entrapment—frozen figures in a never-ending frieze of storytelling.

But if the McCaslin ledgers and the continuous threads they spin suggest the totality of a master narrative, the seven individual stories making up *Go Down, Moses* offer unceasing resistance to all attempts to establish unity and continuity. As James Snead has suggested, the volume's *histoire*, or sequence of events, exists in radical opposition to its *récit*, or the manner in which those events are presented.[22] Juxtaposing tales of runaway slaves, recalcitrant tenant farmers, black grief, Indian lore, hunting stories, love affairs, and funerals, those stories pose narrative strategies of interruption and discontinuity in marked contrast with the stifling bondage of the McCaslin ledgers. No sooner does one tale begin, it seems, then it is interrupted, sidetracked, discontinued, and backtracked.

In story after story, in fact, certain narrative expectations about sequence and culmination are offered, only to be abruptly snatched away. "Was," for instance, begins with a brief reference to Ike and then asserts quite openly that the following story is not about Ike at all but only what was told to him by his cousin McCaslin Edmonds. In a like vein, events in the stories appear to lead to dramatic conclusions and then more often than not suddenly shift perspective altogether. One of the most intensely charged scenes in all the stories, the fight between Lucas Beauchamp and Zack Edmonds in "The Fire and the Hearth," abruptly dissolves at its height, when the gun in Lucas's hand misfires. At that moment the narrative suddenly shifts to the harvest conditions that year and Lucas's memories of that confrontation. Perhaps most disorienting of all is the disruption in narrative sequence characterizing "The Bear." The first three sections appear orderly enough, but they are followed by the dense, labyrinthlike meditations of the fourth section, in which Ike McCaslin formally renounces his patrimony, and then by the fifth section, returning in time to Ike's eighteenth year. The narrative patterns and sequences emerging in these individual stories, in short, are far more disorderly and puzzling than the relentlessly ordered storytelling emerging from the McCaslin ledgers.

Also undermining the foundations of McCaslin storytelling is the possibility of retrieving submerged or forgotten tales posed by some of the individual stories, especially in "The Old People" and "The Bear." Indeed, the tales told by Sam Fathers about the wilderness and about the Indians who lived there teach Ike something of the limits and vulnerabilities of McCaslin storytelling.[23] Even in the dying years of the nineteenth century, the wilderness loved by Ike and Sam seems "bigger and older than any recorded document," too immense to be reduced to an entry in the McCaslin ledgers or to be appropriated by McCaslin storytelling (191). And the tales themselves suggest the possibility of a world completely different from the one created by L. Q. C. McCaslin and his descendants. Listening to them, Ike feels as though "he himself had not come into existence yet, that none of his race nor the other subject race which his people had brought with them into the land had come yet" (171). In the alternative world created by Sam's storytelling, the hold of the McCaslins on their land and their authority appears "as trivial and without reality as the now faded and archaic script in the chancery book in Jefferson which allocated it to them" (171). And so, for that matter, do McCaslin notions of power and of race, class, and gender. From Sam Ike catches a glimpse of much different versions of masculinity and race, premised on "the communal anonymity of brotherhood" rather than the ruthless drive for power defining L. Q. C. McCaslin (257).

Learning about those alternative stories from Sam Fathers, in a manner of speaking, makes it possible for Ike to offer resistance to his family legacy of property, power, and storytelling. In his debate with McCaslin Edmonds in the plantation commissary, the focus of the fourth section of "The Bear," Ike quite simply offers an alternative narrative of Southern history. Like the Mc-Caslin narrative, his version of history is one of white possession and black dispossession, but it is also a history that demands eventual rectification of past sins, like Ike's own renunciation of his patrimony. In that act of repudiation, Ike argues, can be discerned the workings of an immense, divine plan. And when McCaslin Edmonds angrily defends the racial status quo by quoting the Bible and references to the curse suffered by the sons of Ham, Ike replies that not everything in the Bible is "true," that some passages served selfish ends of human beings. It is an indictment, clearly, that can be applied to McCaslin storytelling as well and its self-serving definitions of race and authority.

The greatest resistance to unity and to master narrative presented by the individual stories themselves in *Go Down, Moses*, though, is in the tale each has to tell. For each story in a sense concentrates on the struggle of individuals to break out of the "family chronicle" and its rigid categories of race, class, and gender in which they are imprisoned. "Was," for example, might be an amusing story of two comic courtships, but it is also a deeply felt account of efforts to escape a hierarchy of race, power, and property. As the offspring of incest and as a slave, Tomey's Terrel is as imprisoned as any other character in the web of McCaslin storytelling, but his frequent, illicit visits to his sweetheart on a neighboring plantation and his deft maneuvering during the celebrated poker game suggest that he has managed to achieve some degree of self-control and freedom. Similarly, his white brothers, Uncle Buck and Uncle Buddy, turn out to be covert abolitionists who are, in their own way, as resistant to the legacy they have inherited as is Ike McCaslin himself. Refusing to live in the huge house built by their father, they install their slaves there instead and settle down in a modest log cabin built by their own hands, stubbornly declining to exercise in full the power bequeathed to them by their father.

More resistant still is Lucas Beauchamp, the central figure of the second story, "The Fire and the Hearth." For Lucas, the black grandson of L. Q. C. McCaslin, wages a silent, angry war of will with three generations of white Edmondses who own the land he farms. Looking back on that undeclared war, Roth Edmonds, who owns the property in the 1940s, seems to see nothing but "an accumulation of floutings and outrages covering not only his span but his father's lifetime too, back into the time of his grandfather McCaslin Edmonds" (104). Throughout "The Fire and the Hearth," Beauchamp takes every possible opportunity to assert his own individuality and authority despite the pressing restraints of the racial and economic hierarchy in which he lives. He craftily pursues his moonlighting business despite Roth Edmonds's dire threats, betters a fast-talking salesman over the ownership of a fraudulent gold-finding machine, makes lucrative use of farm animals and equipment belonging not to him but to Roth Edmonds, and unfailingly insists upon the integrity of his family and his own identity. Proud of his descent from L. Q. C. McCaslin, he is also furiously resistant to the authority his grandfather represents, and when he faces down Zack Edmonds to salvage his pride and to keep his family intact, he also faces down L. Q. C. McCaslin. "I got to beat old Carothers," he tells Edmonds. "Get your pistol" (54).

Not insignificantly, even Lucas's name serves as a battlefield of contending narratives and conflicting notions of patriarchal power. His full name, we are told in the fourth section of "The Bear," is Lucas Quintus Carothers McCaslin Beauchamp, and therein lies much of the difference lying between Lucas Beauchamp and his white grandfather. As the narrator of that fourth section ponders, the name is

> not *Lucius Quintus* . . . but *Lucas Quintus*, not refusing to be called Lucius, because he simply eliminated that word from the name; not denying, declining the name itself, because he used three quarters of it; but simply taking the name and changing, altering it, making it no longer the white man's but his own, by himself composed, himself

selfprogenitive and nominate, by himself ancestored, as, for all the
older ledgers recorded to the contrary, Old Carothers himself was.
(281)

Just as disruptive, if not more so, is the black lumber mill
worker Rider in "Pantaloon in Black," driven nearly mad with
grief over the death of his wife. Rider careens through the story
with a furious energy threatening to break down all the boundaries and walls around him, including the very borders of the
short story itself. Trying to hold back the grief by running,
working maniacally, drinking, and finally playing dice, Rider
bounds over the line of every propriety and shibboleth he confronts, from his mad shoveling of dirt into his wife's grave at the
funeral to the knife fight he deliberately courts with the white
dice player. Our last glimpse of him is in the knife fight, and
the fluid motion with which he grasps the dice player and brings
out his razor, described in a seamless, 101-word sentence, suggests nothing so much as angry, rebellious energy spilling over
the boundaries designed to contain it—in this case, the hierarchical relations of race and even the narrative confines of the
story.

Most notable of all, of course, is Ike McCaslin's decision to
extricate himself from the family legacy and its accompanying
storytelling. He has been set free by Sam Fathers, he tells Mc-
Caslin Edmonds, not just from the burdens represented by the
commissary ledgers but from the very narrative embedded in
those ledgers,

> the frail and iron thread strong as truth and impervious as evil and
> longer than life itself and reaching beyond record and patrimony both
> to join him with the lusts and passions, the hopes and dreams and
> griefs of bones whose names while still fleshed and capable even old
> Carothers' grandfather had never heard. (299)

Far more explicitly than any other character in the cycle of stories,
Ike insists that he can step out of imprisoning narratives and their

delimiting roles for fathers and sons, men and women, masters and servants. It is, in fact, in precisely those terms that he defends his decision to repudiate the McCaslin legacy to his cousin. For Ike sees himself, in his own words, as "an Isaac born into a later life than Abraham's and repudiating immolation: fatherless and therefore safe, declining the altar because this time the exasperated Hand might not supply the kid" (283). Just as he refuses to step into the role assigned to him by the Biblical narrative, so too does he refuse to acquiesce to the place assigned to him by the master narrative of the McCaslins. And implicit in his repudiation is a rejection of the way race, gender, and class are defined in that master narrative—all tied, not incidentally, to L. Q. C. Mc-Caslin's own particular version of ruthless masculinity and patriarchal assertion of power.

That the McCaslin narrative nonetheless proves to be too much for Ike McCaslin and other rebels in *Go Down, Moses* is emphasized again and again in story after story. However admirable the abolitionist leanings of Uncle Buck and Uncle Buddy may appear, the fact remains that most of their slaves stay in bondage until emancipation. Moreover, the explicit ending of "Was," the poker game winning Tennie for Tomey's Terrel and temporarily freeing Uncle Buck from Sophonsiba Beauchamp's clutches, is contradicted by the *implicit* ending—the eventual marriage of Uncle Buck and Sophonsiba and their move back into the huge house built by L. Q. C. McCaslin and initially rejected by his sons. Uncle Buck's and Uncle Buddy's rebellion against the narrative begun by their father, it would appear, has largely come to naught. Similarly, Lucas Beauchamp's striking resemblance to his white grandfather is fraught with ambiguities. If his stiff-necked pride and determination to hold his own define his manhood, individuality, and resistance in the McCaslin narrative, those same qualities also bear testimony to the bonds that bind him still. Seeking to author himself, he falls back into patterns of patriarchy, mastery, and conquest set long ago by L. Q. C. McCaslin himself. As Roth Edmonds asserts,

*He's more like old Carothers than all the rest of us put together,
including old Carothers. He is both heir and prototype simultaneously of all the geography and climate and biology which sired old
Carothers and all the rest of us and our kind, myriad, countless, face-
less, even nameless now except himself who fathered himself, intact
and complete, contemptuous, as old Carothers must have been, of all
blood black white yellow or red, including his own.* (118)

Hearkening back to old Carothers himself, Lucas may embody a
fierce and covert rebellion against the restraints of inherited
narrative, but his close resemblance to his grandfather also suggests, unhappily enough, an unwitting reenactment of age-old
stories begun by Carothers. With Lucas, in a sense, Carothers's
story simultaneously repeats itself and begins anew.

If we have any doubt about the all-encompassing power of the
McCaslin narrative and its impact on those who struggle against
its bonds, we have only to look at the ending of "Pantaloon in
Black." For the grief that Rider displays and that threatens to
burst through the story's very boundaries is eventually brought
under control and confined through the storytelling efforts of the
sheriff's deputy. It is the deputy, after all, who sums up the white
perspective of Rider's grief and relates the seemingly inevitable
outcome of Rider's rebellion—a lynching. And it is the deputy,
contemptuous of blacks in general and of Rider's apparently inex-
plicable behavior, who offers the final glimpse of Rider weeping
and fighting in the jail cell. In that last scene Rider's larger-than-
life grief and desperate bid for some sort of emotional release are
finally imprisoned—not just in the jail cell but in the dehumaniz-
ing narration of the deputy whose tale contains Rider within the
confines of racial stereotype. Nowhere else in the stories of *Go
Down, Moses*, I would argue, is the confining power of narrative
more chillingly demonstrated than in the peremptory ending
offered by the deputy.

Above all, of course, the sense of failure defining Ike McCaslin
in "The Bear" and "Delta Autumn" seemingly underscores the
uneven nature of the contest between individual stories of resis-

tance and rebellion and the McCaslins' master narrative. For the lesson that Ike learns from his well-meaning renunciation of the family legacy, it would appear, is that "no man is ever free and probably could not bear it if he were" (281). Having reconstructed the story of the past from the commissary ledgers and having forthrightly rejected that past, Ike nonetheless reenacts the very sins he finds so horrifying in his grandfather. By carrying out the terms of L. Q. C. McCaslin's will and distributing the monetary legacy to the old man's black descendants, Ike to a very great extent does no more than simply carry out his grandfather's wishes and reassert the authority of patriarchy. And as "Delta Autumn" makes clear, Ike appears to reduce his ties to black relatives to a mere cash basis, just as L. Q. C. McCaslin does so many years before. When Roth Edmonds's black lover comes into the camp looking for Edmonds, Ike offers her the money his cousin has set aside and the horn inherited from General Compson. But he cannot, apparently, offer her and her child the one thing truly due them—love and the acknowledgement of family ties. It is with little surprise, then, that we note how closely Ike's handwriting resembles that of his grandfather when Ike records the results of his efforts to distribute the McCaslin legacy to black cousins. Old narrative patterns, apparently, are not so easily circumvented.

Yet, the determination to resist those patterns and to seek out new ones remains. Defeat by the unity and continuity of the intimidating narrative of the McCaslins may be implicit in story after story, but each story nonetheless pursues that struggle anew, contending with the inevitability and rigidity bequeathed by the stories of the McCaslins and the land and people they have mastered. No sooner do Uncle Buck, Uncle Buddy, and their emancipation schemes fade into the ending of "Was" than Lucas Beauchamp takes up the gauntlet and arrays himself against the Edmondses. And if the tale offered by Rider in "Pantaloon in Black" is eventually imprisoned in the narrative related by the sheriff's deputy, the possibility of retrieving alternative stories, Sam Fathers tells us in "The Old People" and in "The Bear," still remains. Even the defeat and weight of history that Ike McCaslin feels so intensely at the end of "Delta Autumn," a story suggesting more than any other the full extent of his failure, are leavened in "Go Down, Moses" by a moment of compassion, hope, and true community. For the funeral of Samuel Worsham Beauchamp, the last and saddest of L. Q. C. McCaslin's black descendants, has been made possible by a brief, fleeting moment of cooperation and understanding among blacks and whites. In that moment can be discerned still one more alternative to the stories of mastery, possession, and dispossession defining the white McCaslins.

To the end, then, *Go Down, Moses* remains a battlefield of contending narratives, an unyielding contest between individual stories of resistance and discontinuity and the all-encompassing narrative of the McCaslins. If those individual stories are never really victorious, neither are they entirely defeated. As each story ends, the struggle is taken up anew by the tale that follows and by the character whose rebellion the story traces. Together the separate stories of Faulkner's short story cycle set themselves in unending opposition to the unity and continuity represented by the McCaslin ledgers, always contending, always attempting to revise and transform the narrative patterns in which they are trapped. And in the unending nature of that struggle is, I would conclude, a small measure of victory, one that questions and subverts the "ending" of white possession and black dispossession, of inflexibly defined categories of race, class, and gender inscribed in the McCaslin ledgers. For the seven individual stories in this volume, bravely struggling against the compelling power of the McCaslin master narrative, even that modest victory is no small achievement.

NOTES

1. Lionel Trilling, "The McCaslins of Mississippi," *Nation* 30 (May 1942): 632–33.

2. Hans H. Skei, *William Faulkner: The Novelist as Short Story Writer* (Oslo, Norway: Universitetsforlaget, 1985), 242.

3. J. Gerald Kennedy has recently observed that discontinuity may be as important as

continuity for examining the "junctures" between stories in a short story cycle. See J. Gerald Kennedy, "Toward a Poetics of the Short Story Cycle," *Journal of the Short Story in English* 11 (1988): 11.

4. James B. Carothers, *William Faulkner's Short Stories* (Ann Arbor, Mich.: UMI Research Press, 1985) 89, 91, and 88–89; Joseph Blotner, *Faulkner: A Biography*, 2 vols. (New York: Random, 1974) 2:1077, 1078, 1089, 1093, and 1087–88.

5. William Faulkner to Robert K. Haas [26 January 1949], *Selected Letters of William Faulkner*, ed. Joseph Blotner (New York: Random-Vintage, 1977), 284 and 285.

6. William Faulkner to Robert K. Haas [28 April 1940], *Selected Letters*, 122.

7. William Faulkner to Robert K. Haas [1 May 1941], *Selected Letters*, 139.

8. "Classroom Statements at the University of Mississippi, 1947," *Lion in the Garden: Interviews with William Faulkner*, ed. James B. Meriwether and Michael Millgate (Lincoln: University of Nebraska Press, 1968), 54.

9. Frederick L. Gwynn and Joseph L. Blotner, eds., *Faulkner in the University: Class Conferences at the University of Virginia, 1957–1958* (Charlottesville: University of Virginia Press, 1959), 4.

10. Kennedy, 10.

11. Quoted in Forrest L. Ingram, *Representative Short Story Cycles of the Twentieth Century: Studies in a Literary Genre* (The Hague: Mouton, 1971), 16.

12. Kennedy, 14.

13. Ingram, 17, 15, 19, and 13.

14. Ibid., 18, 200, and 138.

15. Kennedy, 14.

16. Austin Wright, "Recalcitrance in the Short Story," *Short Story Theory at a Crossroads*, ed. Susan Lohafer and Jo Ellen Clarey (Baton Rouge: Louisiana State University Press, 1989), 115, 117, and 115.

17. Hayden White, "The Value of Narrativity in the Representation of Reality," *On Narrative*, ed. W. J. T. Mitchell (Chicago: University of Chicago Press, 1981), 11, 15, and 10.

18. Wlad Godzich, Foreword, *Story and Situation: Narrative Seduction and the Power of Fiction*, by Ross Chambers, Theory and History of Literature, vol. 12 (Minneapolis: University of Minnesota Press, 1984), xv.

19. Craig Owens, "The Discourse of Others: Feminists and Postmodernism," *The Anti-Aesthetic: Essays on Postmodern Culture*, ed. Hal Foster (Port Townsend, Wash.: Bay Press, 1983), 65–66.

20. William Faulkner, *Go Down, Moses* (New York: Random-Vintage, 1970), 110. Subsequent references to this edition will be cited parenthetically within the essay.

21. Dirk Kuyk, Jr., *Threads Cable-Strong: William Faulkner's "Go Down, Moses"* (Lewisburg, Pa.: Bucknell University Press, 1983), 17.

22. James A. Snead, *Figures of Division: William Faulkner's Major Novels* (New York: Methuen, 1986), 183.

23. John Matthews expresses a similar idea in his discussion of "Was" in relation to the stories Ike eventually hears in "The Old People" and the history that he narrates in the fourth section of "The Bear." See John T. Matthews, *The Play of Faulkner's Language* (Ithaca, N.Y.: Cornell University Press, 1982), 230.

Knight's Gambit: Poe, Faulkner, and the Tradition of the Detective Story

JOHN T. IRWIN

Like the machine gun, the detective story is an American invention. We can assign its origin to a specific author and story. The author is Edgar Allan Poe, and the story the 1841 tale "The Murders in the Rue Morgue." The detective genre has, of course, enjoyed worldwide popularity since Poe's day, but perhaps because of its native roots it has always had a special place in American literature, in both popular and serious fiction. Needless to say, Faulkner is a major inheritor of Poe in this genre, and I would even go so far as to maintain that *Absalom, Absalom!*, with its two young narrators puzzling over the facts of a very old murder trying to understand the motive, represents in some sense the culmination of the gothic detective form.

What I would like to discuss is Faulkner's relationship to the genre's origin (Poe's Dupin stories) in his own practice of detective fiction, that is to say, the way in which Faulkner interprets or inflects various conventions and images associated with the genre, devices that were for the most part invented by Poe. And I would like to center my discussion on Faulkner's 1949 collection *Knight's Gambit.*

Let me begin with a fairly clear cut example of Faulkner's work in the genre, the story called "An Error in Chemistry," first published in *Ellery Queen's Mystery Magazine* in 1946 and awarded a second prize in the magazine's annual contest for the best stories to appear in its pages during the year.[1] (The first prize that year, by the way, went to a writer named Manly Wade

Wellman for a story with an American Indian setting called "A Star for a Warrior.") What I would like to discuss is the story's relationship to the first and third of Poe's Dupin tales—"The Murders in the Rue Morgue" and "The Purloined Letter." As you recall, "The Murders in the Rue Morgue" is a "locked-room" mystery. A mother and daughter have been brutally murdered in their apartment, and when the police arrive at the scene they find that all the apartment's windows and doors are locked from the inside and that the killer has escaped without leaving any trace of his "means of egress,"[2] a puzzle that Dupin must solve on his way to unraveling the still deeper puzzle of the killer's bizarre identity. In "The Purloined Letter," on the other hand, we are confronted with a "hidden-object" mystery. A compromising letter has been stolen from the Queen by the Minister D__, and the police have rigorously searched the Minister's home and person without turning up the missing object. Dupin is certain that if the letter is to be of any use to the Minister in blackmailing the Queen, it must be ready to hand, which is to say that it must be hidden somewhere in the Minister's residence. And the mystery then turns upon the fact that the missing object is undoubtedly present within a finite physical enclosure (the Minister's house) without, as it were, making a physical appearance during the minute searches conducted by the police. Dupin solves the mystery by realizing that the Minister has hidden the letter under the very noses of the authorities by not seeming to hide it at all, by simply turning the letter inside out, readdressing it to himself in a feminine hand, and then leaving it in plain sight in a card rack hanging from the mantelpiece.

As you might conclude from this brief description of the two stories, "locked-room" and "hidden-object" mysteries are structurally related. In the former, a physical body (that of the murderer) is absent from an internally sealed space without there being any apparent means of egress; while in the latter a physical object is present within what we might call an externally sealed space (externally sealed because all the possible hiding places for the object outside the space have been logically eliminated) without the object's making a physical appearance. In the former instance (the locked room) we are certain that what we seek *is not inside a given space*, in the latter (the hidden object) that what we seek *cannot possibly be outside it*. Indeed, part of the peculiar force of the hidden-object and locked-room types of detective stories is that they seem to present us with a physical embodiment, a concrete spatialization, of the very mechanism of logical inclusion/exclusion on which rational analysis is based, present us with this as an apparent confounding of rational analysis.

Now it seems clear that Faulkner had registered the structural resemblance of these two types of mysteries, for in "An Error in Chemistry" he creates his own combination of a locked-room and hidden-object problem. The tale begins with Joel Flint telephoning the sheriff to say that he has killed his wife at the home of his father-in-law, Wesley Pritchel. When the sheriff arrives, he finds the killer Flint and the body of the victim. But Wesley Pritchel has locked himself in his room and won't come out. The sheriff sees Pritchel looking out the window, and the assumption is that Pritchel had witnessed the crime. In the sheriff's account to Gavin Stevens, Faulkner goes out of his way to emphasize the locked-room aspect of the scene by having Stevens ask whether Pritchel's room was locked from the inside or the outside. "On the inside," the sheriff replies.[3] And to compound matters, it seems to the sheriff that Joel Flint, who phones the authorities, waits for them to arrive, and then freely confesses to his wife's murder, is in search of his own locked room. As the sheriff says, "It's like he *wanted* to be locked up in jail. Not like he was submitting to arrest because he had killed his wife, but like he had killed her so he would be locked up" (112). So the sheriff locks Flint up, and the next morning Flint's cell is empty. As the narrator, Chick Mallison, describes it, "He had not broken out. He had walked out, out of the cell, out of the jail, out of town and apparently out of the country—no trace, no sign, no man who had seen him or seen anyone who might have been him" (116). And as he says later, "It was as if Flint had never been here at all—no mark, no scar to show that he had ever been in the jail cell" (120). Concerned about the witness's safety with Joel Flint on the loose, the sheriff sends his deputy out to Wesley Pritchel's place with instructions "not to let that locked door—or old Pritchel himself, if he comes out of it—out of his sight" (117). The deputy reports that Pritchel is still in his locked room and that he doesn't leave it even for his daughter's funeral.

Joel Flint's plan is remarkably simple: The motive is greed. Three Northern businessmen have offered Wesley Pritchel a sizable amount of money for his farm, but Pritchel won't sell. And even if he did, he would never give any of the money to his son-in-law, whom he despises. So Flint decides to kill Pritchel and then use his talents as a make-up artist (Flint had performed for years in vaudeville billed as "Signor Canova, Master of Illusion, He Disappears While You Watch Him" [129]) to impersonate Pritchel, sell the farm, and pocket the money. The only problem with the plan is that while Flint might be able to fool someone like Gavin Stevens, who has only seen Pritchel twice in his whole life, or Chick Mallison, who has never seen him, Flint would never be able to fool his own wife, who is Pritchel's daughter. Consequently, Flint has to kill his wife, who would be a witness not necessarily to Pritchel's murder but the fact of Flint's impersonation (and thus implicitly to the fact that something had happened to remove from the scene the man he was impersonating). And the brilliance of Flint's plan is that he decides to reverse the usual sequence in the murders of an intended victim and a witness, which is to say, he decides to kill the witness (his wife) first and then kill the real victim (Pritchel) later. And he is able to accomplish this plan precisely because he has duped the authorities into misinterpreting the roles of Pritchel and of Flint's wife in the affair. He has created the illusion that his wife was the intended victim (when the sheriff asks Flint why he killed her, Flint says, "Why do men ever kill their wives? Call it for the insurance") and that his father-in-law was the witness.

All of which casts a somewhat different light on the locked-room aspect of the case. The standard locked-room problem requires that the murderer and victim be together at the moment of the crime in the same internally sealed space. But in Faulkner's version of the problem, the locked room has, so to speak, been split and doubled. There are two locked rooms, the jail cell containing the killer Joel Flint, locked from the outside, and Wesley Pritchel's bedroom containing the victim, locked from the inside. At some point during the night after he has been jailed for the murder of his wife, Joel Flint escapes from his cell. Faulkner doesn't say how this was accomplished, but in telling us that Flint had worked in vaudeville as an illusionist and escape artist, he has in effect finessed the question. For unlike Poe, Faulkner is not really interested in the mechanics of how the killer got out of the locked room without leaving any physical evidence of his means of escape.

Once Flint is on the loose, he goes to his father-in-law's farm, makes his way into the locked bedroom, and kills Pritchel. Flint then disguises himself to look like Pritchel and in turn tries to make the victim's corpse look like Flint. He obliterates Pritchel's face with a blow from a shovel and then buries him in a shallow grave with a scrapbook full of Flint's press clippings from vaudeville. Flint then locks himself in the bedroom, and by the next morning when the sheriff discovers Flint's escape and sends the deputy out to Pritchel's farm with instructions "not to let that locked door . . . out of his sight," it is Flint disguised as Pritchel behind that door. And it is Flint who stays there during the funeral of Pritchel's daughter, since he doesn't want to risk having his impersonation discovered by people who might have known Pritchel well. The way Flint has it figured, if he simply stays in the locked room, acting as if he were afraid that the escaped killer might still come back to eliminate the witness to the crime, then the only people that he may ever have to confront in his disguise are the three Northern businessmen who want to buy Pritchel's farm, and they have only seen Pritchel once before.

Flint's illusionary feat is ingenious, and so is Faulkner's. For in the very act of creating Flint's plan, Faulkner has, right before our eyes, reversed the standard structure of a locked-room mystery. When the law arrives at Pritchel's farm the first time, there hasn't in fact been a locked-room murder. Pritchel's daughter has been killed outside the house, and the person inside the locked room is the witness to the crime, who fears for his life. But when the law arrives at Pritchel's farm the second time in the person of the deputy who, after Flint's escape, has been sent to check on the old man's safety, Pritchel's bedroom has now almost certainly become the scene of a "locked-room" murder. But with this difference: it is now the killer who is present in, and the victim's corpse that is absent from, the internally sealed space. And this reversal in regard to the occupant of the locked room grows out of that earlier reversal in the order of the murders, the killing of the witness prior to the killing of the real victim, a trick that Faulkner, like any master of illusion, can't help calling our attention to when he has the puzzled sheriff remark, "It don't make sense. If he was afraid of a possible witness, he not only destroyed the witness before there was anything to be witnessed but also before there was any witness to be destroyed. He set up a sign saying 'Watch me and mark me'" (115). And that is, of course, just what Flint did, because as an illusionist he knows that the way to pull off a trick is to draw the audience's attention in one direction while doing something in another, that is, to make the audience misinterpret what it is that they are seeing.

Flint in effect tricks the sheriff into misreading the roles of the three people at the scene of the crime. When Hub Hampton arrives at Pritchel's farm the first time, he finds a triad of murderer, victim, and witness. He sees, correctly enough, that Flint is the murderer; but he reverses the other two roles in the triad, even though he senses that there is something amiss in his reading of the roles. He says to Gavin Stevens, "The wrong one is dead" (114)—by which he means that if the motive for the murder was greed, as Flint's remark about his wife's insurance suggests, then the amount of money to be gained from the insurance is trifling compared to the amount to be gained from the sale of Pritchel's farm to the three Northern businessmen. But for Flint to get his hands on that money, his victim would have to be Pritchel.

Faulkner's manipulation of the triad of murderer, victim, and witness in the tale has a familiar ring to it. As I argued in *Doubling and Incest,* Faulkner has a predilection for triangular or triadic structures, most obviously for the Oedipal triangle—a structure that he tends to inflect in a variety of ways by substituting different figures in the three roles. Thus, for example, in *Absalom, Absalom!* he substitutes for the standard triad of father, mother, and son the figures of brother avenger (Henry Sutpen), sister (Judith), and brother seducer (Charles Bon), while keeping intact the same structural relationships, the same sexual tensions, associated with the standard triad of the family romance. And as I further argued, the structural principle that governs the dynamics of this triangular relationship is the narcissistic principle of doubling, whereby one figure in the triangle tries to play more than one role within it, as when the son desires to usurp the father's role and thus enjoy a dual relationship to the mother—that of both son and husband.

The ultimate goal of the structural principle of doubling, as it operates within the Oedipal triangle, is the collapsing of all three roles into one. And something very like this is what happens in the triangular structure of murderer, victim, and witness in "An Error in Chemistry." In the sheriff's interpretation of the initial crime scene, Flint's real intended victim Pritchel appears to play the role of the witness, an appearance that deceives the sheriff and that ultimately makes it possible for the murderer also to play the role of the witness when Flint kills Pritchel and assumes his identity. As the narrator says at one point in commenting on the resemblance in physical build of Flint and Pritchel, "he and his father-in-law could easily have cast that same shadow which later for a short time they did" (110), and we know that for Faulkner the image of the shadow almost always evokes the notion of doubling.

Victim as witness, murderer as witness—it is as if the roles of the two people actively involved in the crime (murderer and victim) had been collapsed into that of passive observer (and indeed, the dynamic principle at work here is a kind of death drive that seeks a state of quiescence, of absolute passivity, for the self). Moreover, it is not without significance that the persons who fill these three roles are already linked together in a triangular family relationship as father-in-law, son-in-law, and daughter, the male-male-female structure of the Oedipal triangle. (We might note that in Faulkner's fiction a locked room or a closed door often signifies the site not of a murder but of a primal scene, a fantasized scene of parental intercourse in which the child interprets the sounds of love-making as the sounds of violence perpetrated by the father against the mother.) At one point in the tale, Gavin Stevens gives his own reading of the triangular structure of the crime as a kind of shadow-play, "That triumvirate of murderer, victim, and bereaved—not three flesh-and-blood people but just an illusion, a shadow-play on a sheet—not only neither men nor women nor young nor old but just three labels which cast two shadows for the simple and only reason that it requires a minimum of two in order to postulate the verities of injustice and grief" (121).

But at this point we should pause and ask ourselves if Faulkner hasn't in fact performed another illusion before our very eyes in regard to the "locked-room" character of the story, another disappearing act as startling as the murderer's switching places with the victim in the role of the witness. We suggested a moment ago that when the deputy arrives at Pritchel's home the morning after Flint's escape and stations himself outside the locked bedroom door, he confronts in effect a locked-room mystery, finds an internally sealed space that is the scene of a murder, though in this instance the sealed space contains the living body of the killer rather than the dead body of the victim. Yet isn't it precisely upon that difference in the degree of animation of the room's occupant that the "mystery" in a locked-room problem hinges? Corpses can't lock doors, so to find a corpse alone in a room whose doors and windows have been locked from the inside is mysterious. But where's the mystery in finding the internally sealed space occupied by a living murderer, even if that murderer is disguised as the victim he has done away with in that locked room? The only thing that might resemble a mystery here is how Flint got out of the locked jail cell and then into Pritchel's locked bedroom to kill him, but as we said, Faulkner finesses that problem by making Flint an escape artist. What Faulkner has done in effect is to switch, under the reader's nose, the type of problem that lies on the other side of the locked door. He has set up a situation that bears the obvious marks of a locked-room puzzle, but when we open that locked door we find that it has changed into a hidden-object problem.

Instead of a purloined letter, the object that everyone is seeking in Faulkner's tale is the missing killer. However, like the purloined letter, whose appearance was altered by turning it inside out, readdressing it to the Minister D— in a feminine hand, and then leaving it in plain view in the Minister's drawing room, the killer has also altered his appearance and hidden himself in plain sight. And just as part of altering the purloined letter's appearance was the turning of the letter inside out, so part of altering the murderer's "appearance" in Faulkner's tale is the turning of the locked-room mystery's spatial coding of killer and victim inside out. Which is to say that the person who should be outside the internally sealed space (the killer) is inside it, and the person who should be inside that space (the victim) is outside it (buried under the feed room in the stable).

From what we have said so far it should be clear that Faulkner was a profound student of the origin and conventions of detective fiction and that he wrote his own detective stories with an eye to situating them within the tradition of that genre that had been originated by a fellow Southerner almost a hundred years before. However, what we must add is that while it may be interesting to discuss a tale like "An Error in Chemistry" in terms of its manipulation of traditional detective story devices and thus Faulkner's inflection of the genre's origin in Poe, that is, interesting to give a reading of it in terms of literary history, it is much less satisfying to read "An Error in Chemistry" simply in terms of the pleasures of a standard detective story. For the tale is marred in two important ways.

First, Faulkner's decision to make the killer a former vaudeville illusionist and escape artist inevitably strikes the reader as being itself a kind of vaudeville trick, an illusion that lets Faulkner escape from the traditional challenge of coming up with a solution to the locked-room problem different from the one which Poe originated. As any student of the genre knows, this is a challenge to which detective story writers have consistently addressed themselves over the years. (Indeed, one might note in passing that if the author of a detective story is going to allow himself the liberty of making the killer an illusionist and escape artist, then he might as well go all the way and make his killer the invisible man or superman. A large part of our interest in murder mysteries depends upon the killer's being someone with ordinary human powers like you and me—not a ghost or a creature from outer space.) Second, the way in which Flint's imposture is revealed and his capture effected is not the result of Gavin Stevens's analytic investigations but of an accident: Flint disguised as Pritchel makes the mistake of mixing a cold toddy in Stevens's and the sheriff's presence by trying to dissolve the sugar in raw whiskey, the kind of mistake that a Southerner like Pritchel would never make, but that the Northerner Flint would. Seeing this, Stevens and the sheriff leap upon Flint, wrestling him to the floor and wrestling him out of some of his make-up—a climax that leaves the reader with the feeling that he has witnessed, if not a *deus ex machina*, at least an instance of *iustitia ex ampulla*, justice poured out of a bottle.

All of which leads me to suggest that as a writer of detective fiction Faulkner is most successful when he takes the conventions of the genre and shapes them to his own materials, his own obsessive concerns, rather than when he competes with the genre's originator on terms that are almost wholly Poe's. The reason for this is fairly straightforward. Faulkner's strengths as a fiction writer tend to be in the direction of character and setting and in the poetry of the language, while the detective story is a form that essentially favors plot and has a low tolerance for highly developed characterization or highly evocative language. Indeed, in the history of the genre one finds not great characters but rather great caricatures. From Dupin to Holmes to Poirot, we are confronted not with fully-rendered personalities but with monsters of idiosyncrasy, figures conveyed through one or two odd traits as trademarks. Yet to say that the detective story is a form which essentially favors plot is not to imply that Faulkner has a weakness when it comes to plotting; it is simply to say that the specialized kind of plot which forms the core of the genre demands a type of ingenuity that was the great strength of the genre's inventor, but not of Faulkner, as "An Error in Chemistry" and several of the other tales in *Knight's Gambit* make clear. It is only when Faulkner pushes the detective story to the limits of the short story form that he is able to bend it to his own artistic will, as he did with the tale that gives the collection its title. And it is on the story called "Knight's Gambit" that I would like to focus the rest of my discussion.

Faulkner originally wrote "Knight's Gambit" as a short story, completing it by January 1942. He described it as "a love story, in which Stevens prevents a crime (murder) not for justice but to gain (he is now fifty plus) the childhood sweetheart which he lost 20 years ago" (Blotner, 2: 1097). Some four years later in early 1946, Faulkner began revising and expanding the tale, stretching it from short story to almost novella length before it was completed in November 1948. What I would like to concentrate on is the way that Faulkner took two devices that originated with Poe— the imagery of a chess game used to evoke the battle of wits between detective and criminal, and the notion of the detective's having a personal motive for becoming involved in the solution or prevention of the crime—and, by annexing these devices to standard Faulknerian material, made them his own.

The action of "Knight's Gambit" begins on the evening of 4 December 1941, three days before the Japanese attack on Pearl Harbor. Gavin Stevens and his nephew Chick Mallison are playing chess at home when a young man named Max Harriss and his sister burst into the room. The brother and sister are the spoiled children of Melisandre Backus Harriss, a childhood friend of Chick's mother. Max Harriss has come to demand that Stevens, as the county attorney, take action to get Captain Sebastian Gualdres out of their house, to have him deported if need be. Young Harris says that Gualdres, an Argentine fortune hunter whom the Harriss family had met during their foreign travels, was at first engaged to his sister but has since jilted her and intends to marry his mother. Harriss wants Gavin Stevens to intervene, challenging the older man by asking, "You're the Law here, aren't you?" [4] And Harriss implies that if Stevens doesn't act, then he (Harriss) will take matters into his own hands and kill Gualdres.

The situation is a familiar one in Faulkner's fiction. A young man confronts his father or a father-surrogate (an older man who represents authority, who embodies a patriarchal Law) and demands to know what the older man is going to do about the womenfolk, whether he intends to protect the young man's sister or mother from an interloper, which is to say, to protect the womenfolk from themselves. One thinks of Quentin Compson and his father in *The Sound and the Fury* and of Henry and Thomas Sutpen in the story that Quentin helps narrate, *Absalom, Absalom!* And indeed the father-son analogy certainly applies to the confrontation between Gavin Stevens and Max Harriss. For as we learn in the course of the story Stevens had been briefly and secretly engaged to Harriss's mother when she was a girl of sixteen, and the implication is that, had they married, Stevens would have been the father of her son, much as he is to become her present son's stepfather by the story's end. Moreover, young Harriss's real father, a New Orleans bootlegger, was murdered, and just as the role of Max's father has been violently vacated once before, so now Max is threatening to make it violently vacant once again by killing the man who plans to marry his mother—a state of affairs that, given Stevens's feelings about Max's mother, is not lost on the county attorney. Which is simply to say that when young Harriss presents himself to Stevens in a situation that we recognize from other Faulkner fiction as being that of a son confronting a father to demand that the father exercise paternal authority, he is, from Stevens's point of view, in effect challenging Gavin to exhibit his *own* qualifications to fill the role of stepfather, challenging him to exhibit an authority that is not only able to protect the womenfolk by repulsing the intruder but also able to make the son obey the paternal will by not breaking the law, by not killing the prospective stepfather—a matter of no small importance if Stevens himself ultimately intends to fill that role.

Part of the tale's artistry is that, by having Harriss and his sister interrupt Gavin's and Chick's chess game in order to tell their story, Faulkner is able to assimilate the details of their story to the imagery of chess and thus able to evoke young Harriss's challenge to Stevens in chivalric terms, to present it as a contest, a joust, between a younger and an older knight. As I mentioned earlier, chess is associated with the detective genre from the very beginning. In the first Dupin story, "The Murders in the Rue Morgue," the narrator cites the game as an example, along with draughts and whist, to illustrate the workings of that analytic power which he considers the essence of detection, and in the third Dupin story, "The Purloined Letter," Poe presents us with a scenario that is strongly reminiscent of a chess game—there is a king and queen, and there is a battle of wits between two knights (Dupin is a *Chevalier*, and we must assume that his double the Minister D__ is at least of equal rank), a battle for possession of a letter that concerns the queen's honor and that could, in the Minister's hands, reduce the queen to being a pawn. Given the game's presence at the genre's origin, it is not surprising that the image of a chess game is one of the most frequently used figures for the battle of wits between detective and criminal in the form's history, a figure of the detective's attempt to double the thought processes of his opponent so as to end up one move ahead of him. This doubling of an opponent's thoughts, in which one mentally plays out possible moves, countermoves, and responses against an antithetical mirror-image of one's own mind, at once reflects the kind of thinking that goes on in a chess game and is reflected in turn by the physical structure of the game itself in which the opposing pieces at the start face each other in a mirror-image relationship.

Faulkner would have been exposed to an especially interesting example of the association of chess with both the detective genre and the image of chivalry in the project that he worked on in late 1944—the screenplay of Raymond Chandler's *The Big Sleep*, on which he collaborated with Leigh Brackett and Jules Furthman. Chandler's detective Philip Marlowe always keeps a chessboard in his apartment with a problem laid out on it. At one point in the novel, Marlowe returns home to find that there is another kind of problem laid out in his apartment—his client's daughter, the nymphomaniacal Carmen Sternwood, naked in his Murphy bed with monkey business in mind. Predictably enough, Marlowe's chivalrous nature immediately turns to thoughts of chess: "I went . . . across the room . . . to the chessboard on a card table under the lamp. There was a problem laid out on the board, a six-mover. I couldn't solve it, like a lot of my problems. I reached down and moved a knight."[5] Several moments later, he adds, "The move with the knight was wrong. I put it back where I had moved it from. Knights had no meaning in this game. It wasn't a game for knights" (146). Yet for all his tough talk Marlowe doesn't take advantage of his client's mentally unstable daughter.

Indeed, Chandler had always thought of Marlowe as a kind of modern knight-errant: the detective in search of the solution like a knight in quest of the Grail. Chandler had named an earlier version of his detective Mallory, alluding to the author of the *Morte D'Arthur;* and references to Arthurian romance fill the novels. In *The High Window*, for example, Marlowe is described as a "shop-soiled Galahad";[6] while in *Farewell, My Lovely* Velma Valento, the woman that Marlowe has been in quest of throughout the novel, hides her identity behind the name Helen Grayle. And of course one of the Marlowe novels is even named *The Lady in the Lake*. The tone of Marlowe's slightly ironic, somewhat battered chivalry is set at the very beginning of *The Big Sleep*, when he comes to the home of his client General Sternwood and notices above the front door a "stained-glass panel showing a knight in dark armor rescuing a lady who was tied to a tree and didn't have any clothes on . . . he was fiddling with the knots on the ropes that tied the lady to the tree and not getting anywhere. I stood there and thought that if I lived in the house, I would sooner or later have to climb up there and help him" (1).

It is a short step from Chandler's Marlowe (read Malory), a chessplaying detective and modern knight-errant who uses his wits to uphold his personal code of chivalry, to Faulkner's Gavin Stevens, another chessplaying detective whose own chivalrous nature (as evidenced in his encounters with Eula Varner Snopes and her daughter Linda) is evoked by his Christian name's suggestion of King Arthur's nephew and most famous knight, Gawain. (Recall in this regard that the failed knight in Faulkner's 1926 giftbook for Helen Baird, *Mayday*, is named Galwyn.) But the difference is that where Chandler and Faulkner both use the game of chess, with its kings and queens and knights, to evoke the chivalrous character of their detectives, Faulkner, with an eye to the game's presence at the origin of the genre in Poe's Dupin stories, also uses the game to evoke that basic structure of the analytic act which both chess and detection share—that alogical attempt to project an image of the opponent's mind as an antithetical mirror-image of one's own mind so that one can anticipate the opponent's next move and end up one jump ahead of him, a form of mirror doubling that, as we said, is reflected in the physical structure of the game itself. Indeed, at one point Faulkner alludes to this mirror-image aspect of chess when he has Gavin reply to Chick's apparent dismissal of chess as "a game" by remarking, "Nothing by which all human passion and hope and folly can be mirrored and then proved, ever was just a game" (192).

Faulkner evokes the structure of mirror doubling shared by chess and analytic detection at the very start of "Knight's Gambit." When Max Harriss and his sister burst into Gavin's study, interrupting the chess game, Chick remarks almost in passing that the brother and sister look so much alike that "at first glance they might have been twins" (135). Now there is an obvious appropriateness in having a brother and sister who look like twins interrupt a game whose physical structure involves a mirror-image symmetry in the opening alignment of the pieces, an alignment that evokes the opposing black and white chessmen as antithetical twin images of each other. And this appropriateness was to become even greater some eight years after the appearance of "Knight's Gambit" when, with the publication of *The Town* in 1957, we learn that one of the chessplayers in this scene, Gavin Stevens, is himself a twin.[7] Gavin's twin sister Margaret is Chick Mallison's mother, and as Chick implies on several occasions in *The Town* the twinship of his mother and uncle seems almost to involve their knowing each other's thoughts—apropos the kind of mental doubling associated with analysis in chess. Thus, when the Harrisses burst in on the chess game between Gavin and Chick, a brother and sister who look like twins confront a man who is playing a game of mirror-image symmetries against the son of his twin sister. And what all this twinning and mirroring is ultimately meant to make the reader notice is that the relationship between Captain Gualdres and Max Harriss is the mirror image, the antithetical double, of the relationship between Gavin Stevens and Chick Mallison.

In each case there is an older man and a younger: in one instance the older man is a father-figure for the younger (Gavin and Chick), while in the other the older man aspires to a role that would involve his becoming a father-figure for the younger (Gualdres and Max). And in both cases the father-figure's task is to bring the young man from adolescense to maturity, to conduct a kind of rite of passage by establishing, through a veiled, and sometimes not so veiled, competition with the young man, the older man's authority to instruct him, a paternal authority able to command the young man's respect and thus allow him to learn from the older man. But while this instructive competition or competitive instruction has been eminently successful in the case of Gavin and Chick (Chick not only respects his uncle, he idolizes him), it has been a disaster in the case of Gualdres and Max.

The competition in the latter case turns upon skills that are quite literally knightly—riding, fencing, and romantic dalliance. As Max Harriss's sister describes it to Stevens, her brother is "the rich young earl" and Gualdres "the dark romantic foreign knight that beat the young earl riding the young earl's own horses and then took the young earl's sword away from him with a hearth-broom. Until at last all he had to do was ride at night up to the young earl's girl friend's window, and whistle" (183). One senses a sexual overtone to the first two of these knightly skills (riding a horse and using a sword) that is made explicit in the third, and one further senses that this competition between the older and younger man for the affection of the same woman (the young Cayley girl) is a displacement of the Oedipal struggle initiated by Gualdres's aspiring to marry Max's mother. But where the instructive competition between Gualdres and Max involves skills that are literally knightly, the competitive instruction between Gavin and Chick involves a sublimation of knightly combat into the mental combat of chess and into the verbal fencing that accompanies Gavin's and Chick's games. Indeed, to emphasize the parallel between these two types of combat, Faulkner has Chick momentarily best his uncle in a discussion of the relative sensitivity of younger men and older men and has Gavin reply, "All right. . . . *Touché* then. Will that do?" (174). But then Gavin beats Chick again at chess and becomes sarcastic, and Chick says that Gavin would probably have a better game by playing against himself, "at least you'd have the novelty of being surprised at your opponent's blunders" (176). To which Gavin replies, "All right, all right. . . . Didn't I say *touché?*" (176).

The fact that Chick every so often scores a hit in his verbal fencing with Gavin suggests why this competitive instruction of the nephew by the uncle works so well, for though Chick may come to the end of these encounters feeling chagrined, he never feels hopeless or humiliated, never feels that he hasn't had some degree of success in making his uncle treat him like a man. But it is precisely a sense of humiliation that Max Harriss continually feels in his encounters with Gualdres, for in just those areas in which Max most prides himself (riding and fencing), Gualdres beats him as if he were a child. Or as Max's sister says, "It wasn't even because of Mother. It was because Sebastian always beat him. At everything" (181). It is worth noting here, as regards the kinship of Gavin and Chick, that in those cultures with communal rites of passage for young men, the relative usually given the responsibility for the young man's initiation to adulthood is the maternal uncle rather than the father, the communal wisdom apparently being that the Oedipal tensions between father and son are such that a male relative from the mother's side of the family is a more effective initiator of the son, particularly if the initiation ceremony involves, as is usually the case, the son's symbolic death and rebirth.

The artistry involved in Faulkner's assimilation of the knightly combat of Max and Gualdres to the mental jousting of Gavin's and Chick's chess games depends in large part, of course, upon the fact that the game of chess, according to virtually every psychoanalytic reading of its structure and symbolism, is a ritual sublimation of father murder played out as the checkmating of the king. The word "checkmate" is from the Persian "shah mat," the king is dead. As the psychoanalyst and chess master Reuben Fine points out, since "genetically, chess is more often than not taught to the boy by his father, or by a father substitute," it naturally "becomes a means of working out the father-son rivalry."[8] And as another chess critic has noted, "chess is a matter of both father murder and the attempt to prevent it. This mirror function of chess is of extreme importance; obviously the player appears in both a monstrous and a virtuous capacity—planning parricide, at the same time warding it off; recreating Oedipal fantasy, yet trying to disrupt it. Yet the stronger urge is the monstrous one; the player wants to win, to kill the father rather than defend him."[9]

It is because Gavin has done his work so well in sublimating Oedipal tension, in conducting his nephew from adolescence to maturity through a prolonged rite of passage symbolically evoked by their combative encounters across the chessboard, that Gavin is able to outwit Max Harriss, prevent the son from breaking the patriarchal law by killing the prospective stepfather, and establish his own right to fill the role of stepfather by virtue of his having commanded the son's respect and obedience. And the agency by which Gavin establishes his authority over Max Harriss is in some sense his relationship with Chick, establishes this authority not merely in the sense that he has demonstrated his ability to be an enabling father-figure in his shepherding of Chick from boyhood to manhood, but in the sense that he has literally created through his relationship with Chick a bright young adult who is his devoted helper, an assistant bright enough to know when patriarchal commands must be obeyed and when they must be set aside. And this latter knowledge is crucial, for it is Chick, of course, who brings Gavin the piece of information that allows him to foil Max's plan—the information that Rafe McCallum had sold his wild stallion to Max that afternoon—brings it to his uncle even though Gavin is shut up in his study working on his translation of the Old Testament, that labor of twenty years which no one is allowed to interrupt once he has closed his study door, as Chick says, "nor man woman nor child, client well-wisher or friend, to touch even the knob until his uncle turned it from inside" (207). But Chick has come to maturity as a young man so confident of his own judgment, or rather, so confident of his uncle's respect for his judgment, that he bursts into the study and disturbs his uncle in order to deliver the piece of information that he senses is somehow critical (though he himself doesn't quite know how), disturbs this imposing, white-haired father-figure in the task of translating the patriarchal law.

Together with McCallum, Gavin and Chick hurry to the Harriss mansion aiming to thwart Max's plan, and it is part of the wittiness of Faulkner's plot that the method which Harriss has chosen to eliminate his intended victim constitutes a kind of double en-tendre, evoking that sexual overtone to the chivalric skill of horse-back riding that we mentioned earlier. Gualdres owns a blind mare that he keeps in a separate stable at the Harriss place and that he rides every night, but the people of Jefferson have come to feel that the mare is itself a blind to cover Gualdres's nightly romantic adventures, that Gualdres has trained the mare to gallop around the empty paddock at night at varying gaits as if it were being ridden so as to conceal the fact of its rider's absence in search of young women. The humor of Max's plan turns upon his having removed the mare from its stable and substituted McCallum's wild stallion, so that when Gualdres comes for his (k)nightly ride, he'll find an animal that will jump up and down on top of him rather than the reverse—a switch in the gender of the animal to be ridden that smacks faintly of French farce, as if the seducer had gotten by mistake into the husband's bedroom rather than the wife's. No doubt, Max considers this an appropriate demise for the expert rider and swordsman who had galloped his horse up to the Cayley girl's verandah and tried to beat Max's time. (We might note in passing that horseback riding as a sexual metaphor was used more than once by Faulkner during this period. In the film version of *The Big Sleep*, which Faulkner worked on between writing "Knight's Gambit" as a short story and rewriting it as a novella, Philip Marlowe and Vivian Rutledge, played by Humphrey Bogart and Lauren Bacall, engage at one point in a verbal fencing match in which they appraise each other's romantic possibilities as if they were sizing up the physical abilities of racehorses. Having given her estimate of Marlowe, Vivian Rutledge invites Marlowe to reciprocate, and he says,

"Well, I can't tell till I've seen you over a distance of ground. You've got a touch of class, but uh . . . I don't know how . . . how far you can go." To which she replies, "A lot depends on who's in the saddle." [One recalls that when Faulkner first met Lauren Bacall during the filming of *To Have and Have Not* he told an acquaintance that "Bogie's . . . new girl friend" was "like a young colt" (Blotner, 1156).]

Gavin, of course, saves Gualdres from entering the dark stable and having his brains bucked out, and Faulkner evokes their confrontation as a kind of chivalric combat between the two prospective suitors of the widow Harriss, a duel in which Gualdres's knightly skills are no match for Gavin's prowess in intellectual jousting honed over the chessboard. With a certain *noblesse oblige*, Gavin begins the conversation in the native tongue of his rival, and Faulkner underlines the at once humorous and knightly character of their encounter by having Chick remark that he could understand some of the Spanish because he had read *Don Quixote* and *The Cid*. Gavin structures this verbal exchange as if it were a wager: he bets Gualdres that he doesn't want to enter the darkened stable. And for this life-saving piece of information, Gualdres agrees to marry the young Harriss girl and take her away with him, thus leaving the widow Harriss free for someone else.

And it is with this final ploy of Gavin's that we can see most clearly that other device which Faulkner took from Poe's Dupin stories to use in "Knight's Gambit"—the detective's personal motive for becoming involved in the solution or prevention of the crime. The trajectory of the development of the detective genre within the Dupin stories runs from the pole of physical violence in the first story (the brutal murder of a mother and daughter by a killer ape) to the pole of intellectual violence in the third story (the mental victimization involved in the blackmail of the queen by the Minister D—). And just as the movement from the first to the third Dupin story seems to involve a muting of the form, a sublimation or attentuation of the crime's violence, so this movement also involves a progressive simplification or reduction of what constitutes the mysterious element in the tale. In the first Dupin story, "The Murderers in the Rue Morgue," we are not only confronted with the problem of "who done it," or more precisely "what done it," but also with the problems of "how he done it" (the locked room mystery) and "why he done it" (the senseless savagery of the crime). But by the time of the third Dupin story, "The Purloined Letter," we know at the outset who took the letter, how he took it, why he took it, and what use he intends to make of it. The only mystery is how the Minister D__ has concealed the letter in his home so that the police can't find it.

It is as if the inventor of the genre in producing a series of detective stories had to find an ongoing challenge to his ingenuity in order to spur his imagination to new heights, and that that challenge was to see how much he could pare away or reduce the mysterious element in the tale, the element that needed solution, and still have a detective story. But what happens in "The Purloined Letter" is that with the attenuation of the mysterious element in the crime, its reduction to a single, circumscribed problem, a mysterious element from another quarter enters the story toward the end to fill the vacuum—the mystery of the detective's motive for taking the case. For though at first it seems that Dupin becomes involved in the affair of the letter because he is being well-paid or because he is a supporter of the queen's cause (both of which are true), we learn at the end that the real reason for his taking the case is that he has an old score to settle with the Minister D__. The Minister had done Dupin "an evil turn" once in Vienna which Dupin told the Minister "quite good-humoredly" he would remember (3:993). Consequently, Dupin goes to the trouble of retrieving the letter himself from the Minister's residence, so that he can substitute for it a duplicate letter informing the Minister who it was that made the switch and brought about his downfall.

Something very like this scenario of creating a new source of mystery from the detective's motives, as the mysterious element in the crime is being reduced to a bare minimum, occurs in

"Knight's Gambit." We know at the start by his own admission who the prospective killer is, we know the intended victim and the reason for the crime, and we know that it will be committed within a few days. The only thing we don't know is how it will be done. But as those standard mysterious aspects of the crime are being pared away in the course of the story to a single problem, another mystery is emerging, the problem of the identity of the man who was secretly engaged to Max's mother when she was a girl of sixteen. The realization that it was Gavin Stevens comes about simultaneously with our realizing that Gavin's involvement in preventing the murder has not been simply in an official capacity, but rather has been a personal involvement in order to win the hand of the woman he was once engaged to. For if he allows Max's plan to succeed, then as county attorney he will have to handle the case, and I think that it is still conventional wisdom in the South, as elsewhere, that the best way to advance one's suit with a wealthy widow is not to prosecute her only son for first-degree murder.

But Gavin's problem is more difficult than that, for there are two other obstacles—the lovestruck daughter and the foreign suitor. And the solution that Gavin works out makes us realize how early in the affair he had begun planning to turn matters to his own ends if the situation permitted, how early he had begun to think of the matter not as a chess game but a chess problem, as Faulkner suggests when he has Gavin, at the end of the evening when first Max Harriss and his sister and then Miss Harriss and the Cayley girl interrupt his chess games, sweep the board clean and set up a chess problem "with the horses and rooks and two pawns" (192). Of course, in Gavin's personal chess problem, the object is not to checkmate the king (indeed, it is precisely that Oedipal content he tries to repress), but rather to capture the queen. And the alignment of pieces in his problem is somewhat different from the one he sets up on the board for Chick: there are two dark knights, one older, one younger (Gualdres and Max), one white knight (the white-haired Gavin, read Gawain), a young dark queen (Max's sister), an older white queen (the widow Harriss), and one white rook (the widow's property). The solution goes like this: in exchange for Gavin's saving his life, the older dark knight settles for the young dark queen and half the white rook, or as Gavin puts it, "a princess and half a castle, against some of his bones and maybe his brains too" (218). And in exchange for Gavin's saving Max's life as well, which is to say, for Gavin's preventing him from committing murder and perhaps being executed, the young dark knight acknowledges Gavin's authority and accepts that penalty which small town prosecutors have for years offered to local boys as an alternative to being charged with a first offense—he joins the army. (Indeed, part of Faulkner's wit in setting the story on the eve of America's entrance into the Second World War is the way that this allows him to bundle up all the Oedipal conflict, adolescent mischief-making, and chivalrous yearning for desperate glory and ship it off to the front in the persons of Max, Gualdres, and Chick.) With all the obstacles removed from his path, the white-haired knight rides up to the empty castle and captures the white queen.

But we should have expected this conclusion in a story named "Knight's Gambit," for while there is no chess opening called "the knight's gambit," Chick does tell us that his uncle's favorite opening move was pawn to queen four, that is, the first move of the queen's gambit. And Gavin had said to his nephew during one of their chess games, when Chick had forked Gavin's queen and rook, that in that situation you should always take the queen and let the castle go because "a knight can move two squares at once and even in two directions at once," but "he cant move twice" (176). Chick later applies this remark about the knight's being able to move in two directions at once to Gualdres's attentions to both the widow Harriss and her daughter, but surely Faulkner means for the reader to apply the remark to another knight who in one move was able to carry out his public duty by preventing a murder and at the same time accomplish the most personal of goals, the winning of a wife.

In his reworking of this device of the detective's personal motive for involving himself in the investigation, as in his annexing of the imagery of chess to the detective story, Faulkner shows his debt to Poe, but he also shows how far he could expand and develop such devices when he joined them to the kind of material that was closest to his imagination, thus revealing himself not only as a worthy successor but a formidable competitor of the genre's originator.[10]

NOTES

1. Joseph Blotner, *Faulkner: A Biography*, 2 vols. (New York: Random House, 1974), 2: 1201. All subsequent quotations from Blotner are taken from this edition.

2. Edgar Allan Poe, *Collected Works of Edgar Allan Poe*, ed. Thomas Ollive Mabbott, 3 vols. (Cambridge, Mass.: Harvard University Press, 1969–78), 2: 551.

3. William Faulkner, "An Error in Chemistry" in *Knight's Gambit* (New York: Random House, 1978), 113. All subsequent quotations from "An Error in Chemistry" are taken from this edition.

4. William Faulkner, "Knight's Gambit" in *Knight's Gambit* (New York: Random House, 1978), 137. All subsequent quotations from "Knight's Gambit" are taken from this edition.

5. Raymond Chandler, *The Big Sleep* (New York: Random House, 1976), 144. All subsequent quotations from *The Big Sleep* are taken from this edition.

6. Raymond Chandler, *The High Window* (New York: Random House, 1976), 161.

7. William Faulkner, *The Town* (New York: Random House, 1961), 45, 181, 302, 305.

8. Reuben Fine quoted in Alexander Cockburn, *Idle Passion: Chess and the Dance of Death* (New York: Simon and Schuster, 1974), 42.

9. Cockburn, 101.

10. A version of this essay appears in *Arizona Quarterly* 46 (Winter 1990), 95–116.

Faulkner's Short Stories and Novels in China

Tao Jie

Great writers are not easily recognized, especially when it is someone like William Faulkner whose style is too involved and whose themes too elusive to Chinese readers. It took almost half a century and the concerted efforts of scholars, editors, translators, and university professors to persuade the general reading public to pay serious attention to this great novelist of the American South.

It was in the 1930s and in Shanghai, an important cultural center and the birthplace of many avant-garde literary movements, that Faulkner was first brought to the notice of Chinese readers. Two scholars were directly involved—Shi Zhecun and Zhao Jiabi. The former, very much influenced by Freud and Arthur Schnitzler, was the founder of psychoanalytical fiction in China. He was then the general editor of *Modern Times Magazine*, of which one purpose was "to introduce to our readers the works of foreign writers who have not so far been discussed in China."[1] Zhao Jiabi was mainly an editor of many journals and book series. He became interested in American literature in the 1930s and wrote quite a number of articles on different American writers, many of which appeared in *Modern Times Magazine*.

In 1934 the May issue of *Modern Times Magazine* carried Zhao Jiabi's translation of Milton Waldman's "Trends in Recent American Fiction." For the first time, the name Faulkner appeared in Chinese as 福尔克奈 (Fuerkenai) which in 1958 became 福克纳 (Fukena). The English critic's remark that "Faulkner has taken the

174

road of pure art that is to be developed in the United States" was later quoted by Zhao Jiabi in his own writings.[2]

Five months later, a big event took place and Faulkner was seriously examined in Chinese for the first time. Believing that "our readers know no other names besides those too familiar ones like Gorky and Sinclair,"[3] Shi Zhecun decided to put out special issues to introduce modern literature of different countries and the first such issue was to be one on American literature. In "Editor's Notes," Shi Zhecun explained that he began with the United States, "a country with the shortest history in the world," simply because "gone are the days when the United States was fettered with the British tradition. The modern United States is setting up an example that an independent national literature may still be developed in the twentieth century. What encouragement such an example will offer to our new literature that has severed all its ties with past conventions and is developing independently and creatively!"[4]

In this issue, there are four essays of general interest on American fiction, drama, poetry, and literary criticism, fourteen specialized articles on three literary critics, nine novelists, one playwright, and one poet; translations of fourteen novelists, one playwright, twelve poets, and five essayists; a bibliography of American magazines published since World War I, biographical notes of eighty-seven American writers, and anecdotes or stories about certain writers and books. Faulkner is discussed in an essay entitled "An Experimenter in New Styles" and his short story "Elly" is printed in Chinese. Also, in "The Growth of American Fiction" by Zhao Jiabi, Faulkner is reviewed in the section "The Younger Pessimists" together with Ernest Hemingway. Zhao Jiabi quoted Graham Munson's *Post-War Novels*, Granville Hicks's "The Past and Future of William Faulkner," and Milton Waldman's "Trends in Recent American Fiction" to show that Faulkner was a stylist and a rising star. He applauds Faulkner as a truly native American writer, especially in the use of language: "The dialogues in Black English are the most beautiful part of each of his novels."[5]

"His narrative technique of combining psychological description with dialogues . . . is more worth noting than that of Sherwood Anderson or Ernest Hemingway. He has broken away from the restrictions of English literature and avoided Joyce's defect of incomprehensibility."[6] After stating that Faulkner's themes and plots are all products of American reality, Zhao Jiabi concludes: "As American society is moving towards disintegration, decline, defeat, and chaos, Faulkner has taken the cruelties and miseries of modern society as the subject matter and death as the center of his stories. . . . Faulkner's bitterness . . . , his distress at being unable to find a general solution to all the tragedies, brutalities, and savagery reflects the despair of the modern man who is trying desperately to survive in this crazy world of the 1930s." Fifty-five years later, one still has to admire Zhao Jiabi for his perceptive understanding and shrewd judgment of William Faulkner and his novels.

"Faulkner: An Experimenter in New Styles" examines all Faulkner's novels published before 1934. Ling Changyan, the author, acknowledges his indebtedness to Zhao Jiabi at the end of the essay, and it is therefore understandable to find him repeat some of Zhao Jiabi's viewpoints, such as "Faulkner is a typical writer of modern life,"[7] "he writes about crimes, brutalities, and primitive sexuality,"[8] "his outlook on life is wholly pessimistic,"[9] "Faulkner's writings are actually well-planned beneath the surface of total chaos."[10] His conclusion, however, is rather surprising, especially when we now know that Faulkner did not enjoy much popularity in the 1930s, certainly not in the United States. Ling Changyan suggests that Faulkner tried to win popularity by writing about "immoral matters and unpleasant happenings"[11] and through the use of new techniques so as to cater to the reader's need for sensation and strangeness. He sounds accusatory when he remarks that "Faulkner is not a profound thinker,"[12] "Faulkner has become popular simply because the present time is as unhealthy as the author himself."[13] He concludes that Faulkner was not as good as Sherwood Anderson or Sinclair Lewis.

"Their works force people to think against their will . . . while all that Faulkner gives to the reader is only sensation, an unusual kind of sensual excitement."[14]

In 1936 Zhao Jiabi published a book about American literature, *The New Tradition*, in which the opening chapter is the essay that appeared in the *Modern Times Magazine* and in which there is a separate chapter on William Faulkner. Zhao Jiabi compared Faulkner with writers of primitivism but remarked that he did not write about savages but about "the brutalities of the white people in a corrupted civilized society."[15] He again quoted Waldman, Munson, and Hicks to confirm that Faulkner was a pessimist and a writer of potential. Zhao Jiabi divided Faulkner's novels into three groups: war novels, experimental fiction of psychoanalysis, and naturalistic depiction of brutalities in society. He believed that *The Sound and the Fury* and *As I Lay Dying* were not successful because Faulkner "followed Joyce's way of writing,"[16] that *Sanctuary* and, to some extent, *Light in August* caught the readers' attention because Faulkner used the techniques of the detective story and "catered to the modern reader's need for sensation and sensual excitement." Like Ling Changyan but in a much milder tone, Zhao Jiabi criticized Faulkner for his determinism and for offering heredity as the cause of social cruelties. The most important point, however, is his remark that "both *Sanctuary* and *Light in August* have assured us that Faulkner is a more promising writer than Ernest Hemingway."[17]

Interestingly enough, Faulkner's appearance in *Modern Times Magazine* and in Zhao Jiabi's *The New Tradition* did not seem to stir up any interest. For the next two decades, if we do not count the publication of the paperback edition of *The New Tradition* in 1941, there was no mention of William Faulkner in any of the literary magazines in China and not one piece of his writing was translated into Chinese. In July 1989 I interviewed Zhao Jiabi and Shi Zhecun in Shanghai, trying to find out some explanation for this strange silence. Zhao Jiabi took great pride in being the first and almost the only person to have written about this literary giant in the '30s. He could not, however, explain why there was no interest in Faulkner or why he himself stopped his pursuit of Faulkner's literary career other than saying "Faulkner is not easy to understand." To me, this is very good pretext. Since Faulkner was difficult even to scholars like Zhao Jiabi, few others would take the trouble to read him or to translate him. Without his works in Chinese, it was impossible for people to take any interest in him. Shi Zhecun, also in his eighties and still sharp-minded, was proud of his contribution to bringing Faulkner to China through his magazine. He told me he was to write the essay on William Faulkner and the advertisement for this issue on American literature announced him as the author of the article. However, he gave it up at the last minute as he was busy with the translation of twelve American poets. He gave me two reasons for the neglect of this important American master: Faulkner's novels were too difficult to translate into Chinese. Therefore, very few people had read him or could find his books in Chinese even if they were interested. The other reason was the political situation at the time, especially the threat of Japanese invasion. Most people were concerned about the possibility of China's becoming a colony of some foreign power. As a result, they were more interested in novels about social injustices and the rebellions of the people. The influence of left-wing writers was pretty strong. Books by Soviet writers or by American writers like Upton Sinclair or Michael Gold who wrote about the sufferings of the common people in a more conventional way were widely read and translated. To my question whether there was any Chinese writer who was influenced by William Faulkner or who tried to imitate him, Shi Zhecun answered that he could not recall any names and doubted that there was such a writer. He told me that most writers in the 1930s knew some foreign language and if they were interested in Freudianism or psychoanalysis, they would go directly to Freud or James Joyce or the French Symbolists. To these people, Faulkner was but an imitator. This sounded rational to me as Shi Zhecun himself was trained in a French missionary university and

Zhao Jiabi majored in English literature in his college days and did a lot of translation besides his career as a literary editor. My own guess about this lack of interest is that the general neglect of Faulkner in his home country may have played its part in dissuading Chinese scholars from taking him seriously.

During the twenty-five years between 1934 when Faulkner's name appeared in *Modern Times* to 1958 when he reappeared in another magazine, *Translation,* in Beijing, Faulkner missed two chances of becoming known to the Chinese people. The first time, to make an analogy of Faulkner's determinism, it was Fate that made fun of him. In 1945, just when he was being rediscovered in the United States by Malcolm Cowley, a group of Chinese scholars, translators, and writers gathered together to put out an American Literature Series. The project was initiated at the suggestion of John Fairbank, then the American Cultural Attache in Chongqing, and was partly funded by the American government. Zhao Jiabi was invited to be the general editor and twelve American writers were selected to be translated into Chinese. Unfortunately, Faulkner was not included. When I asked Zhao Jiabi about this, he simply said, "Nobody mentioned him when the names were discussed." Faulkner would certainly have been included if he had won the Nobel Prize for Literature at the time or if he had been more popular in the United States. The second time, it was Faulkner himself who gave up the chance of coming to China not only in books but in person. The People's Republic of China was founded in 1949. In 1955, in order to celebrate the 100th anniversary of Walt Whitman's *Leaves of Grass,* the Chinese government invited a number of distinguished writers from abroad. Faulkner was on the list but he declined the invitation.

Attempts, however, were made from time to time to introduce Faulkner to Chinese readers. In the late 1950s Li Wenjun, a young editor of *Translation,* decided after reading *The Portable Faulkner* and *Collected Works of William Faulkner* that Faulkner was well worth being translated and published. Because of his effort, the April 1958 issue of *Translation* carried two stories: "Victory," translated by Zhao Luorui, a distinguished woman professor of Peking University, and "Death Drag" by Huang Xingxi, at the time an editor of the People's Literature Publishing House. In the introductory notes before the two stories, Li Wenjun states, "Faulkner's novels are mainly descriptions of the declining aristocrats in the American South. But he also writes with great sympathy about people whose lives were destroyed by war. The two stories in this issue reveal to us Faulkner's hatred of war and deep sympathy for the victims of war. His indignation and protest against the cruelties of imperialist warfare have become more bitter and more explicit in *A Fable*, his latest novel."[18] In the early '60s, Li Wenjun made another attempt of having "Dry September" translated into Chinese, but he did not succeed in publishing it because of the political situation of the time.

In retrospect, it is obvious that Li Wenjun selected the stories out of political rather than aesthetic considerations. The antiwar theme and the exposure of racism were politically safe at a time when class struggle was much talked about in China. This was the general situation in the 1960s when political criteria somehow affected criticism of all foreign writers.

In 1962 *Recent Developments in American Literature*, a small booklet, was put out for "inside" circulation, which means it was not sold in bookstores but was put in the library for people who were politically reliable. It was prepared by a Research Group for Academic Reference Material of the Academy of Social Sciences, and the editor admitted in the foreword that the conclusions were based on information from American journals like *Mainstream, Political Monthly,* and *National Guardian.* American writers were divided into three categories: "reactionary," "progressive," and "bourgeois." Faulkner was placed in the group of bourgeois writers together with Arthur Miller, Erskine Caldwell, John Steinbeck, Ernest Hemingway, William Saroyan, and Langston Hughes. He was criticized for "working for a Writers' Committee organized by the Eisenhower government in 1956,"[19] for "insulting" the blacks in February 1958,[20] and for "speaking against" the communists during his visit in Japan. With information from a Soviet magazine, *Soviet Literature*, he was, however, commended for giving up his involved and obscure style in *The Town* and *The Mansion*, for his superficial but well-meant description of the communists in *The Mansion*, and for his disgust with the persecution of progressive people by the FBI as described in *The Mansion*.

In 1964 Faulkner was again examined in a long thesis, "A Review of the 'Stream-of-Consciousness' Fiction in Britain and the United States" written by Yuan Kejia, then an assistant research fellow of the Institute of Literature of the Academy of Social Sciences. (A year later, scholars of foreign literature there formed a separate Institute of Foreign Literature.) The essay makes a careful study of three novels by James Joyce, three novels by Virginia Woolf, and two novels by William Faulkner—*The Sound and the Fury* and *As I Lay Dying*, tracing the growth and development of stream-of-consciousness fiction and pointing out that "with Joyce's *Ulysses*, Woolf's *To the Lighthouse* and *The Waves*, and Faulkner's *As I Lay Dying*, stream-of-consciousness fiction has reached its highest point—the period of symbolism."[21] "After the dead end, Faulkner returned to more conventional way of writing."[22] In the concluding section, Yuan Kejia labels the stream-of-consciousness fiction as "a literary product of the declining bourgeoisie in the West," and mentions *As I Lay Dying* and its interior monologues as a good example of "the psychological reflection of the declining bourgeoisie that is divorced from reality and therefore afraid of confronting it."[23] He severely criticizes stream-of-consciousness novelists for writing about "dreams, sex, madness, and nonconsciousness," which "are but expressions of the perverted psychology and low taste of a decadent class" and which have "power to corrupt the people's minds and their militant will."[24]

Despite the political jargon, Yuan Kejia makes a correct and objective interpretation of *The Sound and the Fury* and *As I*

Lay Dying. Some of his arguments—such as the stream of consciousness as the best technique to depict the spiritual decadence of the Compsons; the decline of the Compsons as represented by Benjy's idiocy, Quentin's suicide, and Jason's greed; the complexity of psychological reaction to experience as reflected in the different characters in *As I Lay Dying*; Addie's distress about the disjunction between words and reality and Anse's belief in abstraction—are still valid twenty-five years later. Although the author criticizes Faulkner for making Dilsey "more slavish than rebellious" and remarks that "it is incredible that this old woman should be so hardworking and so devoted to the white masters that have been exploiting her for years,"[25] he stresses the fact that "Faulkner took part in the 1951 campaign to protect a black man called Willie McGee and denounced the racists in the South in 1955 and opposed segregation in American schools,"[26] to show that Faulkner was not so "reactionary" as James Joyce or so "conservative" as Virginia Woolf.

Political campaigns upset further study of William Faulkner. It was not until fifteen years later, in the late 1970s, when the nightmare of the Cultural Revolution was over that the time was finally ripe for Chinese scholars to remember him and to start a new wave of studying him. After ten years of political repression, the Chinese people felt all the more acutely the significance of personal freedom. They turned to the outside world for clues to the development of individuality. Young people in particular were eager to know what was happening outside China. Their insatiable demand for new ideas, new schools of thought, and new artistic devices brought about a renaissance in the translation of western philosophy and western literature, especially those important but formerly considered "decadent" or "bourgeois" writers like T. S. Eliot and William Faulkner.

Several important events took place towards the end of the '70s which were conducive to the surge of interest in this American virtuoso. In Shanghai in 1978 the Translation Press, which had always been engaged in the publication of foreign writers, put out a new magazine, *Foreign Literature and Art*, whose purposes are to "introduce through careful selection works and theories of contemporary foreign literature and art; to acquaint our readers with representative literary or artistic schools or trends and the important works of their writers; and to provide interested institutions and research workers with up-to-date information about the trends and developments of contemporary foreign literature and art."[27] Believing that Faulkner was unfairly treated both before and after Liberation, Ye Lingliu, a veteran editor, made research on his own and became personally involved in choosing three stories—"A Rose for Emily," "Dry September," and "Barn Burning"—as most representative of Faulkner's themes and techniques, and in inviting two professors of Fudan University and one professional translator to render them into Chinese. Li Wenjun, his colleague in Beijing and editor of a rival magazine *World Literature* (formerly *Translation*), heard about his plan, recommended Malcolm Cowley's famous introduction to *The Portable Faulkner* and did the translation. The three stories and the essay appeared in the June 1979 issue of *Foreign Literature and Art*. In the introductory notes, Faulkner was called "a spokesman of the American South," and praised for his "experimentation with point of view and the dislocation of the time sequence."[28] Zhao Jiabi's argument that Faulkner was a pessimist was refuted by quotations from his Nobel Prize Acceptance Speech to prove that "although Faulkner wrote largely about the ugliness of life and the crimes in society, he was not a pessimist but one who had firm belief in mankind."[29] The publication of these stories heralded a new stage in the criticism of William Faulkner.

While Shanghai took the lead in reintroducing William Faulkner, scholars in Beijing were undertaking steps that were just as important and as unprecedented. The Institute of Foreign Literature was planning to put out a series of collected critical essays on important foreign writers as reference material for academic studies, to edit a set of *Selected Works of Foreign Modernist Writers*, and to write in Chinese *A Concise History of American Liter-*

ature. Faulkner occupied an important place in all three of the projects. Also in 1978 the State Council of the Chinese government decided to compile a multivolume *Encyclopaedia Sinica,* of which there would be one on foreign literature. All these undertakings involved collaboration by research people in institutes of foreign literature, university professors, editors, and professional translators all over the country. Li Wenjun, the editor who, twenty-five years ago, arranged to have Faulkner published in his journal and who was now an established scholar of American literature and a research fellow at the Institute of Foreign Literature, became involved in all the four projects. He was to write the entry on Faulkner for the *Foreign Literature* volume of *Encyclopaedia Sinica,* to translate Quentin's section and provide an analysis of *The Sound and the Fury* for the second volume of *Selected Works of Foreign Modernist Writers,* to select and edit for *Critical Essays on William Faulkner,* and to contribute to the *Concise History of American Literature* a chapter on Southern literature, of which, naturally, Faulkner would be the major writer to be discussed.

Critical Essays on William Faulkner was put on sale towards the end of 1980 with a record impression of 27,600 copies and was reprinted very soon with another 2,500 copies. The preface of the book appeared two months earlier in *Reading,* a magazine that has a wide circulation among college people and the academic world. In it, Faulkner was assessed as "one of the most important novelists of modern America," "an undeniably major writer of the school of Southern literature," "the writer most discussed and most carefully examined in the United States," and "one of the most distinguished modernist writers since James Joyce."[30]

Selected Works of Foreign Modernist Writers was again one of the most popular and the most sought after books in the early 1980s. The first printing of the second volume that includes Li Wenjun's translation of Quentin's section from *The Sound and the Fury* was 40,000 and by the time of 1986 the total number printed and sold had reached 68,500 copies. In the introduction, Li

Wenjun speaks highly of the Yoknapatawpha saga as "reflection of Southern society in the past 200 years,"[31] compares the philosophical depth and emotional appeal of Faulkner's novels to that of the Bible, the Greek tragedies, and Shakespeare's tragedies, enumerates Faulkner's use of stream of consciousness, multiple narration, inverted order, detention, and symbolism, and makes a detailed analysis of the theme and technique of *The Sound and the Fury*, especially Quentin's section.

Li Wenjun's entry for the *Foreign Literature* volume of *Encyclopaedia Sinica* is fairly long as compared with those on Ernest Hemingway, Sherwood Anderson, Theodore Dreiser, or Jack London, writers who were much translated before the Cultural Revolution and even before the founding of the People's Republic in 1949. Besides general information about Faulkner's life, literary career, themes, and artistic devices, Li Wenjun reviews *The Sound and the Fury, Light in August, Absalom, Absalom!*, the Snopes Trilogy, *The Fable*, and the novelettes "Old Man" and "The Bear." These novels and stories are later discussed in greater detail in the chapter "Faulkner and the Southern Fiction" in *A Concise History of American Literature*. There, Li Wenjun concludes the chapter by summing up Faulkner's importance in modern Western literature in three aspects: his depiction of the complicated scenario of the American South; his representation of the major issues that are the chief concerns of the modern man in the twentieth century (actually the middle class and its intellectuals); and his accomplishment in artistic techniques and stylistic devices.[32] With the publication of the *Foreign Literature* volume in 1982 and *A Concise History of American Literature* in 1986, the tone was finally set for the criticism of William Faulkner. Li Wenjun was extremely devoted to the introduction of this great writer to Chinese readers. He published Benjy's section in *Foreign Literature Quarterly* in early 1981 together with an essay, "Stream of Consciousness, Obscurity, and Others," that argues for Faulkner's felicitous skills in depicting the spiritual decline of a social order through the distintegration of a family. He continued to write critical essays and to translate Faulkner's works. His writings about this literary giant are now widely read in China. Like a hard-working farmer, Li Wenjun had plowed the land and sown the seeds.

Li Wenjun was, of course, not the only scholar engaged in bringing Faulkner to China. Efforts were made in the meantime in many of the English departments on university campuses. For years in the past, American literature had not been taught in Chinese colleges or universities as it was not considered an independent national literature and its use of dialects, nonstandard English, and slang was thought to be inappropriate for Chinese students learning good English. There were, naturally, political reasons. After the Cultural Revolution, things were changed because of reform and the open-door policy. Young people became extremely interested in the United States, and demands were great for the teaching of American literature. New courses were set up and Faulkner became one of the major writers discussed in classrooms.

On this front, Americans teaching in English departments in China and Chinese professors who had studied abroad played an important part. In 1980 and 1981 there were two Fulbright programs at Peking University to train English teachers from many colleges and universities in China. The Fulbright scholars taught survey courses on American history, culture, and literature, and special courses on many individual American writers, including Faulkner. The participants were also given anthologies of American literature and works by American writers, among which there were usually Faulkner's *The Sound and the Fury* and *Light in August*. Many of these people later became founders of the American literature program at their home colleges. Professors who had the chance to study abroad were also enthusiastic about offering courses on American literature. I myself was one example. I was one of the translators recruited by Li Wenjun in 1979 for his *Critical Essays on William Faulkner* and became involved in translating this fascinating writer of the human heart. Later, I was sent to study at SUNY at New Paltz and there I took several courses on Faulkner and Southern literature. When I returned to Peking University in 1981, I was immediately asked to teach twentieth-century American literature and to supervise two graduate students who had decided to write about Faulkner's *Absalom, Absalom!* and *Light in August* for their M.A. theses. Since then, I have been supervising graduation and M.A. theses on William Faulkner almost every year.

To meet the need for textbooks, college professors, both Chinese and American, in the early 1980s began to compile anthologies of American literature for Chinese students. The first of such books was *An Anthology of Twentieth-Century American Fiction* edited by Wan Peide and his colleagues, all professors of East China Normal University. This book, written in English, was exactly the same as anthologies put out in the United States, except that there were more notes about backgrounds, allusions, and difficult expressions. The editor invited several Americans then teaching in China to review the manuscripts. The introduction to William Faulkner and his "A Rose for Emily" was actually written by a Canadian professor teaching at Wan Peide's department. This anthology was published in 1981 and immediately 23,000 copies were sold.

Another important book of this kind was *A Brief Introduction to Modern American Literature* published by Shanghai Foreign Languages Education Press in March 1982. The author, Elizabeth B. Booz, was an American serving as a "foreign expert" in the Department of Foreign Languages and Literature of Yunan University in Kunming, a city in the Southwest of China far away from Shanghai, and the book was actually her lectures "presented in 1980 as a course for teachers" at her university.[33] Lecture 14, "William Faulkner, Innovative Stylist, Depictor of the South,"[34] is accompanied by excerpts of about a dozen pages from *Sartoris*. The fact that these lecture notes were discovered and immediately published—the first printing being 20,000—speaks strongly for the earnestness of Chinese students in learning about

American literature. Since then, more anthologies have been compiled by professors of English at universities and institutes of foreign languages, often with the help of some native English speakers working there as "experts."

1984 marked another turning point because of the publication of the Chinese version of *The Sound and the Fury* by the Translation Press in Shanghai. In order to help the reader understand the novel better, Li Wenjun, the translator, provided 421 footnotes about allusions, cultural backgrounds, the clues to the story, and the shift of scenes besides using two kinds of type faces to indicate transition in time order, a device initiated by Faulkner himself. The translation is accompanied with a long preface, in which Li Wenjun remarks that "Faulkner was not merely a provincial writer of local color . . . as he deals with almost all the major issues that confront sensitive intellectuals in the West." [35] In his discussion of the story itself, Li Wenjun warmly applaudes the characterization of Dilsey: "Inexhaustible compassion flows out of her. She protects the weak in defiance of her master's hostility and the prejudice of conventional ideas. She is the only bright spot in the gloomy picture. Her kitchen is the only place that offers warmth in the ice-cold tomblike house. Dilsey is the pillar in the entire tottering world. Her loyalty, endurance, perseverance, and compassion form a striking contrast with the three morbid narrators before her. Through Dilsey, the author acclaims the spiritual beauty of simple and honest people." [36] Li Wenjun also makes the point that Faulkner's repeated use of stream of consciousness is not just out of his belief that "fragments of experience are truer to reality" but is totally subjected to the need of characterization, as "the three narrators are all mentally unbalanced and incapable of logical and rational thinking." [37] These arguments are implicit retorts to Yuan Kejia's viewpoint twenty years before, that Dilsey is too "slavish" and the prejudice of some critics who believe that the stream-of-consciousness technique is but a trick to win popularity.

The first printing o: the Chinese edition of *The Sound and the*

Fury was 87,500 copies, and they sold out very quickly. The book made quite a stir among the academics, college students, and especially writers and literary critics. So far, there had been published in Chinese only critical essays on William Faulkner and the translation of a few stories. Those who were outside universities or research institutes without any access to his works and those who did not know English had only vague ideas about Faulkner's Yoknapatawpha stories, his themes and subject matter, and his use of modernist techniques. The appearance of *The Sound and the Fury* now gave them something graphic to grasp and to ponder upon.

Translations and critical studies of this preeminent American writer are often products of cooperation among research people, university professors, and editors of literary magazines. *Selected Works of William Faulkner* is a good example. After translating R. W. B. Lewis's "Faulkner: The Hero in the New World" for *Critical Essays on William Faulkner* in 1979, I felt strongly that it was not enough to introduce Faulkner to Chinese readers through his criticism and decided to do my part in the translation of his fiction. When I had the chance of studying at SUNY at New Paltz as a visiting scholar, I met Professor H. R. Stoneback, who was a devoted scholar of Southern literature and who was more than willing to help the Chinese people to know Faulkner. I then contacted Li Wenjun, whom I had never met, and worked out a plan for the publication of *Selected Works of William Faulkner.* Professor Stoneback made the choice of stories and wrote the introduction and a group of people were once again recruited by Li Wenjun to do the translation. Included in the book are eighteen stories: "Justice," "Red Leaves," "My Grandmother Millard," "A Rose for Emily," "Spotted Horses," "Barn Burning," "Shingles for the Lord," "The Tall Men," "Shall Not Perish," "That Evening Sun," "Pantaloon in Black," "Ad Astra," "All the Dead Pilots," "A Bear Hunt," "Wash," "Carcassonne," "The Bear," and "Old Man." In addition, there is Professor Stoneback's introduction, "William Faulkner and the Sense of Community," and an

appendix made up of brief notes about individual pieces, Faulkner's Nobel Prize Acceptance Speech, a bibliography of his
works, and a brief chronology of his life and career. At the last
moment, Arthur Voss's "William Faulkner: A Virtuoso Storyteller" was added to give more information about his short stories
and his technical devices. All the stories except "Shall Not Perish"
were chosen by Professor Stoneback as most representative of
Faulkner's concerns and his techniques. I was instrumental in
bringing in "Shall Not Perish" although this is not considered one
of his best stories. It seemed to me at the time that the stories to
be selected should be reflections of not only Faulkner the artist
but the man himself. "Shall Not Perish," although not on the same
footing as other stories in either depth of thought or sophistication
of artistic skill, is an expression of his patriotic spirit. This was one
aspect that should not be neglected by Chinese readers. After
many twists and turns, the book finally came out in 1985. With the
publication of *The Sound and the Fury* and *Selected Stories of
William Faulkner* in Chinese, more interest was stirred up for
Faulkner studies. From then on, the translation and criticism of
William Faulkner have been growing steadily and the name of this
great genius has become known to a wider reading public.

Since 1979 more than twenty of Faulkner's stories and two of his
novels—*The Sound and the Fury* and *As I Lay Dying* (in *World
Literature*, no. 5, 1988)—have been translated into Chinese and
some of them have more than one version. Several more of his
stories and novels are being translated or in the process of being
printed. For instance, Lijiang Press, a new publishing house that
has been in the vanguard of publishing foreign literature in recent
years, is to put out very soon a collection of Faulkner's works as
one of its Nobel Prize Winner Series. The book includes a long
introduction written by Li Wenjun, *As I Lay Dying*, *The Unvanquished*, the short story "Delta Autumn," the essay "Sherwood
Anderson," Maurice Coindreau's "Translating Faulkner," and
Faulkner's Chronology by Michael Gresset. In Shanghai, the
Translation Press is issuing *The Bear*, with a long introduction by

Li Wenjun, Cleanth Brooks's "William Faulkner," which is originally a chapter of *The History of Southern Literature* edited by Louis Rubin, the full text of Faulkner's "The Bear," a chronology of the story, and a genealogy of its characters. Another publisher, the Hebei Education Press in North China, is publishing *The Portable Faulkner* as one of its Classical Writer Readers Series. The collection is aimed at high school students and college undergraduates. It includes "Red Leaves," "Dry September," "That Evening Sun," "Delta Autumn," "A Rose for Emily," "An Odor of Verbena," "Benjy's Section" from *The Sound and the Fury*, "Spotted Horses," "Centaur in Brass" from *The Town*, "The Tall Men," "Wash," "Percy Grimm" from *Light in August*, and "The Bear" from *Go Down, Moses*. Also included is Faulkner's essay "On Sherwood Anderson," his Nobel Prize Acceptance Speech, and *The Wishing Tree*, the only story he wrote for children. What is more, the book will have as its inside back cover the map of Yoknapatawpha County that Faulkner drew for Malcolm Cowley's *The Portable Faulkner.* The format of the book is structured in such a way as to help young people to have a better understanding of this difficult writer. There is a long introduction describing Faulkner's Yoknapatawpha saga, the different aspects of the saga, Faulkner's artistic devices in relation to his themes and messages, and his position in and contribution to American literature. In front of each story, there are notes and analyses either on the book from which the story is taken or on its theme or style. It is hoped that with these publications, more interest will be aroused in appreciating William Faulkner and his literary achievements.

Translating Faulkner is a strenuous task that requires courage, patience, and determination. In his article "Random Thoughts after Translating *The Sound and the Fury*" that appeared in the March 1985 issue of *Reading* magazine, Li Wenjun described the difficulty of the job. Between the spring of 1980 when he first started the translation to April 1984 when he finished reading the galley proofs, "*The Sound and the Fury* haunted me day and night for almost two years. I felt as if I were living in a dream, sometimes sweet, but more often nightmarish."[38] In order to be prepared for the job, he had collected and studied a great many important critical works on Faulkner, reminiscences by Faulkner's friends and relatives, readers' guides, and other reference books such as Brown's *Glossary* and the dictionary about characters in Faulkner's works. He tried to find out about the characteristics and developments of stream-of-consciousness fiction. He read the novel so many times that he felt he knew the story inside out. He went to scholars and specialists for help and advice and snatched every opportunity to ask American scholars visiting his Institute of Foreign Literature questions about American (or rather, Southern) culture and customs and to confirm or correct his understanding of certain details in the novel. He found out from Daniel Aaron that, for a period of time, Harvard students did have to go to the chapel for service early in the morning. Over a banquet of roast duck, he questioned H.R. Stoneback whether the razor the blacks used as a weapon was put in front of or behind the neck. Even after he had handed in the manuscripts, he did not stop his research in William Faulkner. He visited Michael Millgate in Toronto, searched in the library there for the two prefaces Faulkner wrote for *The Sound and the Fury*, went to the building where Faulkner, as a cadet, stayed in 1918 and tried to peep into a room he imagined to have been once occupied by the romantic young man who later developed into a great writer. Undoubtedly, Li Wenjun is now one of the few people in China who are well versed in the study of William Faulkner.

My experience in translating Faulkner's stories or criticism on Faulkner is similar to Li Wenjun's. I share with him the view that Faulkner's language, his use of the Southern dialect, and his involved and unpunctuated sentences are not insurmountable obstacles in the process of translation. The Southern dialect can be transcribed into standard English with the help of dictionaries, particularly Calvin S. Brown's *A Glossary of Faulkner's South*. The long and involved sentences can be understood because there are no punctuation marks in classical Chinese writing and one exercise all of us had to do in high school was to put in punctuation in the process of figuring out the meaning of a poem or an essay written in the classical Chinese language. The question is whether one should put back the punctuation that Faulkner took out deliberately. There have been different opinions. Li Wenjun did not break up Quentin's long passages of stream of consciousness into separate sentences. However, he put a dash at places where he felt should be a full stop. Yu Ning, a veteran translator who was engaged in the translation of *Absalom, Absalom!*, told me a few years ago that he would certainly put in punctuation marks, "just to help the readers." There are others who believe as I do that there should be no punctuation marks or dashes in order to be faithful to Faulkner's style and his artistic intentions. However, at the present stage, renditions of this kind may forestall readers from reading Faulkner as people nowadays are no longer so well used to the classical Chinese language.

Another issue that confronts most translators is whether he/she should use a Chinese local dialect for the Southern dialect Faulkner used so skillfully. So far, no one has ever used a local dialect in his/her translation as there is only one written language in Chinese but numerous dialects that differ from region to region and that are only understood by people of the locality. The transcription of any vernacular language into standard Chinese characters would only create more difficulty for the reader, as the sound suggested by the character may be meaningless or hard to understand if he does not speak the dialect.

The greatest obstacle, it seems to me, usually lies in small details that have a lot to do with American, and more importantly, Southern history, culture, customs, and habits, even life styles, and ways of thinking. For example, one translator made a blunder while rendering the story "Justice" into Chinese as he took it for granted that only white people in the South had Negro slaves and arbitrarily concluded that the story is about "the inhuman treatment of the Negro slaves by the white ruling class as represented by the character Doom." A simple dialogue like the one between

Quentin and the old man he sees outside his train window on his way home for Christmas may offer tremendous difficulty to the translator as he/she has to wonder why the black old man says "You done caught me" to Quentin's address of "Christmas gift."[39] Also the connotations that go with a word or an image may not be the same to a Chinese reader as they are to an American because of our different cultures. For instance, the flower honeysuckle that Quentin connects with sexuality evokes no such feelings in our readers. In China, the flower is often used as medicine to do away the excess of "fire" in one's body. Another problem is allusions. Most Chinese readers do not see the implications when they come across the passage in *Light in August* where Faulkner describes Lena's travel on the road as "something moving forever and without progress across an urn."[40] One solution is to provide the reader with footnotes as Li Wenjun has done in his translation of *The Sound and the Fury*. But then, there is the danger of offering too many. When everything is explained to the reader, the fascination of the story is lost. Therefore, it is no easy job to handle Faulkner in translation. It has to be combined with in-depth research into many aspects of American life and American society and into Faulkner himself. It has to be done through trial and error.

Why has there been so much interest in William Faulkner in recent years in China? Why are we so eager to translate him and publish his works? What is there that so fascinates us among the dark, devious, and even dangerous labyrinths of the Yoknapatawpha County? What is it in those troubled, perverted, even mean and sadistic inhabitants that so appeals to us Chinese living a totally different life in a totally different world?

When Li Wenjun, one of the masterminds in this campaign to bring Faulkner to China, accepted an interview by a reporter from *Encounter Book Review Weekly* in February 1988 and was asked why he was so interested in this American writer, he responded, "Because I am also a Southerner." He feels that Southerners all over the world share some common elements.

(Interestingly enough, about 90 percent of the writers involved in the translation of Faulkner's works are people from the South of China, and several of them, such as Li Wenjun, Ye Lingliu, Yu Ning, come from big families.) The temperament of people in the South tends to be more passionate and may even be excessively romantic or sentimental. Therefore Southern translators in China do not find it an excruciatingly difficult task to understand Faulkner, also a Southerner, though an American. They are not alienated by the extremity of despair or the intensity of emotion as depicted by Faulkner among his characters. Also the decline of the aristocratic family is a traditional theme in Chinese literature from *The Dream of the Red Chamber*, one of our ancient classics, to the modern trilogy of *Family, Spring*, and *Autumn* by Bajin. In the former, the heroine who pines away because of the betrayal of her lover is born in the beautiful city of Suzhou in the South of China. The story of Bajin's trilogy is laid in Sichuan, also in the South of China. In these Chinese novels as in Faulkner's fiction, the woman is also put on a pedestal and her chastity is closely connected to the disgrace or honor of the family. As many of the translators have undergone the disintegration of their own families, they are able to understand Quentin's sense of hopelessness or Emily Grierson's refusal to accept the change of time.

It may also be said that Faulkner depicts country people, and China is a country made up mainly of village people. There is common ground from thinking to action between the village people under Faulkner's pen and their counterparts in China. Chinese peasants behave in exactly the same way as Armstead or others in "Spotted Horses," always eager to pick up a bargain that makes something out of nothing. Like the poor whites in Frenchmen's Bend, they are often cheated and tricked by a Chinese Flem Snopes who acts on principles different from theirs. Gossip carries on in very much the same way in Chinese communities as Faulkner describes in "A Rose for Emily" or *Light in August*, and the convention and prejudice of a Chinese community can be as deadly as that in "Dry September." Chinese peasants share the same kind of stubbornness as the Bundrens in carrying out their promise to their wives/mothers and will appreciate Anse's pragmatism in getting a new set of teeth and finding a new wife. Even the way Cash makes the coffin outside the bedroom of his dying mother is not outrageous to the Chinese. It is always the duty of a filial son to have a nice coffin made long before the death of his father or mother and to have it nicely laid in the house for everyone to see as an expression of his love.

Moreover, the "old verities and truths of the heart" that Faulkner advocates and repeats in his stories and novels correspond, to some extent, to the Confucian doctrine that is deeply rooted in the minds of the Chinese people. Long before Faulkner, the Chinese sage Confucius was concerned with the past and the continuity of tradition. To restore social order and save society from further degeneration, Confucius put forward a theory on the basis of a moral order whose essence is benevolence. This benevolence is further demonstrated in the five duties of universal obligation—those between the ruler and the subject, between the father and the son, between the husband and the wife, between the elder and the younger brothers, and between friends. Out of a firm belief that a harmonious social order had to be achieved through the moral harmony in man himself, Confucius developed the benevolence in moral cultivation into three universally recognized qualities—wisdom, compassion, and courage. Such benevolence, it seems to me, coincides with the measures with which Faulkner judges society. He often traces the cause of the decline of the Old South to man's failure in fulfilling the responsibilities imposed by society and man's loss of the essential moral qualities. This is most evident in *The Sound and the Fury*, in which the disintegration of the Compson family mirrors the decline of the old system. No one in this family carries out the duties laid down by Confucius and supported by Faulkner. Mr. Compson is not the pillar of strength to his wife nor the guidance in life to his children. Neither is Mrs. Compson the ideal "helpful wife and wise mother" according to either the Chinese sage or the Southern standard advocated by Faulkner. Nor do the children live up to the expectation of being filial or loving. Jason bullies his mother and has only contempt for his father. Quentin, obsessed with his own despair, never tries to understand the agony and anguish that is tormenting his father and his sister. There is little fraternal love between the siblings. Jason hates Caddy and Benjy and is contemptuous of Quentin. Benjy's and Quentin's sense of possessiveness toward Caddy is so abnormal and suffocating that it finally drives Caddy to desperation. Evidently, Caddy is not a truly dutiful daughter, despite her love for the family. Interestingly enough, the solution Faulkner offers for the restoration of a new social order also conforms to Confucius's five duties and three moral virtues. Faulkner offers Dilsey as a contrast to the Compsons and as the hope of mankind by extolling her sense of compassion and sacrifice. Is she not, judged with the Confucian doctrine, doing her duty as the servant of the family and taking care of her masters with wisdom, compassion, and courage? Maybe that is why Chinese writers often create a faithful servant in their novels about the decline of the family.

A more important reason for Chinese interest in Faulkner is that he knows the human heart and his stories of the South in the United States carry meanings that transcend the locality to reach people all over the world. My personal experience may offer as a good example. It was in the early 1960s that I first came across Faulkner's works. I was then a young teacher full of idealism, working very hard to do good and to serve the people. An American professor who had lived in China for many years gave me a copy of *The Sound and the Fury* and told me it was great literature. But I did not like the book at all and could not understand what it was all about. I read at most fifty pages and never wanted to finish it. About ten years later, I picked up the book again. This time, I suddenly found I could understand the story and share the poignancy of anguish, confusion, even rage of its characters. The story somehow reflected the bewilderment, misery, hopelessness

I felt during the Cultural Revolution when I tried my best to be "revolutionary" but was always denounced for not being a revolutionary. As I had lived through the years of turmoil in "sound and fury" I now found Benjy's cries and moanings full of meaning. I shared his confusion and his longing for something to fill the void, something to give order to chaos. Unfortunately that something was not only forever lost but could not even be described or named. I understood Quentin's concerns and worries as a sensitive young man full of romantic ideals, his self examination and his fear that he might be the cause of the decline and degeneration of his world. I knew what bothered Quentin most was his inability to keep the good old days or to change things for the better. I believe Faulkner appeals to many Chinese readers just because they see themselves in the fate of his characters and because Faulkner depicts so well the emotions and feelings they too share but are unable to articulate. This is what Li Wenjun meant at the interview when he remarked that he knew very well the sense of loss suffered by descendants of big families and the constant soul searching and the struggle for self-perfection on the part of sensitive intellectuals. That was why he knew almost intuitively what kind of feeling he was to convey in the course of translation and what kind of language and style he should use while he was translating Faulkner.

Since the revival of interest in William Faulkner in the late 1970s, about forty essays have been published about his novels or short stories. They touch upon topics from general discussion to the function of time, the use of stream of consciousness and other techniques, and the theme of individual stories. Most of the writers are people working in institutes of foreign literature or in English departments of different colleges and universities, as they know English and have more access to Faulkner's works and his criticism in English. Very often, their theses play the role of introducing Faulkner to the common reader who does not know much about Faulkner. For instance, when asked to give advice to students of foreign literature, Zhou Jueliang, a distinguished professor of the Beijing University of Foreign Studies, recommended Li Wenjun's translation of *The Sound and the Fury* as one of the two books (the other being Byron's *Don Juan* in Chinese) every student of foreign literature has to read because of its "profound message and consummate skills" and because "it helps you to understand why 20th-century American fiction has occupied the leading position in contemporary world literature."[41]

The greatest influence Faulkner has exerted in China is among writers and literary critics. Young writers have been imitating him in earnest. Veteran writers have been paying tribute to him. And no critic can afford to neglect his name in his/her evaluation of the developments of Chinese literature in the past ten years. Wang Meng, a renowned writer who loves to experiment with techniques and who is said to be the first writer since 1976 to have used the stream-of-consciousness device, placed Faulkner's *The Sound and the Fury* with *Don Quixote*, *War and Peace*, *The Red and the Black*, among others, as books he had read but was unable to understand.[42] Liu Baiyu, one of the most distinguished writers in China, spoke highly of Faulkner's achievement in artistic skills and his accomplishment as a human being. He pointed out that the starting point for Faulkner studies should be "how he used different devices to express a great but tragic theme." It seems to me that Liu Baiyu was thinking of the recent situation in which more and more young Chinese writers became interested only in the mechanism of techniques and in writing about crimes and sex when he stressed that "Faulkner did not give up the essential principle of the form being decided by the content; . . . Faulkner never did away with the experience of reality in his works; . . . he did not take sex as the only subject of his writing; . . . and he did not use stream-of-consciousness technique or other artistic devices just to show off."[43]

The imitation of William Faulkner by young Chinese writers, it seems to me, has gone through different stages. The first stage might be called formal imitation. For example, a lot of young writers nowadays are interested in writing page-long sentences without punctuation. Zhang Kangkang, a young woman writer, used two kinds of typesetting for her novel *An Invisible Companion*, the italicized characters for the stream of consciousness of the heroine, exactly in the same way as Faulkner did in *The Sound and the Fury*. Another woman writer, Li Zhenyu, arranged her novelette "The Women's Apartment" in four sections of unchronological time order just like *The Sound and the Fury*. The heroine helped her lover, Jie, to translate *The Sound and the Fury* and "like Quentin, he killed himself during the Cultural Revolution."[44] Mo Yan, a young writer who has been extremely successful in recent years and who writes mainly about the peasants in his home village, openly admitted: "In 1985 I wrote five novelettes and about a dozen short stories. They were all undoubtedly influenced by foreign literature in theme and in art. The two novels that had the greatest impact on me at the time were Garcia Marquez's *One Hundred Years of Solitude* and Faulkner's *The Sound and the Fury*."[45]

Some of these young writers, however, have gone through the period of pure imitation and are pondering on the lessons that they should learn from the great master. In the same article, Mo Yan tells how he has come to understand that the best lessons he should learn are not actually Faulkner's techniques, but how "past history and the present world are closely intertwined," how "time, like the soft taillight of an automobile, keeps disappearing yet continues to blink up in the next second." He feels that he has to stay away from Garcia Marquez and Faulkner and to discover his own "small postage stamp of native soil" so as to "reproduce the history of the collapse and destruction of the human heart, and to represent the spiral development of the human society."[46]

Chinese writers and scholars will continue to ponder upon William Faulkner, each taking what he/she likes and going his/her own way.

NOTES

1. Shi Zhecun, "Editor's Notes," *Modern Times Magazine* 1 (1932): 198.

2. As I have not been able to find Waldman's article in China, I have translated into English Zhao Jiabi's rendition of the title and the statement.

3. Shi Zhecun, "Editor's Afterword," *Modern Times Magazine* 6 (1934): 834.

4. Ibid., 835–36.

5. Zhao Jiabi, "The Growth of American Fiction," *Modern Times Magazine* 6 (1934): 842.

6. Ibid., 856.

7. Ling Changyu, "Faulkner: An Experimenter in New Styles," *Modern Times Magazine* 6 (1934): 1003.

8. Ibid.

9. Ibid., 1004.

10. Ibid., 1005.

11. Ibid., 1006.

12. Ibid., 1009.

13. Ibid.

14. Ibid.

15. Zhao Jiabi, "William Faulkner," *The New Tradition* (Shanghai: Liangyu Press, 1934), 248.

16. Ibid., 266.

17. Ibid., 255.

18. Li Wenjun, "Editor's Notes," *Translation* 4 (April 1958): 181.

19. See Michael Gresset's *A Faulkner Chronology*, 99. In September 1956, "Faulkner lets himself become involved in the 'People-to-people program' of the Eisenhower administration. The aim of the program is to promote American culture behind the Iron Curtain. On 11 September, he attends a meeting in Washington at which President Eisenhower, Vice-President Richard Nixon, and Secretary of State Foster Dulles speak. Then, with the help of Harvey Breit, an informal committee meets in New York. On 30 September, the steering committee composed of Faulkner, John Steinbeck, and Donald Hall draws up some 'resolutions,' including one supporting the liberation of Ezra Pound. Three months later, Faulkner withdraws from the committee."

20. It may refer to Faulkner's talk "A Word to Virginians" given at Peabody Hall, University of Virginia on 20 February 1958. See Blotner's *Faulkner: A Biography*, 2:1685–88. According to Blotner, the talk "was at once a repetition of what he had said before and a further hardening of attitudes that would seem reactionary to liberals."

21. Yuan Kejia, "A Review of 'Stream-of-Consciousness Fiction' in Britain and the United States," *Essays on Foreign Literature* (Beijing: People's Literature Publishing House, 1964), 1:164.

22. Ibid., 165.

23. Ibid., 210.

24. Ibid.

25. Ibid., 199.

26. Ibid., 202.

27. "Editor's Afterword," *Foreign Literature and Art* 1 (1978): 311.

28. "Editor's Notes," *Foreign Literature and Art* 6 (1979): 5.

29. Ibid.

30. Li Wenjun, "Preface," in *Critical Essays on William Faulkner* (Beijing: Social Science Press, 1980), 1.

31. Li Wenjun, "Introduction" in *Selected Works of Foreign Modernist Writers*, ed. Yuan Kejia et al (Shanghai: Art and Literature Publishing House, 1981), 2:127.

32. Li Wenjun, "Southern Literature," in *A Concise History of American History*, ed. Dong Hengxun et al. (Beijing: People's Literature Publishing House, 1986), 288–89.

33. Elizabeth B. Booz, "Preface," in *A Brief Introduction to Modern American Literature* (Shanghai: Shanghai Foreign Languages Education Press, 1982), 1.

34. Ibid., 238–59.

35. Li Wenjun, "Foreward," *The Sound and the Fury* by William Faulkner (Shanghai: Translation Press, 1984), 2.

36. Ibid., 7.

37. Ibid., 17.

38. Li Wenjun, "Random Thoughts after Translating *The Sound and the Fury*," *Reading* 3 (1985): 99.

39. William Faulkner, *The Sound and the Fury* (New York: Vintage Books, 1956), 106.

40. William Faulkner, *Light in August* (New York: Vintage Books, 1959), 5.

41. Zhou Jueliang, "Some Suggestions about American Literature," *World Literature* 4 (1987): 296.

42. Wang Meng, "To Tell You the Truth," *Foreign Literature Review* 4 (1988): 115.

43. Liu Baiyu, "Faulkner," in "Three Pieces of My Journals," *Art and Literature Weekly*, 14 May 1988.

44. Li Zhenyu, "The Women's Apartment," *Flower City* 1 (1988): 181.

45. Mo Yan, "Two Burning Furnaces: Garcia Marcus and William Faulkner," *World Literature* 3 (1986): 298.

46. Ibid., 299.

FAULKNER NOVELS AND STORIES TRANSLATED INTO CHINESE

1934
"Elly" in *Modern Times Magazine* 5:6.

1958
"Victory" and "Death Drag" in *Translation* 4.

1979
"A Rose for Emily," "Dry September," and "Barn Burning" in *Foreign Literature and Art* 6.

1981
"Two Soldiers" in *Foreign Literature* 4.
"Justice" in *Spring Wind* 4.
"Benjy's Section" in *Foreign Literature Quarterly* 2.
"Quentin's Section" in *Selected Works of Foreign Modernist Writers*, ed. Yuan Kejia et al.
    Shanghai: Art and Literature Press.

1982
"Red Leaves" in *American Literature* 3.
"Centaur in Brass" and "Mules in the Yard" in *Contemporary Foreign Literature* 2.
"Spotted Horses" in *Literature Abroad* 2.
As I Lay Dying in *Ugly Duckling* 11.

1983
"Dry September" in *World Literature and Art* 4.
"Dry September" in *Foreign Fiction* 5.
"That Evening Sun" in *American Literature* 1.
"Evangeline" in *Foreign Literature Quarterly* 2.

1984
The Sound and the Fury. Shanghai: Translation Press.

1985
"A Rose for Emily" in *Appreciation of Foreign Literature* 1.
Selected Works of William Faulkner. Beijing: China Art and Literature Publishing Company. Contents: "Justice," "Red Leaves," "My Grandmother Millard," "A Rose for Emily," "Spotted Horses," "Barn Burning," "Shingles for the Lord," "The Tall Men," "Shall Not Perish," "That Evening Sun," "Pantaloon in Black," "Ad Astra," "All the Dead Pilots," "A Bear Hunt," "Wash," "Carcassonne," "The Bear," "Old Man," "Nobel Prize Acceptance Speech"; two critical essays: "William Faulkner and the Sense of Community" by H. R. Stoneback and "William Faulkner: A Virtuoso Storyteller" by Arthur Voss.

1986
"Spotted Horses" in *Lotus* 2.
"Dry September" in *Spring Wind* 1.
"Funeral Sermon for Mammy Caroline Barr" in *World Literature* 4.
"Old Man." Guangzhou: Guangdong People's Press.
"Dry September" and "Spotted Horses" in *Selected Stories by Nobel Prize Winners.* Guiyang: Guizhou People's Press.

1988
As I Lay Dying in *World Literature* 5.

1989
"The Bear" in *Daisy Miller/The Bear.* People's Literature Publishing House.

1990
Portable Faulkner. Hebei Education Press. Contents: "Red Leaves," "Dry September," "That Evening Sun," "Delta Autumn," "A Rose for Emily," "An Odor of Verbena," "Benjy's Section," "Spotted Horses," "Centaur in Brass," "The Tall Men," "Wash," "Percy Grimm," "The Bear," *The Wishing Tree*, "On Sherwood Anderson," "Nobel Prize Acceptance Speech," "Map of Yoknapatawpha County."
As I Lay Dying and Others. Lijiang Press. Contents: *As I Lay Dying, The Unvanquished,* "Delta Autumn," "On Sherwood Anderson"; also includes "Translating Faulkner" by Maurice Coindreau and *A Faulkner Chronology* by Michel Gresset.
The Bear. Translation Press. Also includes "William Faulkner" by Cleanth Brooks.

CHINESE ESSAYS ON FAULKNER

1934
Ling Changyan, "Faulkner: An Experimenter in New Styles," *Modern Times Magazine* 5:6.

1936
Zhao Jiabi, "William Faulkner" in *The New Tradition.* Shanghai: Liangyou Press.

1964
Yuan Kejia, "A Review of Stream-of-Consciousness Fiction in Britain and the United States," *Essays on Foreign Literature,* vol. 1. Beijing: People's Literature Publishing House.

1980
Li Wenjun, "Preface to *Critical Essays on William Faulkner*," *Reading* 8.
Qiu Xiaolung, "Random Thoughts Elicited by the Word 'Cuckold' in 'A Rose for Emily,'" *Reading* 9.

1981
Li Wenjun, "Stream of Consciousness, Obscurity, and Others," *Foreign Literature Quarterly* 2.

1982
Bu Zhenwei, Jiang San. "Time in Faulkner's 'A Rose for Emily.'" *Foreign Literature Studies* 1.
Ding Shan. "A Brief Introduction to Some of Faulkner's Novels," *Contemporary Foreign Literature* 2.
Tao Jie. "The Theme and Style of 'Spotted Horses,'" *Literature Abroad* 2.

1983
Qing Xinwei. "The Uniqueness of Faulkner," *Northern Literature* 11.
Tao Jie. "Faulkner's Humor and Some Chinese Writers," *Thalia* 2.

1984
Li Wenjun. "*The Sound and the Fury*: Its Characterization and Artistic Devices," *American Literature* 2.

1985
Han Haiyan. "The Young Women in Works of Cao Xueqin and William Faulkner," *Seeking Truth Magazine* 2.
Lan Renzhe. "An Analysis of Faulkner's 'A Rose for Emily,'" *Appreciation of Foreign Literature* 1.
Li Lisui. "An Elegy of the American Southern Society," *Foreign Language Teaching* 4.
Li Wenjun. "Random Thoughts after Translating *The Sound and the Fury*," *Reading* 3.
Zheng Dawei. "The Relationship between a Writer's Artistic Outlook and the Prose Style of His Works: On *To the Lighthouse* and *Sanctuary*," *Foreign Languages* 5.

1986
Gu Ershi et al. "Truth and Beauty behind Grotesqueness: On 'Dry September,'" *Spring Wind* 1.
Li Wanjun. "On Faulkner's Masterpiece *The Sound and the Fury*," *Foreign Literature* 9.
Li Wenjun. "Faulkner and His 'Bear,'" *Studies in Art and Literaure* 2.
———. "The Heart of Yoknapatawpha County," *Literature Abroad* 2. (Later revised and incorporated into *Modern American Novelists* edited by Dong Hengxun and published by Social Science Press in 1988.)
Li Yakuang. "'Spotted Horses': A Typical Case of Consummate Skills," *Lotus* 6.
Mao Xinde. "On Faulkner," *Academic Journal of Henan University* 3.
Wang Xiaoying. "Faulkner's Fugue," *Literary Gazette* 10 May.
Yang Guobin. "The Symbolism of the Shadow in *The Sound and the Fury*," *Teaching Studies* 6.
Zhu Ye. "'A Rose for Emily': An Exploration of Ethics and Aesthetics," *Foreign Languages* 4.

1987
Jiang Meiqi. "Techniques of *The Sound and the Fury*," *Academic Journal of Shanghai Normal University* 1.
Li Dingjing. "The Phoenix from the Ashes: On Caddy's Tragic Beauty," *Foreign Languages and Literature* 2.
Li Jirong, Wu Guoqiang. "Elegy of the Southern Aristocrats," *Foreign Literature Studies* 2.

Shi Shaoping. "'A Rose for Emily': A Thought-Provoking Modern Tragedy," *Seeking Truth Magazine* 4.

Wang Xiaoying. "Faulkner's Narrative Art: The Point of View in *Absalom, Absalom!*," *Foreign Literature Review* 1.

Zhang Xian'ang. "*The Sound and the Fury:* A Tragedy of the American South," *Academic Journal of Jilin University* 6.

Zhao Xiaoli, et al. "The Theme of 'The Bear' and Its Aesthetics," *Academic Journal of Northwest University* 4.

————. "On Quentin's Awareness of Death," *Foreign Literature Review* 1.

1988

Chen Kai. "Language in Faulkner's 'The Bear,'" *Foreign Languages* 2.

Fu Jun. "On the Stream of Consciousness in *The Sound and the Fury*," *Foreign Literature Review* 2.

Gu Sheng. "On the Style of Faulkner's 'The Bear,'" *Foreign Literature Review* 3.

Guo Shumei. "Home of the Outsiders: On Racial Consciousness in Faulkner's Mid-Career Novels," *Foreign Literature Review* 3.

Kong Genghong. "'The Human Comedy' and 'The Yoknapatawpha Saga,'" *Foreign Literature Review* 4.

Li Wenjun. "They Endure: On *As I Lay Dying*," *World Literature* 5.

Liao Caisheng. "The Language and Cultural Signifiers in Faulkner's *Sartoris*," *Academic Journal of Fujian Normal University* 3.

Liu Baiyu. "William Faulkner," in "Three Pieces of My Journals," *Literary Gazette*, 14 May.

Wang Rencai. "Characteristics of Southern Fiction as Seen in Faulkner's Novels," *Appreciation of Foreign Literature* 3.

Zhao Duojian. "The Theme and Artistic Skills of *The Sound and the Fury*," *Academic Journal of Shenyang Teachers' College* 2.

Zhao Xiaoli, Qu Changjiang. "Stylistic Devices in *The Sound and the Fury*," *Foreign Literature Studies* 1.

1989

Kong Genghong. "Elegy of the Declining French Aristocrats and Love Song of the Disintegrating American Southern Aristocrats," *Academic Journal of Anhui University* 1.

Lu Daofu, "Time and Space in *The Sound and the Fury*," *Academic Journal of Fu Yang Teacher's College* 1.

Tang Wenfei. "A Unique Writer and a Profound Story: An Interpretation of Faulkner's 'The Bear,'" *Academic Journal of Shijiazhuang Education College* 3.

Zhao Xiaoli, Qu Changjiang. "Nature in Faulkner's Sense of Community," *Academic Journal of Qinghai Nationality Institute* 1.

Go Down, Moses and the Ascetic Imperative

ROBERT H. BRINKMEYER, JR.

In an interview at the University of Virginia, William Faulkner identified Isaac McCaslin as a type of person who when faced with a serious problem says, "This is rotten, I don't like it, I can't do anything about it, but at least I will not participate in it myself, I will go off into a cave or climb a pillar to sit on."[1] Faulkner's words here, suggesting that Ike's renunciation of his patrimony echoes the ancient Desert Fathers' renunciation of the world for the spirit, points to the significance of the ascetic ideal in Ike's life and more broadly in the stories of *Go Down, Moses*. Besides Faulkner's own observation, there are a number of striking parallels between the early Christian ascetics and Isaac. In my brief discussion here, I can merely touch upon these parallels, but I think sticking with the general is advantageous, for I am sure that Faulkner never meant these parallels to be understood otherwise—that is, he did not construct Ike as a modern embodiment of a specific saint and his or her teachings.

As Peter Brown in *The Body and Society: Men, Women, and Sexual Renunciation in Early Christianity* has shown, early Christian ascetics differed markedly in their understanding of the ascetic ideal. "The Early Church was so creative largely because its most vocal members so frequently disagreed with each other," Brown writes, suggesting the healthy theological dialogue generated by asceticism's multiplicitous voices.[2] (One hesitates to call these doctrinal disputes otherwise healthy—they frequently led to prison and martyrdom.) Despite their disagreements, Christian ascetics nonetheless shared the basic desire to emulate Christ through self-denial and dispossession. William James's elaboration in *The Varieties of Religious Experience* of the theological logic supporting asceticism in the Catholic Church in large part defined the thinking of the early Christian ascetics:

> The dominant Church notion of perfection is of course the negative one of avoidance of sin. Sin proceeds from concupiscence, and concupiscence from our carnal passions and temptations, chief of which are pride, sensuality in all its forms, and the loves of worldly excitement and possession. All these sources of sin must be resisted; and discipline and austerities are a most efficacious mode of meeting them.[3]

Other ascetic ideas and ideals, particularly when keeping in mind Ike McCaslin's ascetic renunciations, stand out. Many Christian ascetics, for instance, saw the individual body as a microcosm for the embattled Christian Church struggling to survive and maintain its purity in a hostile world. Constant vigilance and control were needed in both temples of the Lord—the body and the Church—to resist temptation and suppress unruly desires in order to keep distinct the boundaries enclosing Christian life from foul pagan taint.

Chastity was of course a crucial weapon for protecting these sacred boundaries from penetration, and indeed chastity's perceived power was influential in other ascetical strivings as well. For some ascetics, continence was a means to bring to a halt the transmission of original sin which they believed occurred during sexual intercourse. This idea was particularly appealing for those ascetics who saw Adam's and Eve's fall as resulting from sexual desire. Chastity was also understood to be an effective force for undermining, if not totally ending, the secular structures of family and community that ascetics saw as alien to humanity's original and unfallen condition. As Geoffrey Galt Harpham points out, all Christian ascetics found inspiration in Luke 14:26: "If any man comes to me and does not hate his own father and mother and wife and children and brothers and sisters, yes, and even his own life, he cannot be my disciple."⁴ By giving up their inheritances and their possessions, ascetics struck a blow at the economic order underpinning society; by taking vows of chastity, ascetics went even further, calling, as some but not all did, for the end of society through the deliberate choice not to propagate. Even those ascetics who made no such explicit calls for society's destruction nonetheless set examples of the holy life that many of the most powerful individuals of the Roman world followed, at times drastically disrupting the established order by drawing these figures away from public life and their financial estates.

In all of these actions, the early Christian ascetics set out, on one level, to destroy history—that is, to achieve the purity of humanity's prelapsarian condition before its drastic fall into time. Negating time meant destroying the continuity from one generation to the next so that one's destiny was determined by free choice rather than by capitulation to the pressures of inherited values and conventions of family and society. For the ascetic this liberation specifically entailed embarking on a quest of disengagement from the civilized world, and, as Peter Brown underscores, the myth of the desert became central to this quest. "It was," Brown writes of the desert legend, "above all a myth of liberating precision. It delimited the towering presence of 'the world,' from which the Christian must be set free, by emphasizing a clear ecological frontier. It identified the process of disengagement from the world with a move from one ecological zone to another, from the settled land of Egypt to the desert. It was a brutally clear boundary, already heavy with immemorial boundaries."⁵ Disengagement, along with the rigors of self-mortification and chastity, was a means to exert free choice in a fallen world; ascetic practices allowed people brought up in rigid societies independently to construct their own identities and destinies. Ascetics were in this regard paragons of self-made heroes, striving to configure their selves into Adam's original and uncorrupted state—to humanity's truly "natural" condition.

These struggles by the early Christian ascetics reverberate, as Faulkner himself later suggested, in Isaac McCaslin's decision to repudiate his inheritance and then later, when challenged by his wife, to give up his marriage. Ike's actions at their most fundamental level of motivation link him explicitly with the Desert Fathers, for like them he seeks to emulate Christ, a point that Donald Kartiganer makes much of in his discussion of Ike in *The Fragile Thread: The Meaning of Form in Faulkner's Novels*.[6] Ike sees himself—the suffering consciousness struggling with matters of morality that drastically challenge his inherited place within family and society—as vessel or microcosm of his family's and the South's accursed fate. He hopes to redeem both through his act of expiation—his renunciation of his inheritance. Kartiganer suggests that Ike, driven by a mythic consciousness, sees his decision as a fulfillment of God's plan to redeem humanity after its fall and later suffering, thus wrapping up a comprehensible ceremony of divine history. But one might also see Ike's repudiation as his attempt to destroy history, to disrupt the endless repetition of transgressions that plague humanity's existence and thereby free people to begin anew, pure of heart and freed from the past, new Adams and new Eves in the Southern Eden. By repudiating his patrimony, Ike strives to halt what he sees as the continuity of the curse on the McCaslins initiated by his grandfather; likewise, he hopes to free the South from its punishment for its sinful enslavement of black people and its wanton destruction of the land. "Don't you see?" Ikes asks Sophonsiba's husband after he has tracked the couple down in Arkansas. "This whole land, the whole South, is cursed, and all of us who derive from it, whom it ever suckled, white and black both, lie under the curse."[7]

On a more personal level, Ike sees his repudiation as his own stepping free from the constraints and demands he suffers under as a McCaslin and a Southerner. It allows him, a self-made man, to configure his own identity and to chart his own course for the future, instead of merely following the dictates of family and society. Freedom entails disengagement from the familial and social, presenting Ike, in his isolation, with the authority and responsibility to act according to his own conscience rather than to the responsibilities placed upon him by others. He tells Mc-Caslin during their conversation about his decision: "I could say I don't know why I must do it but that I do know I have got to be-cause I have got myself to have to live with for the rest of my life and all I want is peace to do it in" (288). Like the early Christian ascetics, Ike strives toward a radical individualism that itself threatens the stability of society—traditional Southern society, as we all know, being founded less on principles of individual free-dom and mobility than on those of settled order of community and tradition.

The wilderness is of course Ike's "desert," an ecological zone where the primal forces of nature, rather than the everyday conventions and pursuits of humanity, reign. Isolated from town and farm, the woods are a haven from time and social respon-sibility; here Ike retreats annually to hunt and here he develops his ascetic perspective on the world and his place—or nonplace—in it. Particularly when Ike is young, the towering force of the wilderness is palpable, always at work and always there, bearing in upon the boy with a pressure that pushes aside all else, even the stature of the elder huntsmen. In "The Old People" the narrator describes the hunting party's journey out of the woods, "the wagon winding on among the tremendous gums and cypresses and oaks where no axe save that of the hunter had ever sounded, between the impenetrable walls of cane and brier—the two changing yet constant walls just beyond which the wilderness whose mark [Ike] had brought away forever on his spirit even from that first two weeks seemed to lean, not quite iniminical because they were too small, even those such as Walter and Major de Spain and old General Compson who had killed many deer and bear, their sojourn too brief and too harmless to excite to that, but just brooding, secret, tremendous, almost inattentive" (176–77). Later, in that same story, the narrator characterizes the wilder-ness as the "ancient immortal Umpire" forever leaning inward

upon the hunters, "tremendous, attentive, impartial and omniscient" (181). Awed by this spirit when pursuing Old Ben in "The
Bear," Ike experiences his own minuteness, described by the
narrator as "an abjectness, a sense of his own fragility and impotence against the timeless woods" (200).

If the wilderness humbles Ike, preparing him for a life of the
spirit, it is Sam Fathers who trains the boy and initiates him into
the wilderness's priesthood. Sam is himself a committed ascetic
who, after his fellow hermit and friend Jobaker dies, lives alone in
the woods. With Jobaker, Sam apparently had shared an intimate
spiritual brotherhood. Ike occasionally found them squatting together, "talking in a mixture of negroid English and flat hill dialect
and now and then a phrase of that old tongue which as time went
on and the boy squatted there too listening, he began to learn"
(172). As his "desert" father, Sam likewise communes with Ike,
leading him through what the narrator characterizes as his "noviti-
ate to the true wilderness," a growing up so profound that when
Ike begins going along on the hunting trips, "it seemed to him that
at the age of ten that he was witnessing his own birth" (195).

Sam Fathers teaches Ike, in the words of Mr. Compson in
Absalom, Absalom!, "the hard celibacy of riding and hunting"[8]—
not merely the technical skills of tracking and shooting but also
the code of conduct and the psychological underpinnings of this
code: the patience, humility, pride, and honor of the hunter. For
most Indian tribes of North America, hunting was a ritual cele-
brating the intimate ties between humanity and the divine forces
permeating all of nature. "The hunter," writes Richard Slotkin in
*Regeneration Through Violence: The Mythology of the American
Frontier, 1600–1860*, "comes to appreciate and worship the power
of nature and its spirit through the killing and eating of the beasts
who carry that spirit in the world."[9] For Sam Fathers and then
later for Ike hunting is precisely this ritual, and when Sam smears
on Ike's face the blood from his first buck, he is marked forever,
joined in a spiritual identity with Sam, the wilderness, and this
and all his future prey. Although he cannot put it precisely in

words as he stands over the fallen buck, the young Ike nevertheless knows his duty: "*I slew you; my bearing must not shame your quitting life. My conduct forever onward must become your death*" (351).

If other hunters from Jefferson embrace the code of the hunt, none gives themselves to it as fully as Ike; for him the code becomes the foundation for his everyday life, not merely the two weeks a year when he takes to the woods. His hunting in large part defines his asceticism, for the ritual of the hunt calls above all for self-abnegation, the "hard celibacy" of which Mr. Compson speaks. On one of his solitary journeys into the forest after Old Ben, Ike abandons his watch and compass, relinquishing himself entirely to the "markless wilderness" (208). His giving himself here utterly to the woods, abandoning all ties to society, points to his later willingness to deny his inherited identity in order to embark on a spiritual quest that others see as a foolhardy shirking of his responsibilities and duties to family and society. In this regard, both as a hunter and a seeker, Ike renounces his "self"— his identity in the social world—and so enters, at least in his own eyes, a wilderness of boundless freedom and eternal verities. "Sam Fathers set me free," he claims to McCaslin (300)—free to roam the wilds of nature and spirit without the burdensome ties of history and community. By the light of this freedom, all else appears trivial, even his marriage, as his wife unhappily finds out. "Woe to the wives of these men!" says the wife of Moses in one of the Jewish legends, after her husband has returned from the mountain, consumed with a passion more for God than for her.[10] Indicative of what Flannery O'Connor would call Ike's prophetic vision—"of seeing near things with their extensions of meaning and thus of seeing far things close up"[11]—is his response as a boy to Sam Fathers's tales about his ancestors and the old ways of wilderness life. So consumed is Ike by these stories, that the reality of the narrative becomes more real to him than that of his own presence. As Ike listens, the narrator writes, "gradually to the boy those old times would cease to be old times and would

become a part of the boy's present, not only as if they had
happened yesterday but as if they were still happening, the
men who walked through them actually walking in breath and
air and casting an actual shadow on the earth they had not
quitted." Ultimately, Ike disappears, erased by the narrative: "it
would seem to the boy that he himself had not come into
existence yet, that none of his race nor the other subject race
which his people had brought with them into the land had
come here yet; that although it had been his grandfather's and
then his father's and uncle's and was now his cousin's and some-
day would be his own land which he and Sam hunted over,
their hold upon it was actually as trivial and without reality as
the now faded and archaic script in the chancery book in Jefferson which allocated it to them and that it was he, the boy, who
was the guest here and Sam Fathers' voice the mouthpiece of
the host" (171). Here is the working out of the ascetic logic
that later dominates Ike's adult life: in becoming "dead" to the
world, to the time-bound history of family and society, he becomes alive to the spirit, to the universal history of the desert
wilderness.

As much as Faulkner undeniably found meaning and magnifi-
cence in the hunt and its rituals, it is also clear, recalling his
criticism of Ike in his Virginia interview, that he saw Ike's asceticism as too extreme, an abdication of social and familial
responsibilities. In this same interview, Faulkner went on to
characterize Ike by saying that in a crisis he would say, "This is
bad, and I will withdraw from it." "What we need," Faulkner
added, "are people who will say, 'This is bad and I am going to do
something about it, I'm going to change it.'" [12] An admirer of
Edward Gibbon, Faulkner may have had Gibbon's observations
on Christian ascetics in *The Decline and Fall of the Roman Empire*
in mind when he made his comments on Ike. Gibbon argues that
the rise of ascetic practice in late antiquity was a factor in the
demise of the Roman empire, its vibrancy sapped by fanatic
thinking that drew many away from active involvement in society.

In Gibbon's words, "all the manly virtues were oppressed by the servile and pusillanimous reign of the monks."[13]

As we have seen, Ike's repudiation of his patrimony certainly does suggest a withdrawal from responsibility, an escape from rather than a commitment to the community. It is precisely this appearance that so disturbs General Compson who believes, knowing firsthand Ike's skill and dignity in the woods, that there must be a good deal more than merely moral cowardice behind Ike's repudiation. General Compson offers Ike a place in his bed, determined to understand Ike's motives. "You sleep with me and before this winter is out, I'll know the reason," he says to Ike. "You'll tell me. Because I dont believe you just quit. It looks like you just quit but I have watched you in the woods too much and I dont believe you just quit even if it does look damn like it" (309). Perhaps we, too, should follow General Compson's lead and ask ourselves if Ike's repudiation of the world and worldly desire is as simple as it first appears. Is Ike's renunciation, for instance, an utter abandonment of social responsibility and power, or is it perhaps at the same time an attempt to achieve these ends? Could his withdrawal from society be both a repudiation *and* an affirmation of Southern culture? And is his asceticism free from desire or in fact driven by it? These are of course loaded questions that in their very asking suggest the complexity that I see at work in Ike's repudiation—a complexity much more profound than Faulkner suggests in his comments on Ike in his Virginia interview, and a complexity that I would like briefly to explore by first taking another look at the early Christian ascetics.

As Faulkner's allusion suggests, in his comment linking Ike with early Christian ascetics, many devoted Christians withdrew from the settled world to live in desert caves or atop pillars. Yet most of these ascetics did not merely disappear into the desert or into the sky never to be seen or heard from again. Quite the contrary. As Peter Brown establishes, Christian ascetics in late Roman society wielded a great deal of influence and power throughout the villages of the empire. "Above everything, the holy man is a man of power," Brown writes, and he explains that the ascetics' disengagement from society, making them "strangers" to the community whose lives stood outside the everyday demands and pressures of village life, paradoxically gave them significant influence within the community.[14] Deliberately striving to be other than human in their isolation and self-mortification, the ascetics came to be seen as semidivine creatures, "angelic" beings mediating between God and humanity. Their actions symbolized God's presence and power in the world and their words carried divine force and objectivity. For this reason, ascetics were actively consulted by villages for advice, healing, and arbitration; and in all of this they thus helped structure community life. Indeed, their cohesive power was crucial, for during this time much of the empire was struggling to cope with the collapse of old ways of thinking and the increase of freedom, developments that for many signaled a dangerous drift toward social, economic, and spiritual chaos. As community leaders, the ascetics gave villages identity and direction, fulfilling the function once served by now discredited social traditions and rituals.

The Desert Fathers' empowerment through withdrawal and disengagement suggests that the dynamics of asceticism may be much more complex and problematic than generally conceived. Indeed, Geoffrey Galt Harpham argues that such tangled complexity lies at the heart of ascetic ideology, an ideology he says is best defined as "self-denial undertaken as a strategy of empowerment or gratification."[15] Harpham states that asceticism is never a singleminded venture but is always marked by ambivalence and resistance to itself. The forcefulness of asceticism lies precisely in its unresolvability, entailing a structuring but not collapsing of opposing views; out of this opposition emerges a dynamic interplay of self-observation and self-criticism that prohibits simple affirmations or denials. This ambivalence, what Harpham calls a "compromised binarism," helps explain how the apostles of Western culture could at the same time be so outspokenly anticultural. "Asceticism neither simply condemns culture nor simply endorses it; it does both," writes Harpham. "Asceticism, we could say, *raises the issue* of culture by structuring an opposition between culture and its opposite. . . . To contemplate the ascetical basis of culture, for example, is to recognize that an integral part of the cultural experience is a disquiet, an ambivalent yearning for the precultural, postcultural, anticultural, or extracultural."[16]

From this thickened perspective of asceticism, we might suggest that embedded in Ike's renunciation of his patrimony and heritage, working in resistance to it, is actually his affirmation of his family and society. Indeed, his repudiation and disengagement can be seen as a strategy of empowerment, his effort to procure influence and power in the society that he openly rejects. And certainly both his family (his extended family, the three lines of descent from Old Carothers—McCaslin, Edmonds, and Beauchamp) and the South are in sore need of leadership. As Eric Sundquist underscores, the lines of the McCaslin family suffer miserably in isolation without a mediating force to bring them into some sort of generous harmony; and likewise the South of Ike's generation, like the society of late antiquity, reels in the midst of profound social change and disquiet, lacking strong leadership and direction in a fast-changing world.

In some ways Ike succeeds in his efforts at achieving power and influence. Faulkner said in another of his Virginia interviews that Ike was able to pass the wisdom he had learned from Sam Fathers—"I mean wisdom as contradistinct from the schoolmen's wisdom of education," Faulkner clarified—and the hunt on to countless others in the community. "In a way," Faulkner said, "every little eight- or ten-year-old boy was his son, his child, the ones he taught how to hunt. He had passed on what he had. He was not trying to tell them how to slay animals, he was trying to teach them what he knew of respect for whatever your lot in life is, that if your lot is to be a hunter, to slay animals, you slay the animals with the nearest approach you can to dignity and decency."[17] Thus is Ike, in the often-quoted line from "The Bear," "uncle to half a county and still father to none" (300). One thinks here not only of Ike's barrenness, but also of his visibility and influence within the community, recalling that spokespeople of society, both symbolic and real, are frequently designated in familial roles, as in our own "Uncle Sam."

But how much power does Ike ultimately wield and how effective is his leadership? If, as Faulkner said, Ike instructs the youth of Yoknapatawpha in the ways of the hunt, his influence is apparently short-lived, judging from the hunt in "Delta Autumn" where the old ways of conduct are precisely that—old ways, with little relevance to current practice. Roth's question in this same story—"where have you been all the time you were dead?" (345)—suggests that at least in Yoknapatawpha society a person's striving for the ascetic ideal of becoming dead to the world means becoming that and nothing more. Most people in the community apparently see Ike as an anachronism, worthy of humoring but not of emulating. His asceticism diminishes rather than inflates his stature; Lucas's interpretation that Cass somehow beat Isaac out of the patrimony is not atypical of the community's sentiments. Ironically, when Ike confronts Sophonsiba's husband in Arkansas, a man who in the name of freedom has shunned his duties as family provider, lives in a broken down hut, and speaks with the "sonorous imbecility of the boundless folly and the baseless hope," Ike fails to see that his future life is mirrored, if distortedly, in this deluded man's. His own anger and disgust is not unlike the response forthcoming from his own people to his repudiation of the McCaslin patrimony. "Freedom from what? From work? Canaan? . . . What corner of Canaan is this?" he upbraids the man (279), sounding a good bit like Cass will in their conversation about Ike's refusal to accept his inheritance. Ike, too, of course, will give up a farm and will fail as a husband, and his declaration to Cass that he has achieved freedom echoes Sophonsiba's simple statement amidst her obvious suffering, "I'm free" (280). Much of Ike's failure to achieve significant stature within the community derives from the underlying guilt and grief that fosters his asceticism—feelings that cut against the grain of the community's prevailing spirit. Bertram Wyatt-Brown's observation on ante-bellum Southern culture applies just as well to the South of Ike's day: "Honor, not conscience, shame, not guilt, were the psycho-logical and social underpinnings of Southern culture."[18]

If Ike fails in his bid for leadership and influence, he also, as numerous commentators have noted, fails to halt the McCaslin family curse initiated by Carothers's sexual abuses. Roth's affair with and then abandonment of his black kinswoman in "Delta Autumn" of course echoes Old Carothers's deeds; and Ike's up-braiding of the woman in some ways is every bit as cruel as Roth's treatment of her. Particularly damning is Ike's commandment to the woman (a person, we need to remember, related to him by blood) to leave the South and move to the North; his words here further link him to Roth, as they look ahead to Molly Beauchamp's accusation in "Go Down, Moses" that in banning Butch from the farm, in effect sending him north, "Roth Edmonds sold my Ben-jamin. Sold him in Egypt. Pharoah got him—" (371). Ike's ascetic renunciations clearly have freed neither the family nor himself from the sins of Old Carothers. Although not driven by the same desires as Old Carothers or Roth, Ike in his cold-heartedness (no doubt resulting in large part from ascetic withdrawal and self-denial) is capable of abusing people, even kin, as they did. "Old man," Roth's mistress indicts Ike, "have you lived so long and forgotten so much that you dont remember anything you ever knew or felt or even heard about love?" (363).

Another indictment of Ike, this on the larger scale of commu-nity, comes in his inability to inspire any positive response, ideological or actual, to the ongoing decline of Southern society that is most clearly manifested in the progressive destruction of the wilderness. Michael Grimwood has persuasively argued that with "Delta Autumn," Faulkner's overall conception of *Go Down, Moses* changed significantly, the primary focus shifting from the theme of race to that of depletion, both of Southern society in particular and of human history in general.[19] Rather than acting as a counterforce to this decline, as one might expect, given his forceful commitment to his ascetic ideals and his love of the woods, Ike actually is an embodiment of exhaustion, particularly in his failure to mount any activist response to the wilderness's diminishment. This is not to say that we should indict Ike for not spiking the trees to foul up the loggers or for not dynamiting the logging train and its tracks; and yet for a person whose existence is so integrally tied to the wilderness, his inaction toward the forests' destruction seems striking and problematic. His logic for not attempting to arrest the inroads being made by progress is profoundly ascetic: that by repudiating all complicity in what is happening to the wilderness, by not becoming involved in either its destruction or saving ("there was just exactly enough of it," he rationalizes at one point [354]), he hopes to achieve a purity of spirit, untainted by worldly desire, that mirrors that of the pristine woods. Ike envisions himself and the wilderness coexisting in an everlasting spiritual virginity, the woods uncut, he living the celibacy of the hunt. "He seemed to see the two of them—himself and the wilderness—as coevals," the narrator reports him thinking, and he sees the spans of their existences "running out together, not toward oblivion, nothingness, but into a dimension free of both time and space." There he sees "the names, the faces of the old men he had known and loved and for a while outlived, moving again among the shades of tall unaxed trees and sightless brakes where the wild strong immortal game ran forever before the tireless belling immortal hounds, falling and rising phoenix-like to the soundless guns" (354). Meanwhile, as Ike muses of a world out of space, out of time, the wilderness is fast disappearing; the narrator of "Delta Autumn" observes that it draws yearly inward just as Ike's life does: both approach total depletion—death—no matter what timeless paradise Ike dreams they are heading toward.

But what is the alternative to Ike's withdrawal? At the other extreme from Ike's ascetic strategy of empowerment through disengagement is the forthright seizing of power by force, a means identified in Roth's comment in "Delta Autumn" about the threat of dictatorship in an enervated America. What will happen to America, he asks, "after Hitler gets through with it? Or Smith or Jones or Roosevelt or Willkie or whatever he will call himself in this country?" (338). Roth's comments here, followed by Ike's confident downplaying of Hitler's threat, point I believe to the German dictator as a crucial if absent figure in *Go Down, Moses*. The figure of Hitler shadows Ike and his ascetic strategy of disengagement, and in fact embodies another form of asceticism just as radical and obsessive as Ike's.

The parallels between Ike's and Hitler's psychological obsessions and struggles are nothing if not striking. Like Ike, Hitler was profoundly concerned with his family's genealogy, particularly his paternal grandfather's sexual misdeeds.[20] Hitler's father was illegitimate, and apparently Hitler's grandmother never told, or perhaps never knew for sure, who her son's father was. Evidence suggests that throughout his life Hitler was obsessed by his lineage, and particularly with the possibility that his grandfather was Jewish. (One story had it that his grandmother worked as a domestic for a Jewish family, the Frankenbergers; Herr Frankenberger, the story goes, gave Hitler's grandmother a monthly child support allowance for fourteen years after her son's birth.) Further evidence suggests that Hitler on several occasions had associates look into his genealogy—a genealogy that one commentator later characterized as a "tangled web of family intermarriage, incest and illegitimacy, as well as name changes and incomplete or altered baptismal records,"[21] a description that might just as well describe the McCaslin family. Far more significant than the identity of Hitler's grandfather, a man who will probably never be identified, is Hitler's obsessive concern about his genealogy and his fear that his own blood might be, in his view of racial mixing, poisoned by Jewish impurities.

Hitler's obsession with race, leading initially to the establishment of racial laws requiring people to document their lineage back through their grandparents and then finally to the death camps, may in large part derive from his doubts about his own ancestors. Whatever the cause, there is no doubt that Hitler saw what he characterized as the bastardization of Aryan blood as perhaps the gravest threat to the future of German civilization. The decline of all superior races, he declared in *Mein Kampf,* occurred through racial mixing: *"Blood sin and desecration are the original sin in this world and the end of a humanity which surrenders to it."* [22] Hitler's religious imagery here is not unusual. According to his view of history, the Aryan race, once racially pure, had long ago created a paradisial civilization. With racial intermixing, however, came decline: "The Aryan gave up the purity of his blood and, therefore, lost his sojourn in the paradise which he had made for himself. He became submerged in the racial mixture, and gradually, more and more, lost his cultural capacity, until at last, not only mentally but also physically, he began to resemble the subjected aborigines more than his own ancestors" (296). Hitler did not see this fall as irreversible, however; by restraining what he saw as the diseased sexual compulsion to mate with inferior races, a person could follow his or her racial instinct, "the part which has still remained pure will at once strive again for mating among equals, thus calling a halt to further mixing" (401). Eventually, by the purity of blood, paradise could be regained.

While certainly not on the scale of Hitler's plans or with anything like his ferocity, Ike, likewise, in his own quiet but nonetheless prophetic way, hoped to reverse the South's fall from God's grace and to inspire, through his example, a new era freed from the sins of the past. But here a crucial difference emerges between Ike's and Hitler's racial obsessions: although Ike hoped to stop the consequences of the incest and miscegenation committed by his family and more generally the South, he was not seized by a rage and hatred toward blacks that Hitler was toward Jews: his focus on the South's troubles resided on what his people had sinfully committed against the alien race, not on what the alien race had committed against them.

Besides their obsessions with genealogy and race, Ike and

Hitler also share a profound distrust of modernism and a dismay at the societal decline they saw resulting from it. We have already noted that the movement of *Go Down, Moses* suggests history's progressive decline and depletion—a pattern Ike is fully cognizant of, even if his passive resistance to it itself represents an aspect of this decline. Hitler, too, saw his own society in decay, floundering in what he called, in one of his milder moments in *Mein Kampf,* "humanitarian bilge" (266). Fostering this decay, Hitler believed, was "the absence of a definite, uniformly acknowledged philosophy and the resultant general uncertainty in the judgment and attitude toward the various great problems of the time." In an age lacking convictions, the heroic was utterly lost; and without the heroic, people now strove merely for what Hitler called the "hollowness of comfortable life" (21). The modern era, Hitler wrote, "is stifling in the pettiest utilitarianism or better expressed in the service of money" (266).

This discussion is not meant to assert some simple equation such as Ike = Hitler. What intrigues me, however, is how Ike and Hitler, sharing similar obsessions, end up going such different directions, both essentially ascetic. Ike's solution to humanity's fallen condition is that of the eremite—withdrawal from society into the wilderness by a fanatic individual; Hitler's is that of the cenobite—creation of a community, based on the monastic model, whereby the populace submits to, in Geoffrey Galt Harpham's words, "extraordinary regulation, discipline, and obedience," lives lived "under a Superior in strict adherence to a Rule which prescribes [the followers'] conduct, their attitudes, their food, and even their thoughts."[23] Whatever psychological motives drove Hitler in his lustful pursuit of power, his concepts both of the National Socialist leader and of society were profoundly ascetic in their calls for self-renunciation and sacrifice to further the ideals of the state.

Throughout *Mein Kampf,* Hitler repeatedly describes his ideal society as one in which the citizen foregoes individual desire to fulfill society's needs. Hitler argued that while the Aryan race did not necessarily possess the most highly developed mental capabilities, it did have the strongest will of self-sacrifice, an attribute crucial to the development of culture and society, since "this state of mind, which subordinates the interests of the ego to the conservation of the community, is really the first premise for every truly human culture. From it alone can arise all the great works of mankind, which bring the founder little reward, but the richest blessings to posterity" (298). Hitler added that this ascetic will was in fact the primary shaping force of Nature: "Without this idealistic attitude all, even the most dazzling faculties of the intellect, would remain mere intellect as such—outward appearance without inner value, and never creative force. But, since true idealism is nothing but the subordination of the interests and life of the individual to the community, and this in turn is the precondition for the creation of organizational forms of all kinds, it corresponds in its innermost depths to the ultimate will of Nature" (299). Thus Hitler called for a society where people lived "*in a spirit of sacrifice and joyful renunciation*" (423) and one where the populace, like the members of his political party, followed the leadership with "blind discipline" (483) and "*disciplined obedience*" (457).

Underscoring the ascetic ideology structuring his political vision is the fact that a primary model Hitler looked to for the creation of his nation state was the Catholic Church. Hitler happily admired what he saw as the Catholic Church's rigid and authoritarian structure, particularly—and predictably—the infallibility of the Pope. So, too, did he see strength in the Church's unbending defense of dogma; in an era otherwise given to momentary convictions, the Church, by its doctrinal integrity, remained strong and cohesive, its identity and mission never in question. Hitler also celebrated the discipline the Church demanded from its faithful; so taken was he by Church discipline that he at times reportedly ordered units of the SS to study the *Spiritual Exercises* of Ignatius of Loyola for instruction in loyalty and obedience.

Ike and Hitler, the eremite and the cenobite (or at least Hitler as celebrator of a cenobitic order), thus stand at opposing extremes of ascetic thinking in *Go Down, Moses*, both embracing radical solutions for the ills they see threatening society. Neither is successful in his efforts. Ike, as we have seen, fails to gain the respect and leadership of his community and does little, if anything, to stop the destruction of the way of life he loves. Hitler, as we all know and so did Faulkner and his original readership, created a totalitarian state fueled by destructive fanaticism that trampled upon all matters of human justice and decency. Between these poles of radical asceticism fall the actions of the other central characters in the stories of *Go Down, Moses*, and one might even argue that on some deep level, underlying the problem of race that *Go Down, Moses* obviously explores, the struggles in embracing and/or resisting ascetic ideology structure the text. "Was," for instance, describes the comic efforts of Buck and Buddy to repudiate slavery by abandoning the plantation house to the slaves and also documents their efforts to protect their celibacy before the wiles of women, particularly Sophonsiba. "Pantaloon in Black" portrays a man so passionate in his love for his wife that no ideology of grief or renunciation can control his emotions at her death. If Ike's demise on one level suggests the depletion resulting from fanatic asceticism, Rider's death points to the dangers of a life without any ascetic self-control, any resistance to the power of unbridled emotions. And in "The Fire and the Hearth," Lucas renounces his wife, his happiness, and his work to pursue money—money he doesn't need, and thus money as excess, as abstract desire, a pursuit recalling Max Weber's contention in *The Protestant Ethic and the Spirit of Capitalism* of the ascetic basis of modern capitalism, a way of life where people live by a "hard frugality . . . because they [do] not wish to consume but to earn,"[24] the pursuit of money entirely as an end in itself. Much has been made about Lucas's resemblance to Old Carothers and his difference from Ike; but in the episode with the metal detector Lucas ironically reenacts Ike's renunciation of family and responsibility.

Is there a mean in *Go Down, Moses,* a form of asceticism whereby attention to one's own needs and to the needs of others, particularly one's immediate community, are in some type of healthy balance? Perhaps two figures point to something close to what Faulkner saw as such a mean—Molly Beauchamp and Gavin Stevens, both of whom are central figures in the title story. Molly is a sturdy and generous individual, a person deeply alive to her own emotions and one who is willing to sacrifice for the well-being of the community. In "The Fire and the Hearth," for instance, she cares without complaint for Zack Edmonds's baby after his wife dies, and later, when she sees how the metal detector is depleting Lucas's life, she takes it upon herself, even risking death, to get rid of it. In "Go Down, Moses" she demands that her grandson be treated with the respect and dignity due him in death, no matter what burden, financial or otherwise, she may ultimately have to bear. Her judgment upon Roth Edmonds for sending Butch away—"Roth Edmonds sold my Benjamin. . . . Sold him to Pharoah and now he dead" (380)—underscores her scorn for those who refuse to sacrifice immediate desires for the larger good, in this case the providing for one's kin.

Perhaps even more crucial to the ascetic ideal in *Go Down, Moses* is Gavin Stevens and more generally the system of law he represents as county attorney. Gavin is certainly not a paragon of virtue or clearsightedness; like all of us, he is a flawed individual, and he at times fails miserably in his assessment of character and situation. Moreover, his project of translating the Old Testament back into classic Greek, as my colleague Jay Watson pointed out to me, smacks of monastic excess, suggesting that Gavin suffers from the ascetic temptation of withdrawal and disengagement. But Gavin, unlike Ike, never completely gives in to this temptation; nor does he, like Hitler, seek utterly to transform society around his own individual vision—a temptation that he must at times have felt, given his sophisticated education (law degree from Harvard and Ph.D. from the University of Heidelberg—a hint of the German connection). Instead, Gavin remains committed to working within the community and its structures, doing his best at helping others and making sure that the law works fairly. If he at times blunders in his consideration of Molly's feelings, he nonetheless is instrumental in getting Butch back home and buried in the way Molly wants it done—much more instrumental than the newspaper editor or the typical townsperson, from whom Gavin must beg for change to help pay for the expenses.

It may be that the law itself, a system of normative ideas around which a society organizes its structure and vision, is the ascetic mean Faulkner endorses in *Go Down, Moses*, a notion packed with some urgency given the time of the text's publication when the world was coming undone in war. Although the law can be used insensitively (witness the deputy's interpretation of Rider's actions in "Pantaloon in Black") or openly abused (in the law officers' failure to prevent Rider's lynching in this same story), nonetheless its authority is crucial for holding together a society, particularly one like that depicted in *Go Down, Moses,* in the throes of change and transformation. In ascetic terms, people must sacrifice desires of the ego for those of social stability and justice. Something along these lines is what Lucas learns when he stands before the judge in "The Fire and the Hearth" during his divorce hearing; the law and its ascetic demands bring Lucas around to his senses and back to his marriage. Ike and Hitler, however, in their radical asceticism, seek not to uphold but to undo the law: Ike repudiates the law of inheritance and so undermines the structure of his traditional community; Hitler dismantles the law in order to recreate it according to his mad vision, and in the end brings chaos and destruction. Gavin as attorney for his community and Molly as plaintiff work within the law and the traditions that uphold it, and achieve victories that may not immediately usher in an ideal world but that move society that much closer to justice and dignity. They are the truly empowered ascetics of *Go Down, Moses.*

NOTES

1. *Faulkner in the University: Class Conferences at the University of Virginia, 1957–1958,* ed. Frederick L. Gwynn and Joseph L. Blotner (Charlottesville: University of Virginia Press, 1959), 246.

2. Peter Brown, *The Body and Society: Men, Women, and Sexual Renunciation in Early Christianity* (New York: Columbia University Press, 1988), 429.

3. William James, *The Varieties of Religious Experience* (New York: The Modern Library, n.d.), 298.

4. Geoffrey Galt Harpham, *The Ascetic Imperative in Culture and Criticism* (Chicago: University of Chicago Press, 1987), 23.

5. Brown, *The Body and Society,* 216.

6. Donald M. Kartiganer, *The Fragile Thread: The Meaning of Form in Faulkner's Novels* (Amherst: University of Massachusetts Press, 1979), 131–32.

7. William Faulkner, *Go Down, Moses* (New York: Vintage, 1973), 278. Further references are cited parenthetically in the text.

8. William Faulkner, *Absalom, Absalom!* (New York: Vintage, 1987), 135.

9. Richard Slotkin, *Regeneration Through Violence: The Mythology of the American Frontier, 1600–1860* (Middletown: Wesleyan University Press, 1973), 49.

10. Brown, *The Body and Society,* 67.

11. Flannery O'Connor, "Some Aspects of the Grotesque in Southern Fiction," in *Mystery and Manners: Occasional Prose,* ed. Sally and Robert Fitzgerald (New York: Farrar, Straus and Giroux, 1969), 44.

12. *Faulkner in the University,* 246.

13. Edward Gibbon, *The Decline and Fall of the Roman Empire* (New York: Modern Library, n.d.), 2:363.

14. Peter Brown, "The Rise and Function of the Holy Man in Late Antiquity," *Journal of Roman Studies* 61 (1971): 87.

15. Harpham, xiii.

16. Ibid., xii.

17. *Faulkner in the University,* 54.

18. Bertram Wyatt-Brown, *Southern Honor: Ethics and Behavior in the Old South* (New York: Oxford University Press, 1982), 22.

19. Michael Grimwood, *Heart in Conflict: Faulkner's Struggles with Vocation* (Athens: University of Georgia Press, 1987), 254–79.

20. A number of Hitler's biographies discuss Hitler's obsession with his genealogy. See particularly Robert G. L. Waite, *The Psychopathic God: Adolf Hitler* (New York: Basic Books, 1977), 124–31. Faulkner, except perhaps imaginatively, could not have known about Hitler's concern about his ancestors. In all likelihood, he also had not read *Mein Kampf* before he wrote *Go Down, Moses,* but he certainly knew the thrust of Hitler's ideology. *Mein Kampf* was published in America in an abridged version in 1933 and in two different complete translations in 1939; all three versions were widely reviewed.

21. Waite, 124.

22. Adolf Hitler, *Mein Kampf,* trans. Ralph Manheim (Boston: Houghton Mifflin, 1943), 249. Further references are cited parenthetically in the text.

23. Harpham, 21.

24. Max Weber, *The Protestant Ethic and the Spirit of Capitalism,* trans. Talcott Parsons (London: George Allen & Unwin, 1930), 68.

"He Come and Spoke for Me": Scripting Lucas Beauchamp's Three Lives

Philip M. Weinstein

Who is Lucas Beauchamp? What does it mean to ask that question? In the remarks that follow I want to explore the subjective identity of Lucas Beauchamp not as an unchanging essence but rather as a conflictual space. Conflictual, theoretically, because subjectivity itself is not an essence but a stance shaped by one's position within a signifying economy: as the economy alters, so does the subjectivity. Conflictual, practically, as well, because Faulkner produces Lucas Beauchamp three different times, within three different signifying economies: first, in a cluster of short stories that appeared in 1940 in *Collier's* and the *Atlantic Monthly;* then a second time in the sifted and revised versions of those stories that, two years later, make up *Go Down, Moses;* then a third time, six years later, in *Intruder in the Dust.*[1]

To pursue the subjectivity of Lucas Beauchamp, to ask who he is, is to analyze the language games Faulkner activated in producing this character. Yes, a question not of essence but of language: a discursive strategy, not a brute event. Yet this discursive strategy, while language, is never only language. It is rather the medium through which Faulkner predicts and solicits the response of middle-brow and high-brow audiences (the readers of the popular magazines, the more select novel readership) as he articulates racial difference in the mid-South in the 1940s. To say who Lucas Beauchamp is is to map the career of his creator, William

Faulkner, within a ten-year history of trying in different ways to say black, and always failing. To say who Lucas Beauchamp is involves, irreducibly, charting the racial identity of William Faulkner.

Subjectivity: for at least 200 years we have wanted to see in this word the arena of human freedom, that uncoerced interiority from which voluntary thoughts, feelings, and actions emanate. "A conscious and coherent originator of meanings and actions," the human subject maintains a saving autonomy, a fragile sanctuary, an interiority within which—however turbulent the external conditions that affect him—he remains recognizably himself.[2] Subjectivity is thus the Imaginary answer to objectification, it is that deep unmappable space of the essentially human within an otherwise charted world of Newtonian necessity. Within his own subjectivity, if nowhere else, the self remains an individual: literally, an undivided entity.

It is by now a well-known story how Marx, Darwin, and Freud—among others—have challenged this liberal notion of the autonomous subject by proposing a variety of networks—of class, of biology, of the unconscious—upon which subjecthood is constructed as a fissured entity but which subjecthood refuses to acknowledge. To recognize its constituent dependency upon such transpersonal structures is to see that the subject is not self-generative but rather produced: and (according to recent claims of French critical theory) it is produced in and by *language*. The subject, in other words, is subjected, thrown beneath, "something at the behest of forces greater than it."[3] This embattled subject—one precisely not undivided, not master of his own house but beleaguered from within by "greater forces"—is of course the myriad focal figure of William Faulkner's greatest novels. It is as though Faulkner knew himself most intimately and powerfully as a figure of tragic discord—a subjectivity irreparably fissured—and his memorable characters share this divisive and ennobling trait. Lucas Beauchamp, we shall see, attains such disturbing resonance in only one of his three avatars.

To say who Lucas Beauchamp is, I shall be looking at the language Faulkner provides for indicating how he looks, thinks, talks, and acts. What representational schema governs Faulkner's deployment of Lucas's body, what discursive practice accounts for his speech, what kinds of access do we have to his unspoken and unacted subjectivity? Michel Foucault alerts us to the ways in which the human body moves incessantly through channels of social inscription: the body, Foucault proposes, is "an inscribed surface of events (traced by language and dissolved by ideas), the locus of a dissociated Self (adopting the illusion of a substantial unity), and a volume in perpetual disintegration."[4]

If the body is everywhere tracked by social coding, branded by discursive rituals, the voice is equally a register of a lifetime of social training. How we speak announces who we have and haven't listened to, what "internally persuasive" accents of others we've made our own, what vocal communities we belong to as well as the ones we define ourselves against. As Mikhail Bakhtin writes, "the ideological becoming of a human being . . . is the process of selectively assimilating the words of others."[5] Utterance is inseparable from ideology, and thus the key to selfhood— the language we use to articulate our inner selves—is simultaneously the trap of subjecthood: our often involuntary affiliation within larger groups whose language has become our own. "He come and spoke for me," Lucas says to Zack at a climactic moment in "The Fire and the Hearth." He is referring to old Carothers McCaslin, but we may overhear a larger dynamic: that subjectivity is generated by the assimilation of the words of others, that Lucas becomes Lucas by speaking Carothers. More resonant yet, we may hear in these words Faulkner's own capacity to articulate Lucas—to speak for him—only in the ideologically laden accents of the white progenitor.

Faulkner and the Short Story: I have probably already said enough to indicate that I am approaching this conference topic tangentially. My focus is not Faulkner's deployment of specific genres—short story and novel—but rather his (and my) pursuit of

Lucas Beauchamp across three different forms: magazine stories, revised stories turned into a novel, and finally a novel "proper." I hope to shed light on the literary forms, but my deeper interest is in the produced figure moving across them: Lucas Beauchamp, the crucial character through whom, for almost a decade, Faulkner wrestled with his culture's discursive resources for representing racial difference. How he came and spoke for Lucas is my topic, for his speaking Lucas becomes his way of speaking his own racial identity, and our responses to these speakings—submissive or resistant—emerge as so many figurations of our own fluctuating racial identity.

The Lucas Beauchamp of "A Point of Law" has not yet come into the patrimony of his own name.[6] "Beauchamp" is as yet an inert patronymic—there is no Hubert Beauchamp/Uncle Buck/Tennie's Jim/Tomey's Terrel nucleus for his name to refer to; these figures won't be invented for at least another year—and Lucas is regularly shortened in conversation to "Luke." It could be any name; it is not yet talismanic, speaking of and summoning to the mind the absent old one. This story moves briskly and remains within the spatial and temporal confines of its plot: the comic trouble-making of "niggers" who run illegal stills on Roth Edmonds's land. There are no resonant memories here that escape the exigencies of plot.

Lucas is clearly a sharecropper in this early version, and Roth is unproblematically identified on the first page as his "landlord." When Lucas speaks, his dialect is thick: To his wife's (here, still unnamed) demand: "Whar you gwine dis time er night?" he responds, "Gwine down the road." He may be "gwine down the road" but we never see it; rather, the text tends to limit Lucas's appearance to three main spaces: his own house, the veranda of Edmonds's house, and offices within the courthouse in Jefferson. All three of these spaces are constructed by whites; each constrains Lucas in such a way that we are watching him perform under pressure. The proportion of dialect utterance to narrated plot is high. And while Lucas is clever, he is also seen around; even the deputies can chart his machinations: "So we set down and thought about just where would we hide a still if we was one of Mr. Roth's niggers . . . and sure enough . . ." (217). "Niggers" are figures of fun here, and their behavior finally confirms rather than disturbs this cultural epithet. Lucas Beauchamp emerges as wily in the way that "niggers" are wily: we read him in silhouette against George Wilkins but even more, perhaps, with George Wilkins: two black men negotiating domestic and nondomestic interests, one of them just foxier than the other.

Foxier in Faulkner's text, perhaps, but the *Collier's* readership would have been encouraged visually to remain within comfortable racial stereotypes while encountering this material. William Meade Prince's illustrations to "A Point of Law" (two huge drawings, each taking up a half-page of magazine space) stress not Lucas's agility but the play of bumbling black shenanigans. Prince's first illustration shows a tiptoeing Nat and a bottle-burdened George Wilkins trying to keep their illegal booze hidden from the authoritative gaze of white officers. The caption to the drawing—"About daylight, we see George and that gal legging it up the hill with a gallon jug in each hand"—neatly sabotages their aim, inasmuch as "we see" (we as white deputies, we as white readers: the positioning is identical) exactly what they are clumsily trying to keep from our gaze. The second illustration foregrounds the bottles and worm and jug of a homemade still, with Lucas and Molly stationed above this paraphenalia, their eyes and mouths wide open in astonishment. The caption reads: "'Git the ax!' Luke said. 'Bust it! We ain't got time to git it away.'" Once again the magazine version emphasizes the moment of comic ineptitude, in which the deputies, illustrator, writer, and reader join in a single, cliché-enforcing gaze: black as befuddlement, black as harmless antics, charted by a bemused and superior white intelligence.

"Gold Is Not Always" was written and published at about the same time as "A Point of Law." The same dynamics—prankish black men maneuvering within the confines of judgmental white men—activate this narrative.[7] As Roth says, "As soon as you niggers are laid by trouble starts" (231), and the story delights in providing the trouble. Roth is still identified on the first page as Lucas's landlord, and Lucas's language remains heavily marked by dialect: "He done fotch the machine with him; I seed hit work" (227), Lucas says as the plot gets under way. Part of the comedy here resides in the racially pertinent move of Lucas's pretending to *own* Roth's mule. A certain measure of the ideological work of this tale consists in getting Roth's valuable mule back to Roth— restoring thus the racial norms of ownership—while it transfers the worthless treasure-finder from the foreign salesman to the clever black man. Lucas's admiration for this toy makes him childish; at the same time the salesman who trafficks in such useless fantasy-objects receives his well-earned duping.

At stake here seem to be two options for the right management of the land itself: either a juvenile fantasy of discovering buried treasure that is figured in the machinations of a local black man outsmarting a foreign white one; or, in opposition to this scenario (with its comic but potentially disturbing image of a white man enslaved by a black one), the proper relation to the land—hard work, no miracles. The trouble starts, as Roth says, once the "niggers" are "laid by" and the land does not properly occupy their energies. The implicit fantasy enacted by both these tales is that the blacks are idle and have plenty of time on their hands for such games; indeed, Lucas is envisaged as better off than Edwards "since he owned nothing he had to pay taxes on and keep repaired and fenced and ditched and fertilized" (214). A hoary cliché speaks here—one that at his most astute Faulkner puts in the mouth of a Jason Compson: namely, that the responsible handling of property and goods is a burden borne only by mature white men.

The Lucas Beauchamp of these stories is subordinated to a swiftly moving plot, and that plot cannot afford to dilate upon Lucas's subjectivity. Faulkner provides minimal interiorizing that might counteract the simplifications of Lucas's spoken dialect. His astuteness is never in question, in both senses: it is assured throughout the stories (the reader knows that Lucas's aplomb is not going to be disturbingly contested), and its lineaments hardly escape the containing outline of the trope of the wily black man. To put it more directly, the language that generates Lucas Beauchamp is not itself in question in these two stories. As a corollary, the stories are not likely to foment questions of racial identification in their readers. Complacent ideological alignments remain securely in place; the stories are, in their chosen and narrow way, extremely skillful. [8]

As Faulkner's commentators have noticed, we encounter a sea-change when we move from these stories into the revisionary world of *Go Down, Moses*. [9] Virtually the same passages take on a new aura of implication and value, as in the following pair of quotes:

> Edmonds stared at him [Lucas Beauchamp] as he leaned against the counter with only the slight shrinkage of the jaws to show that he was an old man, in his clean, faded overalls and shirt and the open vest looped across by a heavy gold watch chain, and the thirty-dollar handmade beaver hat which Edmonds' father had given him forty years ago about the face which was not sober and not grave but wore no expression whatever. ("Gold Is Not Always" 237)

> He [Edmonds] sat perfectly still, leaning forward a little, staring at the negro [Lucas Beauchamp] leaning against the counter, in whom only the slight shrinkage of the jaws revealed the old man, in threadbare mohair trousers such as Grover Cleveland or President Taft might have worn in the summertime, a white stiff-bosomed collarless shirt beneath a pique vest yellow with age and looped across by a heavy gold watchchain, and the sixty-dollar handmade beaver hat which Edmonds' grandfather had given him fifty years ago above the face which was not sober and not grave but wore no expression at all. ("The Fire and the Hearth" 97)

The difference between these two passages tells us much about the genesis, procedure, and aims of *Go Down, Moses*. In revising the earlier stories so as to make them cohere as parts of a larger narrative, a transformation takes place. Lucas Beauchamp's clothes take on a new register. What they register is the value-charged patina of time itself. Grover Cleveland and President Taft enter the "aura" of Lucas, his clothes become more luminously fine as they emerge from their long journey into the motley present moment, and the beaver hat undergoes a kindred rewriting. Its original value doubles, its age increases ten years, its source retreats another generation into the past.

"Lucas Beauchamp" is a new signified here. He has become a prism upon time itself, a departed time of heroes, of honorably crafted materials, of valuable bequests given in recognition of sustained service and worn talismanically. The first Lucas Beauchamp, as we saw, was a shrewd black man maneuvering on a largely contemporary stage, the second Lucas Beauchamp—time-immersed—is constructed as an extension into the 1940s of a set of nineteenth-century practices signifying honor, integrity, and determination. Time's mark on him has become his glory, not his scar. The representation of Lucas signals the degree to which *Go Down, Moses* has invested its energies in the survival—often critical but more deeply celebratory—of older modes of being and doing within a diminished present. The telos of *Go Down, Moses* is arche.

"The Fire and the Hearth" dilates upon Lucas's face—the face "which had heired and now reproduced with absolute shocking fidelity the old ancestor's entire generation and thought—the face which . . . was a composite of a whole generation of fierce and undefeated young Confederate soldiers" (118). As Myra Jehlen remarks, "it is a tortuous process by which a black man comes to look most like a Confederate soldier."[10] This throw-back face—incredibly old yet perfectly intact—is antebellum in its undefeat: what, we may ask, is Faulkner doing here? Perhaps an answer emerges when we notice that Lucas's face is twice described as "Syriac," with this gloss added: "not in a racial sense but as the heir to ten centuries of desert horsemen" (108). Systematically exoticised, Lucas's face is being rewritten. The rewriting proposes an identity to be understood "not in a racial sense." Lucas's heroic status is conditional upon his being figuratively removed from his own black heritage.

If a suspect logic governs this rewriting of Lucas's face, an odder one governs the writing of his blood:

> Yet it was not that Lucas made capital of his white or even his McCaslin blood, but the contrary. It was as if he were not only impervious to that blood, he was indifferent to it. . . . He resisted it simply by being the composite of the two races which made him, simply by possessing it. Instead of being at once the battleground and victim of the two strains, he was a vessel, durable, ancestryless, non-conductive, in which the toxin and its anti stalemated one another, seetheless, unrumored in the outside air. (104)

It seems to me that this passage proposes a desperate resolution. The two races are said to stem from incompatible bloods—a toxin and its anti—yet Lucas is imagined as overcoming this racist opposition by some sort of sublime indifference. "Ancestryless," Faulkner calls him here—intransitive, self-sealed—but "The Fire and the Hearth" tirelessly draws upon—what else?—Lucas's ancestry in order to establish his stature. For reasons that lie deep within the culture's racist ideology, Faulkner simply will not imagine the two bloods as merging in time—Lucas must be seen as nonconductive, raceless—yet this figure's clothes, gestures, and habits of thought are soaked in the passage of time and have now become a source of irreplaceable value. One might speculate that the text wants all of Lucas's history, on condition that it be cleansed of its racial coloration. I shall return later to the mystified scripting of Lucas Beauchamp in *Go Down, Moses* and *Intruder in the Dust*, but now I want to move from the problematics of his face and blood to the elaboration of his body and mind; here Faulkner goes beyond cultural givens and generates perhaps the most compelling black portrait in his entire oeuvre.[11]

This new Lucas of *Go Down, Moses* is a figure in intimate relation to the land itself. "He knew exactly where he intended to go, even in the darkness" (36), and when he hears the almost inaudible sound of Nat following him, he whirls not toward her sound but parallel with it, "leaping with incredible agility and speed among the trees and undergrowth" (40–41). Like Sam Fathers, like Rider, like the elaborately trained Ike McCaslin, Lucas Beauchamp reveals a bodily agility beautifully attuned to natural setting and obstacle. Rather than "performing" on a white-constructed stage, as in the stories, he lives in *Go Down, Moses* as a woodsman as well, incandescent in the body whatever shackles have been placed upon his mind. Indeed, the land itself knows him here, striking him a blow as the earth about him suddenly heaves, "a sort of final admonitory pat from the spirit of darkness and solitude, the old earth, perhaps the old ancestors themselves" (38).[12] Finally, this Lucas's intimacy with the land is beyond any white deputy's mapping. When they find his concealed still this time, it is because he has chosen to have them find it so as to keep them ignorant of the buried treasure.

The body is new here; more important, so is the mind. "A Point of Law" moves within three to four lines to plot and dialogue, but chapter 1 of "The Fire and the Hearth" takes nine pages to establish Lucas Beauchamp's interiority: his views about George Wilkins, his complex plans for the two stills, his many-generational history with Cass and Zack, his sense of possession of his land ("it was his own field, though he neither owned it nor wanted to nor needed to" [35]), his dignified position as "the oldest living person on the Edmonds plantation" (36), his strenuous maneuvers with the land itself (trying to bury his still) leading to the earthslide, the glimpse of gold, and the pursuit of Nat, and finally his revision of his plans. Within these nine pages we enter a subjective drama more compelling than any plot it may release. The tensions are not centrally between white landlord and black sharecropper (Roth is never referred to as landlord in the revised version); rather, they open inwardly, subjectively, into the inexhaustible genealogical history of Lucas Beauchamp himself.[13]

For he has now come into his name: not only a new signified, but literally a new signifier. No Luke here: this is the offspring of Lucius Quintus Carothers McCaslin, and the text knows him as Lucas with a near-religious scrupulousness. (That is, the "Lucas" part of the name may be undiluted McCaslin, but the limitation of this genealogical inheritance surfaces in his matrilinear surname. He is not McCaslin but Beauchamp: the matrilinear surname suggests his slave/distaff descent, inasmuch as slave mothers and children were kept together for economic purposes and the off-spring of Tomey's Terrel and Tennie—at least those born before 1865—would be given the name of Tennie's owner, Hubert Beauchamp.) His voice too has altered; he speaks dialect but not (like Rider) barely articulate dialect. "He done fotch the machine with him; I seed it work" has become "He brought it with him; I saw it, I tell you" (79). The changes that matter most, of course—the ones that all commentators on *Go Down, Moses* are drawn to—involve not Lucas's enlarged setting, altered voice, or agile body. They involve his tragic memories of the battle with Zack over Molly, when Zack's wife died at childbirth and Molly replaced her.

These scenes have been richly interpreted already; my aim is less to celebrate than to problematize them. Problematize, not attack: for I too am moved more by this remembered agon than by anything else in "The Fire and the Hearth" (unless it be the mirroring agon of Roth's tragic alienation from Henry, his black alter ego). Why are we so moved? The answer lies embedded within the white male psyches of the writer, the reader, and (paradoxically) of Lucas himself as he rehearses these memories. The scenes are of enacted and failed male bonding. Females drop out of the drama once their purpose as catalyst for the encounter has been served. We never even learn the name of Zack's dead wife. Her narrative purpose is simply to produce an heir (naturally male) and then to disappear so that her widower Zack can meet his rightful mate on the other side of that matrimonial bed: Lucas. As with Roth and Henry later (also a question of beds not taken, intimacies forsworn upon entry into the culture's racist ideology), the bonding that matters is between men. Roth registers the loss of Henry with an intensity of grief starkly absent from his tight-lipped evasion of the "doe" in "Delta Autumn."

It is a male scene; it is also a white one. On the evidence of Lucas's memories in "The Fire and the Hearth" we could take him to have only one progenitor, white and male and two generations removed. The remembered struggle is doubly articulated as an affair of males: Lucas and Zack, Lucas and old Carothers. It unfolds as a chivalric ritual of honor-bound moves, advantages offered but not accepted, the enemy cherished even as he is pursued. It is essentially a love scene—the most concretely represented and intensely narrated in the entire novel—and it dramatizes not desire (in which the boundaries of subjective identity risk being overwhelmed) but respect coupled with aggression (a coupling that exalts selfhood even as, in its intimacy, the one man draws murderously near to the other). We white male critics have been lauding this scene for decades now. Is it because it sublimates eros into principle, turns the stickiness of a self-altering exchange into the ritual of a self-affirming one, and locates in the male-male encounter and the white male grandfather the sources of Lucas's indestructible dignity?

"He come and spoke for me" (58) indeed; Lucas thinks of this accession to the progenitor's voice as the final understanding earned from this identity-enshrining encounter. He has been, as the French theorist Althusser would say, "interpellated." A bid for his identity has been made, and he has accepted it. This is the moment in which he fully assumes the ideological frame of his own subjectivity. As Althusser puts it:

> I shall then suggest that ideology 'acts' . . . in such a way that it 'recruits' subjects among . . . individuals . . . by that very precise operation which I have called *interpellation* or hailing, and which can be imagined along the lines of the most commonplace everyday police . . . hailing: 'Hey, you there!' Assuming that the theoretical scene I have imagined takes place in the street, the hailed individual will turn round. By this mere 180 degree physical conversion, he becomes a *subject*. Why? Because he has recognized that the hail was

'really' addressed to him, and that 'it was *really* him who was hailed' and not someone else.[14]

Who is Lucas Beauchamp? He is who he sees in his subjective mirror, who he allows to speak for him, he becomes himself by saying himself within the signifying economy of McCaslin. Rednecks and white trash may think him a nigger, but the dearest move of "The Fire and the Hearth" is to refuse that outward appellation, to move inwardly and replace it with McCaslin. Not just any McCaslin, but the old man himself: through him Lucas accedes to an empowering identity consolidated by the passage of time. That is, he attains a genealogical memory.

To possess a memory is not only the essential human privilege celebrated by *Go Down, Moses;* it has also been, at least since the Enlightenment, the sign of humanity itself. Henry Lewis Gates argues persuasively that during the eighteenth century memory was certified by the presence of writing, and that a people who could not write (in European languages of course) had no memory—and therefore were not quite human. "Without writing," Gates proposes, "no *repeatable* sign of the workings of reason, of mind, could exist. Without memory or mind, no history could exist. Without history, no humanity . . . could exist."[15] We know with what tenacity many slaveholders resisted the notion of slaves becoming literate, and we know as well the attempts to deny that nineteenth-century slave narratives were really written by the black subject in question. For reading, writing, and remembering powerfully promote subjecthood itself. I refer to this passage of cultural/racist history in order to suggest what is at stake in Lucas Beauchamp's attainment of a genealogical memory. He becomes a full participant in humanity, a blood-brother to Faulkner's brood of resonant, memory-laden, white protagonists.

Lucas can join them, however, only as a white man. Virginia Woolf's haunting phrase—"For we think back through our mothers if we are women"—tells us how pinched and conditioned Lucas Beauchamp's liberated humanity is. He cannot think back through his mother; he cannot think back through his blackness. He speaks himself—or he allows himself to be spoken—within a white signifying economy. His moments of supreme authority are thus deprived of their racial component. If you will, he is permitted to become human only universally, not regionally, and his incapacity to think about his black mother surely plays its role in his callous treatment of his black wife.

Finally, the Lucas Beauchamp who attains white stature in "The Fire and the Hearth" also accepts the discourse of white responsibilities, that is, the discourse of the Bible. This Lucas Beauchamp speaks scripturally of his "allotted span" (75) of life, he tells Zack that "even the Book dont ask a man to forgive them he is fixing to harm" (58), and he waxes eloquently, in the privileged last paragraph of "The Fire and the Hearth," upon the Book's injunctions and his obedience: "Man has got three score and ten years on this earth, the Book says. He can want a heap in that time and a heap of what he can want is due to come to him, if he just starts in soon enough. I done waited too late to start. . . . I am near to the end of my three score and ten, and I reckon to find that money aint for me" (131).[16]

Note the inscription here within an interpellative or signifying economy. The Book has "come and spoke for him"; he reads his interiority in the light of its commands. Accepting its script, he voluntarily chastens his wants. It is not only that he ceases to search, but—more sinister—that he inserts himself within a finished and regulatory discursive structure: "that money aint for me." The containment is complete. He has, we are meant satisfyingly to feel, finally grown up. That he does so by relinquishing his wants, by understanding maturity as white, male, and scripturally ordained, by recognizing and accepting his place within such a system: that he does so carries out the ideological work of "The Fire and the Hearth." Lucas can be left alone now; he will behave himself.

This sardonic note is not the right one, though, for completing my discussion of *Go Down, Moses*. Faulkner was never again to imagine black lives so richly intertwined with white ones. If in the magazine stories we find Lucas in the present company of, mainly, George Wilkins and Roth Edmonds, in the novel he lives in the present and absent company of a rich array of reflecting lives. To name a few, we read him against Rider and Samuel Worsham Beauchamp, two blacks whose uncontrollable passion or defective training keeps them from Lucas's open-eyed prudence; we read him as well against Sam Fathers and Ike: a trio of woodsmen, of aged men of integrity, at odds with the culture they must live in. At his most compelling, Lucas rises into the sinister but sustaining force of his McCaslin ancestry. Ultimately he will rise beyond family altogether, and we will read him against Old Ben, solitary, childless, mythic, unapproachable. This will be Lucas's final avatar in *Intruder in the Dust*.[17]

[Lucas] . . . always in the worn brushed obviously once-expensive black broadcloth suit of the portrait-photograph on the gold easel and the raked fine hat and the boiled white shirt of his own grandfather's time and the tieless collar and the heavy watch-chain and the gold toothpick like the one his own grandfather had carried in his upper vest pocket . . . (24)

These six lines are taken from a sentence that occupies thirty more in the early pages of *Intruder in the Dust*. The perspective is Chick Mallison's, and Lucas as seen in his eyes has receded in a number of ways from the mobile figure of *Go Down, Moses*. "Portrait-photograph": the portrait we encounter here is locked into its mandatory legitimizing details—broadcloth suit, raked fine hat, boiled white shirt, tieless collar, heavy watch-chain, and gold toothpick. These details scrupulously accompany Lucas's every appearance in this latest text. Faulkner cannot seem to find him except through such fetishized objects. So powerful is this imprisonment within clothes, watch-chain, and toothpick that we read not so much of Lucas as of the enbalming accoutrements that announce him. And they do "speak" him. They insert him within a sartorial nineteenth-century tradition of white respectability that Chick tirelessly identifies with his own grandfather.

Lucas Beauchamp has here become a congealed icon. How he looks is textually more important than how he may feel. He emerges less as an imagined subjectivity than as an object— reliably unchanging even if impenetrable—of the male gaze that frets and fusses about him for page upon page. A throwback to the past, he is imagined only once as feeling something unpredictable to Chick—grief for the death of his wife Molly—but the text uses this material with an unswervingly single purpose: to open up the mind of Chick Mallison, not to explore the moves of Lucas Beauchamp nor to enter the subjectivity of the dead Molly. Moves are, in fact, just what Lucas does not have in *Intruder in the Dust*. To put it most broadly, the ways in which Faulkner's discourse *frames* Lucas Beauchamp undercut the ways in which Faulkner's plot seeks to free him from a frame-up. Let me elaborate.

Lucas is framed in his immaculate clothes and visible habits; they are all he has. His wife and children have been taken from him; friends he never had anyway; and now he is not only isolated but almost mute. He barely speaks in this novel (the one time he must convey significant information to the sheriff takes place, as it were, off-stage, summarized by Gavin rather than narratively lived into). Vertically he has lost old Carothers to talk to as well as George Wilkins or Nat to scheme with; horizontally he has no peers. The text everywhere insists on his being like Chick's grandfather but like no other black man. A taxpayer now, he proudly accepts this distinguishing difference. He tells Chick that he insisted on Molly's taking her headrag off before the portrait-photograph could be taken because "I didn't want no field nigger picture in the house" (15). "Field niggers" is his implicit discursive term for most other blacks: no wonder they don't make common cause with Lucas's plight.

He is also, in a figurative sense, castrated; only they sort of took both legs too. Lucas hardly possesses legs in *Intruder in the Dust*.

We see him mainly as in a portrait-photograph—from the shoulders up—he has none of that unpredictable physical mobility, that bodily quickness that flares up in "The Fire and the Hearth." The motion denied him is transferred to Chick Mallison. Chick moves incessantly throughout this novel, circling Lucas, trying to come to terms with him, travelling miles upon miles to refute the evidence against him. More, Chick is moving in the figurative sense as well. His feelings are continuously tracked by this narrative; he can still *be* moved; he is meant to move us. The Bakhtinian drama of authoritative dicta being challenged and replaced by others that are more internally persuasive lives in Chick alone.[18] Lucas does not speak, seems hardly to feel, has no subjective discoveries to make. He is already finalized.

This congealed Lucas responds predictably (if with impeccable dignity) to racial threats. Insulted in a white store by a white man as "You goddamn biggity stiff-necked stinking burrheaded Edmonds sonofabitch," Lucas answers: "I aint a Edmonds. I dont belong to these new folks. I belongs to the old lot. I'm a McCaslin" (19). The enraged white retorts, "Keep on walking around here with that look on your face and what you'll be is crowbait." Unruffled, Lucas replies: "Yes, I heard that idea before. And I notices that the folks that brings it up aint even Edmondses." Well, this is sublime, way beyond what the Lucas Beauchamp of *Go Down, Moses* could afford; and we might ask: how can this Lucas afford it? The answer is that now there are inobtrusive whites stationed everywhere to shepherd him. Even as the white racist snatches up a plow singletree in order to smash Lucas's skull, the son of the store-owner intervenes, grabs the racist, is aided by another white man. "Get out of here, Lucas!" the son hisses. "But still Lucas didn't move, quite calm, not even scornful, not even contemptuous," and when finally he deigns to depart, he goes "without haste . . . raising his right hand to his mouth so that as he went out the door they could see the steady thrust of his chewing" (20).

The deeper fantasy-logic of *Intruder in the Dust*'s narrative emerges in such an episode. Pose is allocated to the black man; motion is reserved for the white man. Lucas's splendid demeanor is inseparable from his immobility. He can look free but not act freely. He is imagined here as saying things that no black responsible for his own safety in Jefferson in the 1940s could say because he need not be—cannot be—responsible for his own safety. Rather, he is an icon that the text proudly sports, while its central white figures almost seem to compete with each other to keep him unharmed. Consider this later moment in the text, when Chick, the sheriff, and his black helpers unexpectedly encounter Nub Gowrie at the site of his murdered son's grave. The old man raises his pistol:

> But long before this he [Chick] had seen the sheriff already moving, moving with really incredible speed not toward the old man but around the end of the grave, already in motion even before the two Negroes turned to run, so that when they whirled they seemed to run full tilt into the sheriff as into a cliff, even seeming to bounce back a little before the sheriff grasped them one in each hand as if they were children and then in the next instant seemed to be holding them both in one hand like two rag dolls, turning his body so that he was between them and the little wiry old man with the pistol, saying in that mild lethargic voice . . . (160)

The passage is perhaps more revealing than it knows. Again, motion, protective power, and voice are reserved for the white man. He has anticipated the two blacks' moves, and like a cliff his superior substantiality grounds their aimless terror. Figured as "children" and as weightless "rag dolls" in this passage—offered up to us as testimony to the sheriff's adroitness and resolution—the blacks are safe enough. But they remain safe only within a discursive economy that identifies them as fetishized objects, as predictable children, ultimately as "Sambo." Their moves, in every sense of the word, are scripted in the reifying and limited terms of a white discourse.

Who are the other blacks in this text? Old Ephraim who

delights in domestic wisdom (when you want something done, get the women and children to help you do it); Aleck Sander, Chick's sidekick who is nearly voiceless, accompanying Chick into each dangerous foray, his own construing of this strange adventure largely kept out of the text's narrative. Instead, Aleck Sander is endowed with preternaturally keen senses; he can hear and smell better than whites. The contours of his mind—which might liberate him from this cliché of the hyper-sensed Negro—go almost uncharted. In their place we get vast generalizations about black workers in the fields—naturalized there, since time imme- morial properly at work there—and we get Gavin Stevens's discourse of "Sambo."[19]

The appellation "Sambo" has been attacked by liberal critics almost since the book's publication, and there is no need to rehearse their commentary.[20] Yet my argument does require this observation—that Stevens's desperate attempt to corral the black man within the epithet "Sambo" weirdly repeats the culture's traditional attempt to read him as "nigger," and that this move belies the plot momentum of the text that would spring Lucas free. The *discours* recontains what the *récit* would enfranchise, just as the frantic claim of homogeneity is undermined by the alterity everywhere at work in these pages: the uncrossable bar- rier between a few liberated whites in the foreground and an anonymous mob of racists that surround them as background, as well as the barrier between the unflappably sartorial Lucas Beau- champ and the nameless black workers toiling in the fields (both barriers suggestive of class demarcations).

Finally, why is *Intruder in the Dust* such a safe book on matters of racial identity? Partly because of its Tom Sawyerish aura of security—we know right away that these kids are not going to get hurt, that Lucas is not going to be lynched; but also because Lucas is only superficially connected with the murder itself. He hap- pened to be strolling in the wrong place and to see something he shouldn't have seen. Faulkner goes on, implausibly, to have Craw- ford Gowrie seek to placate Lucas, as well as have Lucas easily

tricked by Crawford's wiles. (This Lucas is so ritualized—his
fetish objects so well known—that Crawford has no trouble strok-
ing his vanity and getting him to fire his 41 Colt at a stump from
fifteen feet distance, thus enabling the 41 Colt to become the
suspected murder weapon.) Perhaps the book's racial discourse is
safe, finally, because we know too surely that Lucas *couldn't* have
done the murder. Perversely, I would like to envisage a Lucas
at least capable of murder, one whose embroilment within the
racism of the South were reciprocal, unpredictable, threatening.
Faulkner will not imagine this possibility in *Intruder in the Dust*.
To glimpse what such a Lucas might have been, we must go
elsewhere, go backwards in Faulkner's career, and conceive a
shadowy tripartite figure composed of Joe Christmas, Rider, and
Samuel Worsham Beauchamp. Such a figure is monstrously unlike Lucas Beauchamp, but what is this to say but that Faulkner's
most disturbing portrayals of racial turmoil have no place in his
novel most explicitly dedicated to thinking through racial turmoil?

My focus here has not been on Faulkner's practice as it activates
the formal possibilities of the short story differently from those of
the novel. Yet the scripting of Lucas Beauchamp seems implicitly
to suggest something important about the writer's treatment of
race and the givens of his form. For Faulkner's genius is juxtapositional, repercussive. He rises into power as he broods upon and
revisits his materials, submits them to new perspectives, finds
in them hidden resources. Outrage—his thematic hallmark—
occurs in the encounter with the unexpected. In his best work
procedure and theme alike overturn expectation; they do so
through unpredictable juxtapositions. *The Sound and the Fury*,
As I Lay Dying, *Light in August*, *Absalom, Absalom!*, *The Hamlet*, and *Go Down, Moses* play off facet against facet, dance from
one subjective point of view to another, set into motion reading
upon reading of the same (but never the same) materials.

"Maybe nothing ever happens once," Faulkner wrote in *Ab-*

salom, Absalom! In turning over his materials he rescripts them, sees them as rescriptable—objects with no inherent meaning but rather capable of taking on new meanings when inserted within new signifying economies. It is not a question of choosing between the short story writer or the novelist: Faulkner becomes a supreme novelist because he is a short story writer as well. It is the revisiting that makes him Argus-eyed, for the repositioning of objects leads to the rethinking of subjects, to the discovery— among others—that racial identity is a matter more of discourse than of biology.

Intruder in the Dust, I would speculate, is a novel that has managed to forget its story origins and has sacrificed the play of juxtapositional possibilities to the insistence of a singular demonstration.[21] We know too clearly how we are meant to take both Lucas Beauchamp and the plot in which he is enmeshed; they come at us with pedagogic urgency. This novel's shrillness, like that of *A Fable,* resides in its knowing too much and its being locked into a single discourse of knowledge. Lucas Beauchamp emerges within such a discourse as mythic, impenetrable, and immovable object; Chick Mallison as a vulnerable and moving subject. Lucas's journey thus comes to an end.[22] A wily "nigger" in the magazine stories, sprung as free as he would ever be in *Go Down, Moses* (his freedom here calibrated in a lithe body and a mind whose surface is black but whose depth is McCaslin), he settles down in this last novel as an antique, a source of his white creator's nostalgic delight.

His final words are a request—"My receipt," he asks Gavin— he has liquidated his debt and wants to depart from his white benefactors, to return to his impregnable, unknowable state. The concept of the debt bristles beyond its immediate usage here, for indebtedness—the ledger-recorded purchase of black men and women as chattel, the payment for their abuse in the form of money but not love—resonates darkly throughout *Go Down, Moses.* But *Intruder in the Dust* prefers to imagine the debt the other way, to have Lucas laboriously count out his quarters, dimes, nickels, and pennies, get his receipt, and disappear into the unnarratable. Such a refusal to continue scripting racial culpability—a refusal wrought into this fantasy-image of debts cleared off, of ledgers audited and approved by both black and white— signals eloquently the weariness of the text. For that debt is of course still not liquidated—only it is we, not they, who owe it— but William Faulkner, for his part, had exhausted in this book his twenty-year attempt to imagine it and—in the revisionary freshness of his racial discourse—to do his part in paying it off.

NOTES

1. The standard account of the genesis of Go Down, Moses remains James Early's The Making of "Go Down, Moses" (Dallas, Texas: Southern Methodist University Press, 1972). Since then, Myra Jehlen (Class and Character in Faulkner's South [New York: Columbia University Press, 1976]), John Matthews (The Play of Faulkner's Language [Ithaca: Cornell University Press, 1982], James Snead (Figures of Division: William Faulkner's Major Novels [New York: Methuen, 1986]), and Michael Grimwood (Heart in Conflict: Faulkner's Struggles with Vocation [Athens: Georgia University Press, 1987]), have been especially informative about the interplay of stories making up this novel.

2. Paul Smith, Discerning the Subject (Minneapolis: University of Minnesota Press, 1988), xxviii.

3. The decentered self is a commonplace of recent theoretically informed criticism, and we are just now beginning to see a productive counterargument to such widely shared claims about the mystified subject. Paul Smith (xxxiii) usefully probes the idea of a subjectivity wholly scripted by its entry into a Symbolic field; he argues that agency— empowerment rather than paralysis—can occur through recognition of one's own subjectivity as a site of conflicting positions within more than one signifying economy.

4. Michel Foucault, "Nietzsche, Genealogy, History," in Language, Counter-Memory, Practice, ed. Donald F. Bouchard (Ithaca: Cornell University Press, 1977), 148.

5. Mikhail Bakhtin, "Discourse in the Novel," in The Dialogic Imagination, trans. Caryl Emerson and Michael Holquist (Austin: University of Texas Press, 1981), 341.

6. William Faulkner, "A Point of Law," Collier's 105 (June 1940): 20–21, 30–31; illustrations by William Meade Prince, 20, 21. Rpt. in Uncollected Stories of William Faulkner, ed. Joseph Blotner (New York: Random, 1981), 213–25. Citations in my essay (with page numbers entered parenthetically in the body proper of my text) refer to this edition.

7. William Faulkner, "Gold Is Not Always," Atlantic Monthly 166 (November 1940): 563–70. Rpt. in Uncollected Stories of William Faulkner, ed. Joseph Blotner (New York: Random, 1981), 226–37. Citations in my essay (with page numbers entered parenthetically in the body proper of my text) refer to this edition.

8. Among recent critics Grimwood provides the most thorough and provocative new reading of the stories as entities conceived at different times and conflicting radically in their stance towards matters of family and race—the two central concerns of Go Down, Moses.

9. William Faulkner, Go Down, Moses (New York: Random, 1942). Citations from this text (with page numbers entered parenthetically in the body proper of my text) refer to this edition.

10. Jehlen, 107.

11. The only challenge to this claim is Dilsey in *The Sound and the Fury*. I would argue, however, that the power of her portrait is suffused in racial "innocence," Faulkner's sense of her as separately blooded from his white Compsons and spared the turmoil (psychic and genealogical) that besets them.

12. As the mythic tenor of this passage suggests, *Go Down, Moses* makes the land itself numinous. The buried treasure of "Gold Is Not Always" emerges in revision within the economy of ancient Indian rituals. The "old Injun's mound" (where Lucas is now digging) marks a considerable departure from the originally unplaced shenanigans about a new-fangled treasure-finder.

13. Roth is no longer referred to as landlord because in *Go Down, Moses* he has been as it were disinherited. He is now seen as five generations removed from the original landowner, and on the distaff side as well. Faulkner repeatedly suggests that the land passes to Roth only because Ike could not rise to its responsibility.

14. Louis Althusser, "Ideology and Ideological State Apparatuses," in *Lenin and Philosophy, and Other Essays* (London: New Left Books, 1971), 174.

15. Henry Lewis Gates, "Writing 'Race' and the Difference It Makes," in *"Race," Writing and Difference*, ed. Henry Lewis Gates (Chicago: University of Chicago Press, 1986), 11.

16. Molly's emergence in chapter 3 of "The Fire and the Hearth" drives home this moral lesson. Touching Roth's heart as the only mother he ever knew, speaking to him (and us) with Biblical authority ("Because God say, 'What's rendered to My earth, it belong to Me unto I resurrect it. And let him or her touch it, and beware'"[102]), Molly is placed by Faulkner so as to articulate decisively—as mother, wife, and religious seer—the text's rebuke of Lucas's rebellious moves.

17. William Faulkner, *Intruder in the Dust* (New York: Random, 1948). Citations from this text (with page numbers entered parenthetically in the body proper of my essay) refer to this edition.

18. Bakhtin develops a major distinction between "authoritative discourse" and "internally persuasive discourse." Our journey as subjects from the former to the latter—from dicta that have been pressed upon us to those that we can internalize and make our own—is, precisely, our ideological maturation. Lucas undergoes no such linguistic trajectory. (See "Discourse in the Novel," 341–49.)

19. Jehlen comments aptly on the naturalized blacks working the fields, figures objectified and "invested with meaning only through the agency of a white observer" (132).

20. Representative commentary can be found in Edmund Wilson (*Classics and Commercials* [New York: Farrar, Strauss, 1950], 460–69), Cleanth Brooks (*William Faulkner: The Yoknapatawpha Country* [New Haven: Yale University Press, 1963], 420–21), Lee Jenkins (*Faulkner and Black-White Relationships* [New York: Columbia University Press, 1981], 272–74), and Walter Taylor (*Faulkner's Search for a South* [Urbana: University of Illinois Press, 1983], 145–65). More recently, Wesley and Barbara Morris (*Reading Faulkner* [Madison: University of Wisconsin Press, 1989], 222–38) have sought to resuscitate *Intruder in the Dust*'s reputation, arguing for it as a morally compelling piece of work.

21. "First, in order to take care of George Wilkins once and for all . . . " (33): this baffled urge to conclude that spawns the opening sentence of "The Fire and the Hearth" is comically explored through Lucas's unavailing plots and tragically worked out in Ike's unwanted autumnal discoveries. Grimwood and Morris both attend fruitfully to *Go Down, Moses*'s reverberations, its resistance to the male desire for willful closure. By the time of *Intruder in the Dust*, however, Faulkner seems unironically to take care of Lucas Beauchamp "once and for all."

22. Lucas was fated to appear one more time: a year later (1949), in another medium, Clarence Brown's film of *Intruder in the Dust*. This last representation arguably does him most credit. The film edits out the most disturbing elements of the novel—Gavin's sermonizing about Sambo and the South, the narrator's exacerbated sensorium and

consciousness—and renders a drama that is sober, surprisingly faithful to Faulkner's text, and moving. The emergent lines of action are simple, but this is one of Faulkner's novels in which the doings *are* simple. The film is quiet enough for us to hear the crickets now, and we *see* what the text itself scants: Lucas walking through the square, Lucas as a figure belonging to the community of Jefferson. Camera angles emphasize Lucas's dignity, showing him almost godlike as he looks down at Stevens and laconically demands his "receipt." In place of the feverish intensity that suffuses the narrative consciousness of the novel, we find a more "democratic" visual entry into all the principal figures in the story. Gavin (here called John) is so strenuously edited that Lucas's speeches—minimized in the verbal onslaught of the novel—take on finally their appropriate weight. It is a fitting last appearance.

Faulkner's Advice to a Young Writer

JOAN WILLIAMS

Joan Williams read her story "The Morning and the Evening" to the conference audience and then recalled the advice William Faulkner gave her when she was a young writer.

I met William Faulkner in 1949. Right away he read my first published story, in fact, the first story I'd ever written ["Rain Later," *Mademoiselle*, August 1949]. Afterwards, he wrote to me:

> I read the piece in Mlle. It's all right. You remember? 'to make something passionate and moving and true'? It is, moving and true, made me want to cry a little. . . . It's all right, moving and true; the force, the passion, the controlled heat, will come in time. Worry because it's—you think—slow; you've got to worry; that's part of it: the suffering and the working, most of all the working, the being willing and ready to sacrifice everything for it—happiness, peace, money, duty too if you are so unlucky. Only, quite often, if you are really willing to sacrifice any and everything for it, everything will not be required, demanded by the gods.

As a hopeful young writer reading these words, I remember feeling a little lost, lonesome, and at sea. What did force, passion, and controlled heat mean? How was I to recognize them when they came? Or recognize the fact if they never did come?

Letters would continue about writing. Faulkner said: "People need trouble, fret, a little of frustration, to sharpen the spirit on, toughen it. Artists do; I dont mean you have to live in a rathole or gutter, but they [artists] have to learn fortitude, endurance."

If he hadn't stayed in Mississippi would he have been a writer, I asked. "If I had lived in the New York Bowery," he replied, "I still would have written Faulkner. I mean by that, that what is worth it in Faulkner would have got itself written regardless. Of course, if I had been the Bowery bloke, I would not have been Faulkner."

In order to write, he told me, it was necessary to have "something burning your very entrails to be said . . . writing is important only when you want to do it, and nothing nothing nothing else but writing will suffice, give you peace."

Thirty-one years in age separated us but we had sprung from the same Southern middle class, the same part of the South. I grew up in Memphis, but the blue hills of North Mississippi were part of my family, my heritage, my life. The same earth was as innate to me as that which would eventually hold his fast and find him breath.

In all those intervening years—the difference between his age and mine—not much changed for young women of our background. Largely, you were supposed to act sweet, look pretty, and for the Lord's sake, get married! So that from the beginning, he warned me about what would be required for me to be a writer: "If you cannot resist the middleclass unaided, you do not have it in you to be a good artist." He thought I would "'save my soul' anyhow, unaided," but he wanted to save me "some of the lacerations and abrasions" he knew. "They didn't hurt me," he wrote. "And I never considered myself especially tough. They were no fun, but I was a better man than they were." "Art is a little stronger than any human passion for thwarting it," he contended. "Art takes care of its own. Takes care of those who are willing, capable of, fidelity to it above everything else."

Already, I've mentioned the two most important things Faulkner really taught me about writing: that it was work, and that I had to be able to resist the scorn of wanting to do something beyond vegetating. He really didn't talk much about technique. I don't know that he thought writing really could be taught. I know he did think that if I wanted to be a writer, being in college was a waste of time. He would have had me quit, except I was already in my last year.

By 1950 Faulkner conceived the idea I'd learn about writing by helping him to write *Requiem for a Nun*. But we must do it, he said, "for simple pleasure, ecstasy. Otherwise, it won't be worth the trouble anyway." He was not trying to compel me to write, he said, was not disappointed if I didn't, and insisted that I had not failed him. Yet, his belief that I would write was partly what drew him initially, he admitted, "or maybe it was vanity: Lucifer's own pride: I dont, refuse to, believe that I can take . . . a young woman . . . into my life (spirit) and not have her make something new under the sun whether she wills or not."

In an article published in the *Atlantic Monthly* ["Twenty Will Not Come Again," May 1980], I stated exactly how Faulkner helped with the story I read you. However, those who have written about him since persist in stating that every scrap of paper that passed between us, at the time, was revision after revision of my story "The Morning and the Evening." Had the story been mailed back and forth so much, I think it would have been in shreds back in that ancient time of carbon paper copies. The story "The Morning and the Evening" was almost as you heard it the first time Faulkner read it in the woods one afternoon and said, "This may be it."

All the things mailed back and forth between us were novice stories of mine that never got made right. One of them was about a child at a grownups' drunken New Year's Eve party. In trying to help it, Faulkner wrote: "A child's loneliness is not enough for a subject. The loneliness should be a catalyst, which does something to the rage of the universal passions of the human heart, the adult world, of which it—the child—is only an observer yet. You dont want to write just 'charming' things. Or at least I dont seem to intend to let you."

The immature stories continued, though finally he said:

You are learning. All you need is to agonise and sweat over it, never to be quite satisfied even when you know it is about as right as it can be humanly made, never to linger over it when done because you dont have time. You must hurry hurry hurry to write it again and better, the best this time. Not the same story over again, but Joan Williams, who has the capacity to suffer and anguish and would trade it for nothing under heaven. . . .

You know: something new, so that it was worth living through yesterday in order to reach today; and since you know you can, will find something new still, it will be worth living through today in order to reach tomorrow.

There was eventually the story which he would turn into the TV script "Graduation Dress." In December 1951, however, he wrote about the story itself: "it doesn't move. It's static. You can write about a lazy, inert character, but the character must be told in motion." After making suggestions about the plot, he continued:

> show all this in action, dialogue which carries action, tell the story from the OUTSIDE instead of the INSIDE. This is not an essay, remember.
>
> Start off by seeing if you can tell the story orally to me, for instance, in one sentence. Any good story can be told in one sentence, I mean, the line, the why of it. . . . A good rule of thumb before writing a short story is to be able to tell in one sentence what it is about. . . . You have got to write the first sentence of a story so that whoever reads it will want to read the second one.

Finally, the day came that I handed him the story about Jake. I don't remember what my own title was. But I have read in Michael Millgate that Faulkner's first thought was to name *The Sound and the Fury* "Twilight." Faulkner took my story home and wrote back from Oxford after a second reading:

> It's still all right. I cant find anything you could leave out. If you could break up the idiot section into shorter paragraphs, even at times a single sentence to a paragraph, it would help the effect: of his simple mental processes, his mental fumbling, his innocence. . . .
>
> I don't like the title. You are writing about a human being, true. But I think the title should refer to a *condition*, some applicable quotation, like a little child should lead them, though that is not quite right. Some word maybe, like Twilight, some tender word, or, for emphasis,

some savage word or phrase out of Hollywood motion picture slogans, about the educational or artistic value or the importance of motion pictures.

I had started my first sentence with "The owner-manager." Faulkner added, in parentheses, "(and ticket-seller and -taker and everything else too, with the exception of the licensed projectionist whom labor union regulations compelled him to hire)." When I asked the reason for the enclosure, he replied that it established right away the proprietor's character, in effect, in a nut shell. He wrote about the story itself: "It's all right, this time. I think you can stop worrying, and just write. The next one may not be this good, but dont let that trouble you either."

About himself, in 1952, he was saying: it's been "a long time now since I have anguished over putting words together, as though I had forgotten that form of anguishment." He thought probably that meant he was "storing up energy or whatever you want to call it, to start again. . . . To have written something once, which you dont need to hate afterward is like having cancer; you don't really ever get over it."

Faulkner gave my story its title saying the mute—Jake—did not know the difference between the morning and the evening. Through that story he believed I had made my choice between art and the middle class. "Jake freed you," he wrote.

> You cant be both, and being an artist is going to be hard on you as a member of the human race. You must expect scorn and horror and misunderstanding from the rest of the world who are not cursed with the necessity to make things new and passionate; no artist escapes it. You have got to say to yourself: Are Jake and Bill and what Bill and I have between us, which produced Jake and, continued, will produce still more beautiful Jakes, more or less important than the conventional approval of me by the mass of people who see nothing but ugliness and even obscenity in Jake's beauty.
>
> That's the choice you will have to make. If you choose Jake nothing can hurt you. It will not be important enough, no jealous husband nor wife nor public smear, anything.

I wrote him in August 1952 about analyzing the story, and he replied:

> that works with the hospital sort: not with Jake. You have to learn how to do ones like Jake from inside yourself, because JAKES are not commercial tricks, which is all anyone, Col[ege] or correspondence or anyone else, can teach from the *outside*. You have to feel Jake from inside, as you did. To write him properly, you must have not instruction nor criticism, but imagination, which you had to have to invent him, and observation and experience. Which you will get partly from reading the best which others have done, and from watching people, accepting everything. . . . accepting them, I mean, not as experiments, clinical, to see what it does to the mind, like with drugs or dead outside things, but because the heart and the body are big enough to accept all the world, all human agony and passion.

Previously, he thought, I had run from my heart and my body, back into my mind, "which is dead matter, nothing, since only the heart, the body, the nerves, are capable of feeling fire, anguish, passion, exultation, happiness, hope. . . . the mind is afraid of fire." He replied to another remark about writing: "No, the fury and the passion are enough. You have just not found them yet, they can't reach you yet because of the wall, the mind, which is afraid of fury and fire and hates them both."

His own big book [*A Fable*], he wrote in 1952, is "going well. I just need something, someone to write not *to* but *for.*"

"The Morning and the Evening" story was published in January 1953. And since then, people writing about Faulkner have assumed that everything we mailed back and forth to each other after that was the manuscript of my eventual first novel by the same title. That was not even once true. Always, what went back and forth were stories that never got off the ground.

One was about a plantation owner named Mr. Howard and a black man named Ottis. I was telling the story from Mr. Howard's point of view, Faulkner said, "but Howard cant keep on telling Doakes [the reader] what he is by repeating himself: he must tell Doakes what he is by letting Doakes see his actions and the

reactions of the other people . . . around him: even Ottis's character emerges from what other people say to Howard."

Faulkner wrote that maybe his comments were "overempha-
sized and burlesqued almost," and explained:

> But from this distance, I dont know how else to do it; I must write
> almost as many words explaining what I mean, as I would need to
> write the story itself, which would be much easier. And I hate to send
> the letter because I'm afraid [of its] result on you: will discourage or
> depress you, because we don't agree on what you have done. . . . You
> worked hard on this story. I know that. Where you didn't work hard
> enough was in using the time I was with you to learn from me the best
> point of view to approach a story from, to milk it dry. Not style: I dont
> want you to learn my style anymore than you want to, nor do I want to
> help you with criticism forever any more than you want me to. I just
> want you to learn, in the simplest and quickest way, to save yourself
> from the nervous wear and tear and emotional exhaustion of doing
> work that is not quite right, how to approach a story to tell it in the
> manner that will be closest to right that you can do.

"The first sentence of the story," Faulkner said "should tell
Doakes that something bad is going to happen. It should be such a
sentence that Doakes has got to read it, then read all the rest of
them, until he cannot put the story down until he finds out what
happened." This is a story about violence. Therefore, the dialogue
should be hard, explicit, bear down on it. Milk it dry. "A short
story," he said, "is a crystallised instant, arbitrarily selected, in
which character conflicts with character or environment or itself.
We both agreed long since, that next to poetry, it is the hardest art
form."

I returned the letter with many jottings. What about my first
sentence? Was it wrong? And how do you milk dialogue dry? This
letter was returned with a few jottings of his own beneath my
multitude of questions. He still worried, however, about his letter, and appended a note: "I may be completely wrong about the
story. . . . It may be that, with one who is himself a writer, since

his own work never quite is right, good enough, nobody else's can ever be."

Faulkner really never did talk about writing in person, and I didn't know enough to ask questions. As I related in my *Atlantic Monthly* article, I wanted to ask about his own work but didn't know what to ask about that either—and said so. And he thought that being in woods in silence was enough—watching together a butterfly brave enough to light on his hand.

When I worried about his influence, he said:

> I learned to write from other writers. Why should you refuse to? . . . The putting of a story down on paper, the telling it, is a craft. How else can a young carpenter learn to build a house, except by helping an experienced carpenter build one? . . .
>
> Have you already forgot what I always preached to you? Never be afraid. Never give one Goddamn about what anybody says about the work, if you know you have done it as honestly and bravely and truly as you could. Sure—some discerning person will holler Faulkner because there will be some Faulkner in it. Every writer is influenced by everything that ever touches him, from the telephone directory to God.
>
> I was in your life at an age which I think you will find was a very important experience, and of course it will show on you. But don't be afraid.
>
> There are worse people and experiences than me and ours to have influenced you. Don't be afraid. Do the work.

Having finished a section of his own work in 1953, he felt: "It's all right. It's good. Too good, for just one person to contain." He needed someone to be with him. To read it, so that it is as if *they* made it. "That's the answer, the reason for it all," he said, "the one and only way you can say No to death: the best, the strongest, the finest, the most enduring: to make something . . . that doesn't just 'move' you, but that will tear your living entrails."

Encouraging me to write a novel by then, he said *I* had worried for a while because *I* was not doing it. Now *it* was beginning to worry and nag me saying, "Come on, write me, make me. I want to stand up and breathe too. Which is as it should be. You're sunk," he said, "You might as well give up. There will be all sorts of pressures to try to make you be the other things first—put other things first before the writing. But you won't. You can't now. That comes first. After it, you will have everything."

When I wrote discouraged that same year, he continued:

> I believe I can give you the help you need, that a writer, a young one, must have. And I know I can give you the help you need, while you are young and new at it, until you don't need help from anyone, because I am an experienced and good writer myself. Because I believe in your honesty and integrity.
>
> It is harder now. You want to grow as a writer. You have passed the prize story of Bard 1949. You have challenged the big time now. Just to *want* to be a writer is not enough, not enough to just sit down and be, a sort of sacred vessel for the Gods to fill from the outside, no effort on your part, and just to sit while the good stuff flows out the ends of your fingers onto the paper. You have to *work* to learn, be willing to work, anguish, sacrifice: not just to want Joan Williams to be a good writer, but to want to get the stuff down, made, no matter whose name is on it.

Suddenly, in writing this piece for the conference, I was drawn to a bookcase in my room and took down a book I will confess I have not really read—and which was given to me by a friend. I remembered Faulkner said, "It helped me." But we never discussed Bergson's *Creative Evolution* further, though inside on the flyleaf I found he had written something I'd forgotten about:

> Don't work too hard at it
> But read it

The critic Cleanth Brooks has stated he feels uncertain about how much influence this book had on Faulkner, but at least we know he read it and was influenced.

I was surprised, too, in rereading the last letter from which I quoted, to think—after so many years—of the words Faulkner used in saying he believed I would be a writer—that he believed in my honesty and integrity.

Not the usual choice of words. Not that he believed in my talent, or ear for dialogue, or my ability to be disciplined.

That is why, I think, we are gathered in this room today with our love and our reverence, to honor Faulkner—the man and the writer—not for his talent alone, nor for his discipline, but for his integrity and his honesty.

Soviet Perceptions of Faulkner's Short Stories

WILLIAM FAULKNER'S SHORT STORIES IN THE USSR: AN INTRODUCTION

Sergei Chakovsky

The topic of this year's conference is of special interest to us for two major reasons. The first is cultural. The genre of the short story (first called novella or tale) has been a favorite in Russia ever since Washington Irving's "Rip Van Winkle" was published in 1825. Thanks to the pioneering work of Mark Twain, Bret Harte, O. Henry, Jack London, and, of course, Ernest Hemingway, the short story during the first decades of the twentieth century came to be regarded by our countrymen as something manifestly American—like jazz music or Model-T cars. The second reason we are especially interested in the conference is that not unlike the rest of the world the mainstay of Russian Faulkner scholarship has traditionally concerned his novels. This may seem peculiar, for unlike the rest of the world we first made acquaintance with Faulkner as a short story author.

Faulkner's introduction to the Soviet public was certainly auspicious. In 1934 an anthology, *American Short Stories of the Twentieth Century*, was published in Moscow under the editorship of A. Gavrilova, I. Kashkin, N. Eishiskina, and A. Elistratova—the best specialists of the day. "That Evening Sun," translated by O. P. Kholmskaya, was heralded by no lesser figures than Stephen Crane, Henry James, Ambrose Bierce, Jack London, O. Henry, Ring Lardner, Sherwood Anderson, and Ernest Hemingway. This alone, however, did not assure a brilliant reception for a newcomer to the Soviet literary scene.

To make a long story short, the Soviet literary establishment of the 1930s did not quite know what to do with Faulkner's stories and had a tough time trying to incorporate them into a rigid set of categories. He certainly was not as "progressive" as John Reed, Jack Conroy, or Michael Gold, who were also present in the anthology, but was he "formalistic," "decadent," or "bourgeois"? He knew and loved the way the "common folk" lived, he hated the imperialist war, and he obviously put his loyalty to the people he told about before his loyalty to the "form." He could hardly pose as James Joyce or Virginia Woolf or even the Faulkner of *The Sound and the Fury*, though, in his short stories.

Even his name was a minor puzzle. It was spelled one way throughout the 1934 volume and then changed in the editorial summary. The next year a third spelling was used when "Artist at Home" appeared in *Literaturnii Sovremennik (The Literary Contemporary)* magazine for 1935, translated expertly by Val. Stenich. The publication of "Victory" in the three-monthly review *Za Rubejom (Abroad)* for 1936 restored the first version of the author's given name, but improvised on his last name.

Granted, this confusion was hardly more typical of Faulkner's reception in Moscow than it was then in New York or even in Mississippi. The characteristic attitude then—not just about Faulkner, but about any author—was an obsessive need to place him or her within a particular ideological mold. The task was not just scholastic but practical, as well. Since literature could be a powerful social force, the idea was to make a writer "work" for a specific political goal. The 1936 publication of "Victory" is quite instructive in that respect.

Even in its abridged form (all of the first section was omitted, and the numbers were accordingly changed) the story occupied a very prominent place in the 25 July 1936 issue of the popular journal, taking up almost all of the first page and running into the median. The presentation of the story implied a message that was hard to miss. The titles of the supporting pieces in the journal were "German Fascism Is Getting Ready for War"; "The Fascist Threat to Danzig"; "The Soldiers' Letters" (a review of the unrest in the Western armies, of soldiers' protest against fascism). All of these made the subject matter of "Victory" as politically relevant as it could be, yet the publication would not have been just right without an optimistic note at the end. Hence the article "Positions of the Friends of Peace Gain Strength," which maintained, "The situation of 1936 is different from that of the August days of 1914. The peoples have become more educated in regard to the military threat." And then the ultimate verdict: "Positions of the friends of peace gain strength. . . . Their power lies in the fact . . . that in the whole world there is no people that would want war" (Stalin's words).

Despite all the decorum observed by politicizing Faulkner, the coeditor of *Za Rubejom*, Mikhail Koltzov, was executed by Stalin the following year as a German-French spy. He had been a great journalist, a hero of the Spanish civil war, and a friend of Garcia Lorca and Hemingway. I will not speculate on whether reprinting a story by a "decadent-fascist-pacifist" American au- thor featured as one of the counts in the indictment. It is just as absurd as it is possible. Yet the fact remains that "Victory" was the last Faulkner published for Soviet readers for almost twenty years.

The process of Faulkner's "rehabilitation" began under Khrus- chev's "thaw" when Elena Romanova's "The Antiwar Motifs in the Work of William Faulkner" was published by the *Foreign Liter- ature* magazine *(Inostrannaya literatura)* in 1955. We then began where we left off: a full version of "Victory" translated by M. Bo- goslovskaya appeared in the same publication in 1956. Two collec- tions came out shortly thereafter, both prepared by Ivan Kashkin: *Seven Short Stories* (Sem' Rasskazov, Moscow, 1958) and *Barn Burning* (Podzhigatel', Moscow, 1959). The contents of the books overlapped somewhat. The first contained "Barn Burning," "A Justice," "Red Leaves," "That Evening Sun," "Smoke," "Percy Grimm," and "Victory." The second forsook "Red Leaves," "Smoke," and "Victory" for two early pieces: "Sunset" and "Yo Ho and Two Bottles of Rum." As welcome as the collections were, they represented an editorial arbitrariness that was typical of the country in those precopyright days.

Faulkner was not consulted, of course, but he likely would not have authorized the arrangement of those books. Yet his compensation was to be given recognition as a major American author. "Taken as a whole," wrote Kashkin in the afterword to *Seven Short Stories*, "Faulkner's work is important as a literary-historical phenomenon and as a social fact." This recognition was still guarded and somewhat ambiguous. "Our reader," continued Kashkin, "has given his due to books as diverse and of different values as *The Sun Also Rises, A Farewell to Arms, Manhattan Transfer, The 42nd Parallel, The Grapes of Wrath, Georgia Boy*, yet so far he hasn't found among Faulkner's novels works of equal attraction and pertinency" (164–65). How could he, one might ask, if none of Faulkner's novels had been translated before 1961? Well, not to worry, Kashkin suggested. The short stories are better—or the Soviet reader will be better off with them—at least for the time being.

Like most Soviet critics up to fairly recent times, Kashkin was paradoxically making a case for Faulkner, waging a sort of rhetorical warfare to make the "defendant" look good. The time simply was not yet ripe for the novels.

"Social significance" remained the password, although translators often had a difficult time convincing their editors of Faulkner's social significance. It was an important argument to make, though, so that the editors could be armed with argument in case their superiors started asking questions. The overall effect was fortunate in that stories did get published from time to time. Unfortunately, they were usually presented as odd thematic pieces: *Ogonyok (A Small Flame)* in 1959 published "Sunset" to tweak Americans on the race issue during Vice President Nixon's visit to Moscow; *Vokrug Sveta (Around the World)* threw in some local color with "Rosary" in 1967 and "The Old People" in 1969; *Selskaya Molodezh (The Country Youth)* published "Hand Upon the Waters" in 1966 and "Two Soldiers" in 1972, stories that are, appropriately, set in the country and tell about youth. A yearly almanac *Okhotnichji Prostory (The Hunting Vistas)* would legitimately print "The Bear" in two installments in 1964 and 1965, but it was hardly fair to the reader to make him wait a year to read the second installment.

The thematic fallacy was all the more unfortunate, for Faulkner's short stories, however occasional some of them might seem, are essentially poetry. Only the best translators—R. Rait-Kovaljeva, V. Hinkis, A. Kistyakovsky, O. Soroka—were aware of this distinction.

I believe it was a sign of a coming breakthrough when the esteemed literary journal *Novii Mir* in 1975 offered a selection of previously untranslated Faulkner stories: "Shingles for the Lord" (trans. V. Golyshev), "Fox Hunt" (trans. Yu. Zhukova), "Uncle Willy" (trans. V. S. Muravjev), and "Honor" (trans. L. Bespalova). All the stories were incorporated into the first Russian edition of *Collected Stories* (Moscow, 1978), initiated and coedited by A. N. Nicolukin and brought to completion by Alexei Zverev. The publication of this fundamental scholarly edition produced by the Academy Press Nauka represented a significant cultural event—a milestone of sorts—in our perception of Faulkner, unveiling as it did "a heap of folks in a heap of situations" that were fresh and challenging to even the most devoted readers of his novels. The latest addition to the canon is the sixth volume *(Short Stories)* of Faulkner's *Collected Works* (Moscow, 1985–87), compiled by B. Gribanov, with a commentary by A. Dolinin (under the general editorial supervision of B. T. Gribanov, P. V. Palievsky, and A. N. Sakharov). Significantly, the grouping of the stories is chronological rather than thematic. It presents, although incompletely, the four books of short stories as Faulkner laboriously composed them. One can only hope that Faulkner's complete works will be published in Russian in the foreseeable future. No political obstacles exist any longer to prevent it—just economic ones.

FAULKNER'S SHORT STORIES IN RUSSIAN

Maya Koreneva

To speak of William Faulkner's short stories in translation into Russian is essentially to tell the story of the writer's introduction to the Russian reader. For many reasons, Faulkner the storyteller preceded by more than a quarter of a century Faulkner the novelist in Russian.

The first Faulkner work translated into Russian was his short story "That Evening Sun" from the collection *These Thirteen*. It was published in 1934 in an anthology, *American Short Stories of the Twentieth Century*, which, besides Faulkner's work, included stories by Stephen Crane, Henry James, Ambrose Bierce, Jack London, John Reed, Sherwood Anderson, Ernest Hemingway, Langston Hughes, Erskine Caldwell, and others. The next year brought a translation of another Faulkner short story, "Artist at Home" (*Literaturnyi Sovremennik*, 1935, #10). One more story, "Victory," was published in Russian in 1936 (*Za Rubejom*, 1936, #21) in an abridged form.

These three stories were all that was available to Russian readers for many years to come. The publication of Faulkner's work in the Soviet Union was interrupted in 1936 and renewed only two decades later. In the mid-1930s, with the growing tensions both in Europe and especially inside the Soviet Union, those who made Soviet literary policies accepted only the writers who shared their ideological bias. Faulkner obviously did not belong to them, so his name, like so many others, disappeared completely from Soviet publications.

The political Cold War that followed World War II aggravated the situation. The Cold War against American literature was proclaimed in 1948 in an article by V. Rubin, who chose William Faulkner and Eugene O'Neill as his main targets. *Intruder in the Dust* and *The Iceman Cometh* were denounced in that article as the embodiment of all the negative, decadent, perverted, and antihumanistic elements to be found in contemporary American literature.

A change was brought by liberalization during the "thaw" in the mid-1950s. Again it was the short story that was used to re-introduce Faulkner to the Russian reader. The same story that closed the short period of Faulkner's publication in Russian dur-ing the 1930s—"Victory"—was published this time in full in the newly founded magazine *Inostrannaya literatura* (1956, #1). The next year the same magazine published "Smoke" (1957, #12).

1958 marked a new phase in the progress of Faulkner's transla-tion into Russian. That year the first Faulkner publication in book form appeared, and once again it was a collection of short stories, entitled *Seven Short Stories (Sem' rasskazov;* Moscow: Izda-telstvo inostrannoy literatury, 1958). Among the stories included in the volume were several that were new to Russian readers— "Barn Burning," "Red Leaves," "A Justice," and "Percy Grimm."

Even at that time the editor of the book, a well-known trans-lator and critic who had done a lot for Hemingway's reputation in the USSR, Ivan Kashkin, felt it necessary to stress important differences between Faulkner's short stories and his novels. De-scribing the latter as "repulsive in subject, difficult from the point of view of form and language" (165), Kashkin concluded that "most of Faulkner's novels will probably stay in the history of literature as documents of the epoch of disintegration, while some of his best novels and especially short stories may survive his inor-dinately inflated reputation" (177).

Evidently Kashkin made these remarks to ensure the book's publication. Even though to some extent the remarks were just lip service and did not express the critic's views, the very necessity of such actions revealed the distance that needed to be overcome before a full understanding of Faulkner's art could be achieved.

Nevertheless, the strategy worked. More translations of Faulk-ner's short stories followed before *The Mansion*, the first of his novels to be translated into Russian, was published in 1961. In fact, every year brought publication of two of Faulkner's short stories in at least one literary magazine. An abridged version of "The Bear" appeared in 1962; two years later it was published in full form. By the mid-1960s most of the stories from *Big Woods* had been translated.

Though there were some excellent translations of Faulkner's short stories, not all of them were of high quality. At times the translator's poor knowledge of English was obvious. For instance, one translator turned "The Rosary" into "The Rose Garden." Inevitably the meaning of the story was completely lost by him and ultimately for the reader as well.

The next major event in this field was the publication in 1978 of Faulkner's *Collected Stories*, which contained many previously translated short stories presented in new versions. This edition was prepared by Nauka, the publishing house of the Academy of Sciences of the USSR. The edition helped to establish a higher standard of translation of Faulkner's short stories into Russian.

The six-volume edition of Faulkner's *Works* should also be mentioned (Moscow: Khudojestvennaya litreratura, 1985–87). Faulkner's artistry as a short story writer is adequately represented in it. The edition included the collection *Go Down, Moses* in its entirety (volume 3, 1986). *The Unvanquished*, whose genre is a mixture of the short story and the novel technique and which first appeared in Russian in 1976, was published in the same volume. The last volume of this edition, given over entirely to short stories, included those from *These Thirteen, Doctor Martino and Other Stories, Knight's Gambit,* and *Collected Stories.*

Now it can finally be said that the Russian reader who is especially interested in Faulkner's short stories has a good number of them at his disposal.

Soviet Criticism of Faulkner's Short Stories

Ekaterina Stetsenko

When Faulkner's first short story published in Russian appeared in *American Short Stories of the Twentieth Century,* this genre of American literature predominated in the USSR, and not simply because short fiction facilitated translation and publication. Condensed and dynamic in form, the short story epitomized the Russian image of America as an active and energetic country. More importantly, however, the short story presented a narrative with well-defined content, which made it easier for the authorities to choose what they considered suitable for the Soviet reader.

The novel, as a rule, is a complex production with many themes, motives, and points of view that often contradict each other and have no strict moral or ideological content. The novel was anathema to the USSR's politicized mentality of the 1930s, which demanded unanimity of thinking. Distinct and simple ideas were absolutely essential to achieve their political goals. The ideal short story chosen for translation had to underscore the horrors of capitalism, illustrate the difficult life of the working people, and be written in simple language and form. Writers who depicted the positive side of American life were denounced as reactionaries, deliberately exalting the American social system and promoting false optimism. The work of writers who abandoned realism was compared to the literature of decadence that reflected the decline of bourgeois culture. The official line represented the American short story as a continuum from the frontier short story of the "democratic" period to the formalistic and decadent short story of the age of declining imperialism.

In that context Faulkner's short stories served as illustrations of the "new tendencies" in American literature. In the introduction to the book containing the first Russian translation of Faulkner, N. Eishiskina describes the writer as a typical representative of the psychoanalytical school and calls his methods "bohemian radicalism," which in her opinion is nothing but "the expression of bourgeois decadent literature in its most refined form."[1] Faulkner was reproached for his overburdening of the "stream of consciousness" school with the motifs of the ugliness and senselessness of life. His style was characterized as "deliberate primitivism" and "the aesthetic tongue-tie." The "childishness" of his narration was attributed to his "special form of aestheticism, revealing a deep and at times strange helplessness of the author."[2]

The same mood permeated Al. Abramov's review, which appeared in the magazine *Inostrannaya kniga* in 1935 and was devoted to Faulkner's collection *Doctor Martino and Other Stories*. The reviewer represented the book as "one of the most striking symptoms of decay of bourgeois literature in general."[3] The critic appreciated the writer's talent but, for him, "Faulkner's giftedness only more sharply, more openly exposes the deadlock in which modern bourgeois art found itself, its ideological poverty, its spiritual bankruptcy, its creative sterility."[4] Abramov considered Faulkner's poetics to be evidence of the decline of American culture and the cynical mocking of all positive social values. He accused Faulkner of a disposition to pathology and a love for "decay, death, stink of a decomposing corpse."[5] He was obsessed with death and wrote about it with a kind of "unhealthy voluptuousness, which is some sort of a cemetery psychopathology." Faulkner's style was called "an absurd mystic delirium" in which the subconscious was hostile to reason and symbolized the helplessness of the writer's mind. Abramov could not deny Faulkner's fidelity to life and truthfulness of characters and circumstances, but he represented those gifts as tactics in a decadent text. For him, "Faulkner's realism was a literary method, an ornament for the self-satisfying play of situations, as if disclosing 'the inmost recesses' of the human soul."[6] The clarity of the writer's language was just "deliberate primitivism" and "infantilism."

Such notions about Faulkner's short stories survived for three decades, during which time his name was encountered in articles under titles like "The Literary Production of the Factory of Lies."[7] The first attempt to consider Faulkner objectively as a storyteller was undertaken by Ivan Kashkin, who wrote an introduction to a collection of seven Faulkner short stories in 1958. Kashkin tried to refute two myths about Faulkner: one, that he was an oracle and a writer of classic twentieth-century fiction, and the other as "the complex, unpleasant, and harmful modernist." "The truth," wrote Kashkin, "is somewhere in the middle."[8] Kashkin, in no way free of the cliches of vulgar sociological doctrines, was rather severe in his assessment of Faulkner, judging his work on the basis of principles of socialist realism—that is, class approach, social analysis, and obligatory optimism. Kashkin doubted whether Faulkner was justified in including himself in the pantheon of the best American writers—Thomas Wolfe, John Dos Passos, Ernest Hemingway, and John Steinbeck. According to Kashkin, it was very easy to explain Hemingway's popularity, for his themes are realistic and his style is clear. But it was very difficult to understand Faulkner's prestige. Faulkner's art was called "abstract," his books were described as "repulsive in theme and too complex in form and language," and his fame was considered "artificial," since it was only critics who seemed to appreciate him. For Kashkin, Faulkner's books were "documents of the epoch of disintegration," contrived and fashionable owing to their pervertedness and sadistic aura. Like his predecessors, Kashkin regarded Faulkner primarily as a historical and literary phenomenon. He ascribed Faulkner's fascination for the human soul to his unwillingness to analyze his society and to understand the forces that would ensure its progress.

Kashkin considered Faulkner's stories to be trite examples of detective and sporting narrative. Nevertheless, he was the first Soviet critic to analyze Faulkner's poetics. He wrote about Faulkner's role as storyteller, about pace and dynamics, about humor and lyricism, about skillfully drawn characters and intricate language. For the first time Faulkner was considered to be an original and gifted artist. That perspective became predominant in the succeeding decades as the political and cultural situation in the USSR changed dramatically.

By the 1960s and 1970s Faulkner was deemed a great writer who should be offered to the Soviet readership, but his writing could be made available only if the censorship that blocked the way to anything resembling modernism could be overcome. That helps to explain why many critics tried to emphasize the realistic side of Faulkner's work, striving to make him a critical realist and to some extent negating the strong modernist influence in his work. *The Modern American Short Story* by V. Oleneva[9] emphasized the depiction of the interdependence of man and his social environment in Faulkner's stories and devoted many pages to describing realistic plot construction. In the introduction to *American Novella of the Twentieth Century*[10] A. Mulyarchik called Faulkner an epic writer, optimistic and confident about mankind. In the course of several decades of Soviet criticism Faulkner was recast from a decadent, a pessimist, and a misanthrope to a realist, an optimist, and a philanthropist.

In the late 1970s and early 1980s the analysis of Faulkner's work became more objective. The critics acknowledged Faulkner's many-sided talent and appreciated the diversity of the traditions and trends he adopted. More and more of Faulkner's novels were translated, and more and more criticism was devoted to them, but the short stories were not neglected, since they were considered to be a fundamental part of Faulkner's work. A. Zverev, the author of the introduction to a volume of Faulkner's *Collected Short Stories*, performed the most detailed analysis of Faulkner's stories. The main theme of the article was the unity of Faulkner's work; the stories were "the strokes on the great canvas" of the Yoknapatawpha saga. That unity, Zverev believed, expressed the concepts of strong ties between man and humanity, past and present, and of the spiritual unity of personal existence and the world that pervades Faulkner's work. Zverev considered Faulkner's vision to be unique in a modern Western culture—and literature—obsessed with the problem of alienation. Zverev defined Faulkner's books as experimental prose that transcends mere verisimilitude and that cannot be described simply as realistic or formalistic. According to the critic, Faulkner's experimentation served "to stop the chaotic movement of life and, not taking away from its real complexity, to create an artistic harmony from the chaos of the everyday world and moral integrity out of disintegration. For Faulkner the aesthetic was never separated from the humanistic."[11] Faulkner's humanism was also emphasized by B. Gribanov, who titled his introduction to Faulkner's stories and novels "About Honor, Dignity, and Endurance of Man."[12] Faulkner exposed violence and evil in order to mitigate vice, Gribanov explained, and that made him the heir to civilization's democratic tradition.

Several dissertations have explored various aspects of Faulkner's stories. M. Danelia[13] wrote about the psychology of Faulkner's heroes, stressing their attitude towards history and time and analyzing Faulkner's character depiction. O. Tangyan[14] and N. Yakimenko[15] turned their attention to the interesting phenomenon of Faulkner's novels that were composed of stories and to the short story cycles. Thus, we have made a good beginning in appreciating Faulkner's short stories as well as his novels.

NOTES

1. *American Short Stories of the Twentieth Century* (Moscow, 1934), 7.
2. Ibid., 8.
3. *Inostrannaya kniga* (1935, #3), 17.
4. Ibid., 18.
5. Ibid., 17.
6. Ibid.
7. Zvezda (1949, #10).
8. W. Faulkner, *Sem rasskazov* (Moscow, 1958), 162.
9. V. I. Oleneva, *Sovremennaya amerikanskaya novella* (Kiev, 1973).
10. *Amerikanskaya novella XX veka* (Moscow, 1976).
11. W. Faulkner, *Sobranie rasskazov* (Moscow, 1977), 97.
12. W. Faulkner, *Rasskazy.* Medved'. Oskvernitel praha (Moscow, 1986).
13. M. S. Danelia, "Amerikanskaya psihologicheskaya novella XX veka" (Moscow, 1974).
14. O. Yu. Tangyan, "Novellistika W. Faulkner" (O soedinenii zhanrov rasskaza i romana) (Moscow, 1987).
15. N. L. Yakimenko, "Stanovlenie zhanrovih traditsiy 'romana v rasskazah' v amerikanskoy prose 10-40-h godov XX veka" (Moscow, 1989).

Between God and Satan: Vision of the Human Predicament in Short Stories by Faulkner and Russian Authors

Tatiana Morozova

William Faulkner's story "A Rose for Emily" has always been a favorite of critics. The obvious reason is that it represents Faulkner at his best. The other is that its ambiguous subject matter and latent symbolism provide critics with ample opportunities for exercising their wits and imagination. In this respect "A Rose for Emily" may be compared with "The Turn of the Screw" by Henry James, for his story, too, provoked a flood of controversial critical interpretations. There are several similar examples in Russian literature: "The Overcoat" by Gogol, "The First Love" by Turgenev, "The Lady with a Dog" by Chekhov, and such lengthy short stories as "The Notes from the Underground" by Dostoevsky and "The Death of Ivan Ilych" and "The Kreutzer Sonata" by Tolstoy.

"A Rose for Emily" has often been interpreted in sociological and historical terms. Thus, Malcolm Cowley suggested that in this story "Faulkner has found one of his most effective symbols for the decay of the old order"[1] in the South. Faulkner, however, was reluctant to admit that "A Rose for Emily" contained any symbolism at all or that it reflected the social conditions in the South. At the University of Virginia Faulkner said, "The writer is too busy trying to create flesh-and-blood people that will stand up and cast a shadow to have time to be conscious of all the symbolism . . . people may read into it."[2] Faulkner also disagreed with the suggestion that Miss Emily was meant to be a symbol for the South while her unfaithful lover Homer Barron, a Yankee, was meant as a symbol for the North, revenged upon by the South. Faulkner said: "It was a conflict not between the North and the South so much as between, well you might say, God and Satan."[3]

Faulkner's remark about the conflict between God and Satan

certainly applies not only to "A Rose for Emily" but has a much broader meaning; it reflects Faulkner's vision of man (or woman) as a person of double nature, of double citizenship, so to speak: he (or she) is a subject of God as well as a subject of Satan, and the conflict between the two creates the essence of human life. The invisible conflict between God and Satan lies at the core of all visible conflicts: social, political, national, personal, and so on. Those authors who write only about the visible conflicts and ignore the invisible ones appear to be superficial; they never attain a status of genius. Faulkner is a much deeper writer than Hemingway precisely because, though both of them were equally gifted artists and craftsmen, they were unequally equipped with the knowledge of human nature and the human predicament.

In Russian literature we have a similar pair: Dostoevsky and Turgenev. Both Hemingway and Turgenev enjoyed greater fame than their rivals during their lifetime, but were overshadowed later when the deeper meaning of Dostoevsky's and Faulkner's works came to be appreciated. By the way, Faulkner's utterance concerning the conflict between God and Satan almost literally corresponds to the famous dictum in *The Brothers Karamazov:* "Here the Devil is fighting with God, and the battlefield is the heart of man." You may dig up all of Turgenev and all of Hemingway, but you'll never find any such statement in their works. They brilliantly depicted the outward manifestations of the conflict but did not give much thought to the investigation of its origin.

This difference between Turgenev and Hemingway on the one hand and Dostoevsky and Faulkner on the other also explains why the former were liberals while the latter were conservatives. Liberals as the heirs of the Enlightenment believe in man's essential goodness and think all the evidences to the contrary to be the result of inadequate social and political conditions. Such a belief can produce good art but it cannot produce great art. Great art is produced by those who perceive that the social order is shaped by man, not vice versa, that the political systems may change but the essential qualities of human nature remain through centuries, modified only externally.

One of the most powerful stories by Faulkner is "Red Leaves," and the secret of its power is that fundamental vision of human nature that draws no distinction between the Indian, the Negro, the Frenchman where certain human essentials are concerned. Faulkner significantly names the Indian chief Doom. On the one hand Doom means "fate"; on the other it is a distorted version of the French word *l'homme* or *de l'homme* (man). From this one may conclude that the doom of man is man himself. Unfortunately, this semantic trick is lost upon a Russian reader in translation.

But the main idea of the story is not lost upon a Russian reader. In fact, a contemporary Russian reader feels it perhaps more acutely than an American one. I suppose that the main idea is again the conflict between God and Satan in the heart of man. It is a clash between love of liberty and lust for power. Both feelings are instinctive and equally inherent to any human being. They came into existence with man, and will be extinguished when man is extinguished. The primeval life, primitive man, and primitive culture are not either idealized or condemned by Faulkner as they had been by the generations of writers since Rousseau. In "Red Leaves" Indians simply don't differ much from the "civilized" people. Their social structure, though not as elaborate and refined as that of the whites, is shaped by the same elemental human drives.

No wonder Doom became friends in New Orleans with a Frenchman, the Chevalier Soeur Blonde de Vitry. Faulkner writes, "They were seen everywhere together—the Indian . . . and the Parisian." A strange couple? Not at all. They became close friends because both had a third close friend—Satan. The great brotherhood of Satan, according to Faulkner, may include anybody, irrespective of race, color, sex, class, intellect, or education.

Lust for power may manifest itself differently in different cultures and societies, but it is as universal as any other human instinct. It works in monarchies and democracies alike, though in different ways and with different consequences. It works in primitive societies as well, and Faulkner shows both the comic and the tragic sides of it. Doom and his son Moketubbe regard as a symbol of power a very curious object, a pair of slippers with red heels that Doom took home from Paris. This symbol seems comical but after all it is no more comical than the crown of any European king. The struggle for the right to wear slippers with red heels is no less fierce and merciless than the struggle for the right to wear a crown. The son poisons his father in order to replace him as a ruler, a situation that is absolutely identical whether it takes place in a king's palace or in a lodging of an Indian chief. The tradition of the struggle for power has been adopted by the rulers of totalitarian states. The triumph of democracies makes the lust for power less evident, but it still remains. The assassinations of presidents and politicians, scandals like Watergate—disclosed and undisclosed—show that Satan is active and that people should be on their guards not to let him win his old battle with God.

The conflict between God and Satan is a predominant theme of Russian literature. In the novels this conflict may be disguised by the social and political forms it takes, but in the short stories the essence of the clash is more transparent if only because the narrative space of the short story is limited, making long historical and social analyses impossible.

There was no problem of happy endings in our literature as distinct from the situation in English and American literature in the nineteenth century. Russian authors usually avoided happy endings. With many American authors the happy ending was predominant. Later, the situation in American literature changed. Faulkner, among others, did away with the tradition of the happy ending. Faulkner is as tragic an author as Dostoevsky because both were aware of the power of Satan while believing in the eternal truth of God.

NOTES

1. Malcolm Cowley, ed., *The Portable Faulkner* (New York: Viking, 1967), 390.

2. *Faulkner in the University*, ed. Frederick L. Gwynn and Joseph L. Blotner (Charlottesville: University Press of Virginia, 1959), 47.

3. Ibid., 58.

FAULKNER AND THE UKRAINE

Tamara Denisova

"Who remembers Ukrainians?" the hero of Walker Percy's *Thanatos Syndrome* asks, meaning that these people had vanished as a nation—as an economic, political, and cultural phenomenon—from the world human community. But I have come to you from the Ukraine and can testify that the Ukrainian people are alive and highly active, that we are part and parcel of world history, and, like every living and developing, progressing and seeking community, we are open to other cultures and peoples. Regaining our own historical consciousness, we are trying to assimilate the experience of all mankind and accept other peoples' methods. For us, American culture occupies a great place in the process of recovering our own heritage. As it turned out historically—or politically—the only phenomenon of the American way of life popularized widely in the Ukraine during, say, the previous thirty years has been classical and modern literature. For many reasons, the most important of which being its high artistic merits, Southern literature has been a very large portion of the American literature that has reached Ukrainian readers.

At first, educated Ukrainian readers were exposed to foreign literature by means of Russian translations issued in the USSR. But, as the general cultural standard of our people increases and as our creative intelligentsia comes to maturity, Ukrainian translations have come to the fore.

For that reason the generation of the 1960s, which includes Ukrainian writers who began their literary activities during the period of the "thaw"—Dratch, Gutzalo, Shevchuk, Scherbak, L. Kostenko, Vingranovsky, and others—take a keen interest not only in folk sources, historical roots, and national originality, but in international culture as well. The achievements of the culture are being imbibed by them and are becoming an organic part of their own creative work. That is why we cannot and do not need to speak about borrowings from other literature, but it is easy to find the influence of modern literature and cultural tendencies— including Faulkner's influence—on these writers' poetry and prose. For example, deepening psychological characteristics, inseparable from stream of consciousness forms, penetrated into Ukrainian literature through William Faulkner rather than through James Joyce, whose translations came to us later than Faulkner's.

The furthering of intellectual development has affected both translators and readers, so that beginning with the 1960s the quality of Ukrainian translations has been constantly improving, expressing the growing interest of the reading public in foreign literature and in American literature in particular. Nowadays not only the so-called traditional writers, such as Mark Twain and Jack London, are published, but new names and books have emerged. Among them are many Southern writers: Thomas Wolfe, Eudora Welty, Erskine Caldwell, Truman Capote, Robert Penn Warren, Harper Lee, Carson McCullers, and, of course, William Faulkner. Faulkner's works are so important, in fact, that they have been recommended for study not only in specialized college departments but in Ukrainian grammar schools as well.

The Ukraine has been the South of the Soviet Union. It is a large and very special country with its own history. Its century-old existence as a colony, when it was in fact divided between Russia, Austro-Hungary, and Poland, was not a bright period of its history. That is why our people are very much aware of the problems of the South—a region that suffered defeat in the Civil War and its aftermath.

Let me give you an example. The Ukraine has been fortunate to have avoided racial discrimination and all the problems connected with racism. But it has come through serfdom, which has its own demoralizing humiliation. Since the days of Shevchenko—a great Ukrainian artist, thinker, poet—the Ukrainian vocabulary has been enriched with the word *pokrytka*, which means a peasant girl who has given birth to a child of her lord, master, landowner.

Such a situation was considered the deepest disgrace, a moral degradation, a deadly sin. It helps us to understand the Southern tragedy of miscegenation, even though we cannot identify with the specifics of it.

The Ukraine was a peasant country in which man and the land—man and nature—have been almost inseparably linked. This typically Ukrainian motif helps us to understand Faulkner. Our literature has always been a literature about the land, about a complex correlation between man and the land, and about the power of land over man. That is the central motif of Ukrainian classical prose of such writers as P. Mirny, Netchuy-Levitzky, O. Kobylyanska, V. Stefanik, M. Kotzubinsky, early Vinnichenko, and with such modern writers as A. Golovko, Senchenko, Gutzalo, and Zemlyak.

To a certain extent, even Faulkner's poetics are not absolutely alien to Ukrainian prose, which is characterized by romantic traditions and is closely associated with folk humor. Faulkner's syntax and the complicated constructions of his phrases with their innumerable coordinations and subordinations are close to the structure of the Slavic languages and of Ukrainian in particular. Faulkner's work is close to us through its symbols based on the Bible, on Christian ethics, and on agrarianism. It is close to us only to a limited extent, though, because Ukrainian literature is based mainly on classical realistic tradition with its priority of description over dramatic tension and its tendency toward reconstructing causative-consecutive relations and temporal succession that organize an external plot. The latter is based on psychologically true and logically convincing characters. The romanticism of Ukrainian literature is expressed mainly in its lyricism and in the softening and smoothing of depicted reality. In so brief an introduction it is impossible to describe completely Ukrainian literature, especially in comparison with Faulkner's works, but I hope to have suggested their correlations in some points, at least.

In recent years some Ukrainian critics have produced scholarly works on Faulkner. A deep penetration into Faulkner's prose has provided a basis for one of the integral concepts of the modern novel, especially as formulated by D. Zatonsky. As for me, I began learning about American literature with a study of Faulkner's novels in the context of twentieth-century prose. American short stories, and Faulkner's in particular, have been the subject of a special investigation carried out by V. Oleneva.

Ukrainian translations of Faulkner should also be noted. The first Ukrainian collection of works by Faulkner was *"The Reivers" and Other Stories* (Dnipro Publishing House, 1972). I wrote the preface to this volume, which contains several works—"Old Man," "Knight's Gambit," and *The Reivers*—previously published in *Vsesvit*, the Ukrainian magazine for foreign literature. D. Zatonsky wrote the introduction to *Red Leaves* (1974), a volume that contains fourteen of Faulkner's best stories from different collections. In 1983 Molod, a publishing house for young people, issued *Go Down, Moses* under the title *At Home*, because we could not then use Biblical expressions. Some years later *Vsesvit* magazine published a translation of *As I Lay Dying*. Up to now, that is all that has been translated into Ukrainian. In general, these versions of Faulkner's works are distinguished by their high quality.

Currently, Dnipro Publishing House is planning to issue two volumes of Faulkner's works, and we plan to have his best novels—*The Sound and the Fury* and *Absalom, Absalom!*—translated for this purpose. It is our hope that they will serve as the basis for a future Ukrainian version of the complete collection of William Faulkner's works.

Contributors

Robert H. Brinkmeyer, Jr., is professor of American literature and Southern Studies at the University of Mississippi. He is the author of *Three Catholic Writers of the Modern South* (1985), *The Art and Vision of Flannery O'Connor* (1989), and a forthcoming book on Katherine Anne Porter. His other publications include numerous book reviews and more than a dozen scholarly articles, some of which have been reprinted in *Walker Percy: Art and Ethics* (1980), *Critical Essays on Erskine Caldwell* (1982), and other collections.

James B. Carothers, professor of English at the University of Kansas, is a member of the editorial board of the *Faulkner Journal*. He is the author of *William Faulkner's Short Stories* (1984) and several essays, among them "The Road to *The Reivers*," "The Myriad Heart: The Evolution of the Faulkner Hero," and "Faulkner's Short Stories: 'And Now What's to Do.'"

Sergei Chakovsky, a research fellow at the A. M. Gorky Institute of World Literature in Moscow, specializes in Faulkner studies as well as literary theory and the depiction of blacks in American literature. As part of a joint USA-USSR project on William Faulkner, he has lectured at six Faulkner and Yoknapatawpha Conferences and presented a paper at a Faulkner symposium held in Moscow. His publications include "William Faulkner" in Soviet Literary Criticism," "Word and Idea in *The Sound and the Fury*," and "Lucas Beauchamp and Jim: Mark Twain's Influence on William Faulkner."

Carvel Collins (14 June 1912-10 April 1990) was one of the first scholars to recognize William Faulkner as a major American writer. In the 1940s, while a member of the faculty at Harvard University, he taught the first seminar devoted entirely to Faulkner. Later, at Massachusetts Institute of Technology, at the University of Notre Dame, and at several institutions where he was visiting professor, Carvel Collins continued to teach Faulkner, to write about his work, and to compile material for a critical biography of the author. Although he left the biography unfinished, Carvel Collins published many scholarly articles about Faulkner's life and work and edited a number of his books. These include *New Orleans Sketches* (1958), *The Unvanquished* (1959), *William Faulkner: Early Prose and Poetry* (1962), *Mayday* (1976), and *Helen: A Courtship* (1981).

Tamara Denisova lives in Kiev, where she is a research fellow at the T. H. Shevchenko Institute of the Academy of Sciences of the Ukranian Soviet Socialist Republic. She is the author of *On the Road to Man: The Struggle of Realism and Modernism in the Contemporary American Novel* (1971), *Ernest Hemingway* (1972), *Jack London* (1977), *Existentialism and the Modern American Novel* (1985), and three other books and numerous essays.

Susan V. Donaldson has published articles and presented papers on many Southern literary and visual artists and is working on a book-length study entitled "Reluctant Visionaries and Southern Others: Writers and Painters in the Modern South." She is also writing a book on Eudora Welty. Among her publications on William Faulkner are "Subverting History: Women, Narrative, and Patriarchy in *Absalom, Absalom!*," "Isaac McCaslin and the Possibilities of Vision," and "Dismantling the *Saturday Evening Post* Reader: *The Unvanquished* and Changing 'Horizons of Expectations.'" She is associate professor of English at the College of William and Mary.

John T. Irwin is the author of *Doubling and Incest/Repetition and Revenge: A Speculative Reading of Faulkner* (1975), which has been described as "an epoch-making book," "a brilliant overview of Faulkner's work," "a classic in Faulkner studies," "one of the most complex, stimulating, and potentially controversial books in the whole range of Faulkner criticism." Among his other publications are *American Hieroglyphics* (1980) and *The Heisenberg*

Variations (1976), a volume of poems. He is professor and chair of the writing seminars at Johns Hopkins University and general editor of the Johns Hopkins University Press series in poetry and short fiction.

Maya Koreneva studied at Moscow State University and at the Gorky Institute of World Literature, where she has been a staff member since 1965. She is the author of "American Drama," "American Literature in the Eighteenth Century," "Spiritual Crisis in Contemporary Society and in American Literature," and numerous other articles. American authors about whom she has written range from Hawthorne and Henry Adams to Denise Levertov and William Styron. A 50,000-copy edition of her translation of Faulkner's *The Unvanquished* sold out in the Soviet Union in a matter of days.

John T. Matthews teaches at Boston University and is editor of the *Faulkner Journal*. Among his works on Faulkner are *The Play of Faulkner's Language* (1982), *"The Sound and the Fury": Faulkner and the Lost Cause* (1991), and essays in scholarly journals and such collections as *Intertextuality in Faulkner* (1985), *Faulkner and History* (1986), and *Faulkner's Discourse* (1989). At the 1987 Faulkner and Yoknapatawpha Conference he presented a lecture on "Faulkner's Narrative Frames."

David Minter, recently appointed Libbie Shearn Moody Professor of English at Rice University, formerly taught and held administrative posts at Emory University. He is the author of *William Faulkner: His Life and Work* (1980), a literary biography that explores "the reciprocities between Faulkner's great art and his flawed life." Among his other publications are *The Interpreted Design as a Structural Principle in American Prose* (1969), *Twentieth-Century Interpretations of "Light in August"* (1970), essays in *Faulkner and the Southern Renaissance* (1982), and *The Norton Critical Edition of "The Sound and the Fury"* (1987).

Tatiana Morosova studied at Moscow State University and at the Gorky Institute of World Literature, where she has been a fellow since 1974. Her many publications include "James and

Turgenev," "Tolstoy and Faulkner," "Faulkner Reads Dostoevsky," "Expatriation: The Essence and Modifications," "Nineteenth-Century American Literature: The Major Trends," "The Artistic World of Henry James," "Emerson's Concept of Self-Reliance and American Individualism," and "The Literature of Modernism."

Hans H. Skei chairs the Department of Comparative Literature at the University of Oslo and edits *NLA*, an annual of Norwegian literary scholarship. He is the author of *William Faulkner: The Short Story Career* (1981; reprinted 1984), *William Faulkner: The Novelist as Short Story Writer* (1985), "Inadequacies of Style in Some of William Faulkner's Short Stories," and other publications. He was a visiting scholar at the University of South Carolina in 1976–77 and has participated in Faulkner meetings held in Tokyo (1985), Bonn (1987), and Rome (1989).

Ekaterina Stetsenko is a researcher at the A. M. Gorky Institute of World Literature. At a symposium on "William Faulkner and the American South" held in Moscow in 1984 she presented a paper on "Time in Faulkner" and has participated in other programs sponsored by the Gorky Institute and the Center for the Study of Southern Culture. Among her many publications are *The Problems of Artistic Time in the Southern School of the Modern American Novel* (1978), essays on Thomas Jefferson and Thomas Paine in *The Sources and Formation of American National Literature* (1985), three essays in *Mark Twain and His Role in the Development of American Realistic Literature* (1987), and a detailed study of William Styron's *Sophie's Choice in Social Content and Its Aesthetic Realization* (1988).

Tao Jie is professor of English and deputy director of the American Studies Center at Peking University. She edited *The Portable Faulkner for Chinese Readers* (1990), has translated works of Faulkner and other American authors into Chinese, and is the author of numerous scholarly articles including "Faulkner's Humor and Some Chinese Writers," "New Trends in American Literature," "Popular Literature in the United States," and "The Difficulties in Compiling a New American Literary History."

Among her translations are Robert Penn Warren's *All the King's Men* (1986), Alice Walker's *The Color Purple* (1986), and three collaborative works—*Critical Essays on William Faulkner* (1980), *Selected Stories by William Faulkner* (1985), and *"As I Lay Dying" and Others* (1990).

Philip M. Weinstein has been a member of the faculty at Swarthmore College since 1971 and served as chair of English Literature from 1980 until 1985. In the fall of 1987 he was Visiting Distinguished Professor at Rhodes College. His publications include *Henry James and the Requirements of the Imagination* (1971), *The Semantics of Desire: Changing Modes of Identity* (1984), and a number of essays on Faulkner and other authors. His most recent book—*Faulkner's Subject: A Cosmos No One Owns*—has been supported by grants from the National Endowment for the Humanities and the American Council of Learned Societies.

Joan Williams has published short fiction in numerous magazines, the collection *Pariah and Other Stories* (1983), and five novels—*The Morning and the Evening* (1961), *Old Powder Man* (1966), *The Wintering* (1972), *County Woman* (1982), and *Pay the Piper* (1988). For her writing she has received the John P. Marquand First Novel Award from the Book-of-the-Month Club, a grant from the National Institute of Arts and Letters, and a Guggenheim Fellowship.

Index

Absalom, Absalom! (Faulkner), 81, 98–99, 101, 185, 187, 211, 285; prostitution in, 52; contradiction in, 79–80; community in, and the story "Wash," 96–97, 100; elements in, 125; father-son analogy in, 160; style in, 193; subjective point of view in, 248
"Ad Astra" (Faulkner), 47–48, 108–27, 189
"All the Dead Pilots" (Faulkner), 69, 125, 189
"Ambuscade" (Faulkner), 3
American Mercury, 3, 8
Armstid, Henry, 21–23
"Artist at Home" (Faulkner), 269
As I Lay Dying (Faulkner), 4, 6, 34, 81, 125, 181, 182, 190, 248, 285

"Barn Burning" (Faulkner), 5, 69, 183, 189, 265, 266, 270
"Bear, The" (Faulkner), 5, 136–37, 142–43, 145, 146; style in, 138–39; southern history in, 141; reviewed in China, 185; published in China, 189, 191; published in Russia, 271
"Bear Hunt, A" (Faulkner), 189
Beauchamp, Lucas, 229–52
Big Sleep, The (Chandler), 162–63, 168–69
Big Woods (Faulkner), 271

"Carcassonne" (Faulkner), 74–75, 84, 88–91, 92, 189
"Centaur in Brass" (Faulkner), 26–29, 191
Chandler, Raymond, 162–63
China, Faulkner's work in, 174–205
Christian ascetics, 207–08, 209, 213, 214–15

Collected Short Stories (Faulkner), 275
Collected Stories (Faulkner), 267, 271
Collected Works of William Faulkner, 179, 267, 271
Cooper, Minnie, 23–25
"Crevasse" (Faulkner), 125

"Delta Autumn" (Faulkner), 130, 145, 146, 147, 190, 191, 218, 219
Dilsey, 188
Doctor Martino and Other Stories (Faulkner), 271, 273
Doom, 20
"Dry September" (Faulkner), 5, 23, 25, 48, 49, 50, 84, 183, 191, 195
Du Pre, Aunt Virginia, 13, 14, 15

"Elly" (Faulkner), 49
Elnora, 14, 15
"Error in Chemistry, An" (Faulkner), 149, 151, 152–53, 158
Existential experience, in Faulkner's short stories, 62–77

Fable, A (Faulkner), 52, 117, 119, 121, 124, 125, 180, 185
Fathers, Sam, 140, 211, 212, 213
Faulkner, Estelle Oldham, 112, 115
Faulkner, William: and mass market magazines, 3, 38; and the occasion and purpose of art, 81–83; as a poet, 84, 86–87; influences on, 85; war fiction of, 108–27; in New Haven, 112–13; works of, in China, 174–205; advice to a young writer, 253–62; works of, in Russia, 263–81; works of, in Ukraine, 282–85
"Fire and the Hearth, The"

(Faulkner), 137–38, 139, 142, 224, 225, 231, 235, 238, 239, 240, 242
Flags in the Dust (Faulkner), 9, 98, 111, 122
Flint, Joel, 151–55
"Fox Hunt" (Faulkner), 267

Go Down, Moses (Faulkner), 78, 81, 121, 191, 229–48; elements in, 125; and the short story cycle, 128–48; renunciation of the world in, 206–28; published in Russia, 271; published in Ukraine, 285
"Golden Land" (Faulkner), 69
"Gold Is Not Always" (Faulkner), 233, 235

"Hair" (Faulkner), 48–50, 52
Hamlet, The (Faulkner), 54, 248
"Hill, The" (Faulkner), 69, 70, 84
Hitler, Adolf, 220–24
"Honor" (Faulkner), 122, 267
Hunting, 212–13

Indians, 19–21
Intruder in the Dust (Faulkner), 229, 237, 243, 244, 245, 247, 248, 249, 269

"Justice, A" (Faulkner), 69, 74, 189, 193, 266, 270

Kashkin, Ivan, 265, 266, 274
Knight's Gambit (Faulkner), 149–73, 271, 285

Light in August (Faulkner), 52–53, 81, 186, 187, 191, 194, 195, 248
Lilacs, The (Faulkner), 122
"Lion" (Faulkner), 130
Li Wenjun, 179, 180, 184, 185, 186, 188, 190, 191, 194, 199
"Lizards in Jamshyd's Courtyard" (Faulkner), 21
"Love" (Faulkner), 120

McCaslin, L. Q. C., 134–35
McCaslin, Isaac, 206, 207, 209–11, 214, 216–22

Mannie, 29–33
Mansion, The (Faulkner), 40, 41, 57, 58, 181, 270
Marionettes, The (Faulkner), 84
Mass market magazines, Faulkner's view of, 3, 38
Mayday (Faulkner), 84
Memory, and William Faulkner, 99
"Mistral" (Faulkner), 74
"Miss Zilphia Gant" (Faulkner), 49
"Mountain Victory" (Faulkner), 71–74
"Mule in the Yard" (Faulkner), 29–33, 34
"My Grandmother Millard" (Faulkner), 189

Narrative, 133, 136, 141–42
Nobel Prize Acceptance Speech (Faulkner), 183, 189, 191
"Nympholepsy" (Faulkner), 84, 87–88, 92

"Old Man, The" (Faulkner), 185, 189, 285
"Old People, The" (Faulkner), 130, 140, 146, 210, 267
"On Sherwood Anderson" (Faulkner), 190, 191

"Pantaloon in Black" (Faulkner), 128, 130, 143, 145, 146, 189, 224, 226
"Percy Grimm" (Faulkner), 191, 266, 270
"Peter" (Faulkner), 44–47, 48
"Point of Law, A" (Faulkner), 130, 232, 233, 238
Portable Faulkner, The, 179, 183, 191
Prostitution, 38, 39, 41–47
Pylon (Faulkner), 51

"Raid" (Faulkner), 3
"Red Leaves" (Faulkner), 6, 7, 19, 69, 189, 191, 266, 270, 279, 285
Reivers, The (Faulkner), 48, 52
Requiem for a Nun (Faulkner), 42, 52
"Rosary" (Faulkner), 267, 271
"Rose for Emily, A" (Faulkner), 5, 49, 84, 183, 189, 191, 195, 277
Russia, Faulkner's work in, 263–81

Sanctuary (Faulkner), 4, 6, 11, 40, 41, 48, 52, 177
Sartoris, Narcissa Benbow, 11–13
Sartoris (Faulkner), 6, 78, 187
Saturday Evening Post, 3, 4, 6, 8, 9, 19, 119, 130
Scribner's, 3, 7, 8, 17, 23
Selected Stories of William Faulkner, 190
Seven Short Stories (Faulkner), 265, 270
"Shall Not Perish" (Faulkner), 69, 189, 190
"Shingles for the Lord" (Faulkner), 189, 267
Short Stories, Faulkner's view of, 38, 48, 59, 60
Short story cycle, 131–32
"Smoke" (Faulkner), 266, 270
Snopes, Flem, 26–28
Snopes, I. O., 29–33
Soldiers' Pay (Faulkner), 124
Sound and the Fury, The (Faulkner), 78, 184, 185, 194, 196, 197, 199, 200, 248, 264, 285; new introduction to, 6; fragmentary nature of, 34; elements in, 42; and the sexual double standard, 52; story versions in, 81; fictional officer in, 114; father-son analogy in, 160; stream-of-consciousness in, 181–82; published in China, 188, 189, 190
"Spotted Horses" (Faulkner), 5, 16–17, 18–19, 189, 191
Stevens, Gavin, 160–61, 163–64, 165–66, 167, 169, 171, 225–26
"Sunset" (Faulkner), 266

"Tall Men, The" (Faulkner), 69, 189, 191
"That Evening Sun" (Faulkner), 5, 41–42, 69, 189, 191, 263, 266, 269
"There Was a Queen" (Faulkner), 11–13, 15, 69
These Thirteen (Faulkner), 269, 271
Town, The (Faulkner), 48, 55–57, 164, 181, 191
"Turnabout" (Faulkner), 119, 125
"Two Soldiers" (Faulkner), 267

Ukraine, Faulkner's work in, 282–85
"Uncle Willy" (Faulkner), 43–44, 69, 74, 267
Uncollected Stories (Faulkner), 5
Unvanquished, The (Faulkner), 3, 130, 190, 271

"Victory" (Faulkner), 47, 48, 264, 266, 269, 270
Vision in Spring (Faulkner), 84

War fiction, Faulkner's sources for, 108–27
"Was" (Faulkner), 130, 138, 146, 224
"Wash" (Faulkner), 51, 93–97, 100, 189, 191
Wild Palms, The (Faulkner), 49
Wishing Tree, The (Faulkner), 191
Writing, Faulkner's advice on, 253–62

"Yo Ho and a Bottle of Rum" (Faulkner), 266